Disappearing War

Disappearing War

Interdisciplinary Perspectives on Cinema and
Erasure in the Post-9/11 World

Edited by Christina Hellmich and Lisa Purse

EDINBURGH
University Press

Edinburgh University Press is one of the leading university presses in the UK. We publish academic books and journals in our selected subject areas across the humanities and social sciences, combining cutting-edge scholarship with high editorial and production values to produce academic works of lasting importance. For more information visit our website: edinburghuniversitypress.com

Edinburgh University Press Ltd
The Tun – Holyrood Road,
12(2f) Jackson's Entry,
Edinburgh EH8 8PJ

First published in hardback by Edinburgh University Press 2017

Typeset in 11/13 Adobe Sabon by
IDSUK (DataConnection) Ltd, and
printed and bound in Great Britain by
CPI Group (UK) Ltd, Croydon CR0 4YY

A CIP record for this book is available from the British Library

ISBN 978 1 4744 1656 6 (hardback)
ISBN 978 1 4744 3752 3 (paperback)
ISBN 978 1 4744 1657 3 (webready PDF)
ISBN 978 1 4744 1658 0 (epub)

Contents

Figures

Notes on the Contributors

Jessica Auchter is Assistant Professor at the University of Tennessee at Chattanooga, USA. Recent work includes *The Politics of Haunting and Memory in International Relations* (2014), and articles in *Review of International Studies, Journal of Global Security Studies, Journal for Cultural Research* and the *International Feminist Journal of Politics*.

Robert Burgoyne is Professor of Film Studies at the University of St Andrews. His work centres on historical representation and film, with a particular emphasis on questions of memory and emotion in film. Currently, he is working on the representation of war in film and photography. His recent book publications include *The Hollywood Historical Film* (2008), *Film Nation: Hollywood Looks at U.S. History: Revised Edition* (2010) and *The Epic Film in World Culture* (2011).

Shohini Chaudhuri is Senior Lecturer at the Department of Literature, Film and Theatre Studies, University of Essex. Her main research interests are world cinema, critical theory and human rights. She has published three books – *Cinema of the Dark Side: Atrocity and the Ethics of Film Spectatorship* (Edinburgh University Press, 2014), *Feminist Film Theorists* (2006) and *Contemporary World Cinema* (Edinburgh University Press, 2005) – and articles in journals such as *Screen* and *Camera Obscura* and chapters in several edited collections. She is currently curating a film programme, titled 'Crisis and Creativity: A Season of Contemporary Films from and about the Arab World', at the Mosaic Rooms, London.

Cora Sol Goldstein is Professor of Political Science at California State University, Long Beach. Her book, *Capturing the German Eye: American*

Visual Propaganda in Occupied Germany (2009) focuses on the American experience in post-war Germany. She is interested in transformative military occupations, and the interplay between culture and politics.

Thomas Gregory is Lecturer in Politics and International Relations at the University of Auckland, New Zealand. His research focuses on civilian casualties, contemporary conflict and the ethics of war and he has published articles in *International Political Sociology*, *European Journal of International Relations* and *International Feminist Journal of Politics*. He is also the co-editor (with Linda Åhäll) of *Emotions, Politics and War* (2015).

Janet Harris is an award-winning documentary producer/director, having worked for many years at the BBC and as a freelancer with experience of working in Iraq in war and in post-war. Her latest documentary was for BBC2 *This World*, 'Iraq: Did my son die in vain?' for the tenth anniversary of the invasion of Iraq in March 2013. Janet holds a PhD from Cardiff University on the media coverage of the British military in post-war Iraq, and teaches modules in international journalism and media theory and practice.

James Harvey is Associate Lecturer in Film Studies at Anglia Ruskin University and the University of Greenwich. His recently completed PhD thesis focuses on the political aesthetics of Jacques Rancière and contemporary art cinema. He is currently researching the relationship between philosophies of 'the human' and the face in close-up, throughout film history and theory.

Christina Hellmich is Associate Professor in International Relations and Middle East Studies at the University of Reading. She is a specialist in Middle East politics, currently based in Abu Dhabi, with a particular research interest in Political Islam, International Security and Women's Health. She is the author of *Al-Qaeda: From Global Network to Local Franchise* (2011) and co-editor of *The Epistemology of Terrorism: Knowing al-Qaeda* (2012).

Agnieszka Piotrowska is an award-winning documentary film-maker and a theorist. She is the author of *Psychoanalysis and Ethics in Documentary Film* (2014). Her new monograph *Black and White: Essays on Zimbabwean Cinema* (2016) deals with postcolonial trauma. She is Reader in Film Practice and Theory at the University of Bedfordshire.

Lisa Purse is Associate Professor of Film in the Department of Film, Theatre and Television at the University of Reading. She is the author of *Digital Imaging in Popular Cinema* (2013) and *Contemporary Action Cinema* (2011), and has published widely on genre cinema, digital aesthetics, and the relationships between film style and the politics of conflict representation in mainstream cinema.

Acknowledgements

This book emerges out of a cross-disciplinary collaboration that has been mutually enriching, and that has repeatedly pondered the relationship between cultural representation and intercultural understanding, between how we are shown war, and how we know war. The book would not have been possible without the generous support of the British Academy, which funded the project from which this edited collection arises, as well as the support of the University of Reading's Research Endowment Trust Fund, the Department of Politics and International Relations, the Department of Film, Theatre and Television, and the Faculty of Arts, Humanities and Social Sciences Rights and Representation Research Theme. We also wish to thank colleagues who offered encouragement and critical insights as the project evolved, including Tarak Barkawi, Alan Cromartie, Dominik Zaum, Andreas Behnke, Susan Breau, Jonathan Bignell, Anna McMullan and Lúcia Nagib. Thanks to the students enrolled on the 'Representing Conflict on Stage and Screen' module, who offered fascinating responses to some of the films examined here, as new ideas were tested in co-taught seminars. Particular thanks are owed to the participants at the interdisciplinary workshop 'Disappearing War: cinema and the politics of erasure in the war on terror', which took place at the University of Reading on 13 April 2015, and to the authors who contributed to this volume. It is through their different perspectives – and the intense discussion that ensued – that this project has come to life. We thank the organisers of the annual BRISMES conference for giving us the opportunity to present several of the contributions to this book at a panel at BRISMES 2016, Lampeter, on 14 July 2016. We are also grateful for the balance of patience and enthusiasm of our commissioning editor at

Edinburgh University Press, Gillian Leslie, and the generous feedback of two anonymous reviewers as this project took shape. This project would also not have been possible without the ongoing support of our respective partners and families.

CHAPTER I

Introduction: Cinema and the Epistemology of War

Christina Hellmich and Lisa Purse

The battles fought in the name of the 'war on terror' have reignited questions about the changing nature of war. Significant attention has been paid to the ontology of war, with arguments both proposing war's disappearance (Goldstein 2011; Pinker 2012) and its increasing presence, especially in previously civilian and domestic spaces (Dillon and Reid 2009; Jabri 2010; Sylvester 2014). Over the same period, cultural and political debate about the motivations, scope and effects of the US and allied nations' 'war on terror'-related military interventions in Afghanistan, Iraq, Pakistan, Yemen, Libya, Somalia, Syria and Cameroon (covert and overt) indicates intensifying public concern about what remains concealed in the reporting of these acts. The title of this volume, 'Disappearing War', seeks to capture these competing conceptions of what exactly is disappearing in this period, and to foreground our claim that what has been 'disappeared' in media representations of the war on terror requires further examination and critical reflection. What is clear is that existing debates often take place from the privileged position of being physically removed from the theatres of war and conflict, a position in which the experience of war is inherently mediated. This is easily overlooked at a time when the accelerations in media technologisation, including social media, seem to provide unprecedented and immediate forms of access. Indeed, at no other point in time have distant locations and peoples seemed so instantly accessible, via the click of a button. But every image or sound that is accessed in such a manner has been produced, framed or selected, and edited by someone else, a partial view that leaves something out of sight, and that may also distort or misrepresent.

Processes of selection and mediation characterise those forms that seem to offer the most immediate access to war and its consequences – news reporting and social media – but it is an equally pressing concern in the documentaries and fiction films that have sought to offer their own perspectives and histories of the war on terror. Films are a significant site of enquiry in this regard not just because cinema is a mass medium with the capacity to engage large numbers of people, but because film form permits rhetorical strategies of framing, selection, narrativisation, immersion and erasure to work on the viewer over longer durations. Film theorists have long recognised the persuasiveness of narrative cinema, its capacity to invite the spectator to share a particular point of view through narrative structure and audio-visual cues, and its capacity to obscure gaps in credibility, logic or conflicts between competing positions in the momentum of narrative unfolding, the elliptical potential of screenwriting and editing, and the movement towards a desired narrative resolution.[1] Narrative, whether in a narrative fiction film or in a documentary, uses the rhetorical force of storytelling to persuade and to elide. But the documentaries and fiction films responding to and attempting to document the war on terror are also all marked to a greater or lesser extent by truth claims that seek to persuade the viewer of the veracity of the depiction offered – from the ubiquitous handheld camera's claim to 'as if you are there' immediacy, to explicit 'based on actual events' statements, to the foregrounding of aesthetic details that create an impression of presence, such as detailed and credible renderings of textures, environments and emotional responses. In this cinematic world of compelling stories and compelling verisimilitudes, from *Standard Operating Procedure* (Errol Morris, 2008) to *Dirty Wars* (Rick Rowley, 2013), from *Redacted* (Brian de Palma, 2007) to *Eye in the Sky* (Gavin Hood, 2015), and from *World Trade Center* (Oliver Stone, 2006) to *American Sniper* (Clint Eastwood, 2014), critical reflection on the partial or partisan nature of a depiction can be challenging. Yet the failure of critical reflection can result in the reinforcement of wider cultural entrenchments, debate replaced by audio-visually compelling 'shorthands' that shape some of the ways Western audiences conceptualise the war on terror and its consequences. As a result, this book places cinema at the heart of its enquiry into how aspects of the war on terror are variously mediated, understood and elided in contemporary Western visual and moving image culture.

The essays in this collection proceed from an acute awareness of the fragmentary evidence upon which knowledge of the lived, on the ground experience of the war on terror is based, and of the distortions and erasures that can mark the audio-visual, ideological and rhetorical framings of the war on terror and its connected military campaigns. The discussions variously focus on three central questions: What is missing from the highly mediated experience of the war on terror? What are the intentional and unintentional processes of erasure that characterise this mediation? And what are the consequences of these erasures for cultural understanding? The authors featured here are most interested not in the question of *what* is known about the war on terror and the wars fought in its name, but *how* one comes to know it. Put another way, the authors collected here examine what has been made visible but also, and equally importantly, the erasures that structure understandings and misunderstandings of the social realities of these wars. As such, the essays in this volume seek to offer critical reflections on an epistemology of the war on terror, and in particular to examine cinema's ongoing significance within this epistemology.

KNOWING WAR AT A DISTANCE

As indicated above, one of the defining features of the post-9/11 relationship between those Western populations both initiating military interventions and attempting to understand their nature and effects, and those living in the territories affected, is geographical distance. Distance, in one sense, is an empirically measurable thing, but it can also, as Edward Said (1978) observed, become imbued with an ideologically freighted 'imaginative geography and history' of difference and distance (2003 [1978]: 55). This has implications for how those who occupy geographically distant locales are imagined and depicted in cultural representation: as David Morley suggests, in the production of imaginary geographies, 'the members of a society locate themselves at the center of the universe, at the spatial periphery of which there is a world of threatening monsters and grotesques' (1999: 161). Said's *Orientalism* offers a compelling account of the ways in which Europeans (and, later, Americans) sought to define themselves in relation to the 'Orient', the 'White Man's vantage point' (2003 [1978]: 236) offering a pseudo-authoritative and pseudo-scientific position from which to assert and mythologise the differences (from him) displayed by the Oriental Other, a typology subsequently deployed to justify imperialist acquisitions of land, people, property and governance. In addition to the material consequences of European and American imperialism, Said's work makes clear the logic of erasure that defined representations of Asian peoples by self-nominated Western 'experts'. For example, in his analysis of a passage from Gertrude Bell's *The Desert and the Sown* (1907), in which she generalises about the persistence of war in 'Arab' society, Said notes that Bell's '"Arab" or "Arabs" have an aura of apartness, definiteness, and collective self-consistency such as to wipe out any traces of individual Arabs with narratable life stories' (2003 [1978]: 229). This book contends that this erasure of lived heterogeneity and shared humanity continues today in the rhetorical divisions marked out by governments and media producers in the 'war on terror'.

Before his death in September 2003 Said took the opportunity in the Preface to the 2003 edition of *Orientalism* to reflect on how the events of 11 September 2001 had impacted on the cultural and ideological tendencies he had mapped so influentially in the 1970s. Here Said decried the extent to which, after 9/11, the long-standing binaries of 'self' and 'other', 'us' and 'them', 'here' and 'there', 'West' and 'Orient', had been marshalled by Western media and governments into a new/old narrative of a 'clash of civilizations, unending, implacable, irremediable', deployed to justify a new set of imperialist wars (2003 [1978]: xii).[2] Said's observations are borne out by media discourses of the time which invoked the language of war,[3] and political discourses framed by George W. Bush's oft-repeated pronouncement, on 20 September 2001, that 'Either you are with us, or you are with the terrorists.' This slogan was both a symptom of America's long-standing capacity for a geographically located exceptionalism and orientalism, and an attempt by Bush to activate the 'architecture of enmity' (Shapiro 1997) that such a worldview implies. Michael J. Shapiro's concept of 'architectures of enmity' asserts that the manner in which 'territorially elaborated collectivities locate themselves in the world and thus how they practice the meanings of Self and Other', provides 'the conditions of possibility for regarding others as threats or antagonists' (1997: xi). This concept illuminates why the then-US president began to talk in such puzzlingly conflationary terms of 'a terrorist underworld', that included not only al-Qaeda but various other groups such as Hamas, Hezbollah, Islamic Jihad, Jaish-i-Mohammed, that 'operates in remote jungles and deserts, and hides in the centers of large cities', and was apparently aided by regimes including North Korea and Iraq that sought to export terrorism and threaten the US. 'States like these, and their terrorist allies,' he says in his 2002 State of the Union address, 'constitute an axis of evil, arming to threaten the peace of the world' (2002). Potential targets of the war on terror would soon include a wide range of Islamist groups and actors, as well as regimes that differ remarkably in their ideological frameworks and political objectives, all united by the fact that they could be accused of having links with al-Qaeda. Though it may at first have seemed surprising that the US government, with all its intelligence resources, should yoke al-Qaeda together with a range of disparate groupings such as Hamas, the 'disputatious schoolmen of Qom', the Deobandi seminaries of northern Pakistan that trained the Taliban, and then, elsewhere, relate these groups to secular Arab nationalist Baath Party regimes (Cole 2006), with hindsight such a conflation constructed an imaginative geography that could serve to justify the Bush administration's programme of military and homeland security interventions. Against the backdrop of an overall political climate of fear that divided the world into 'good' and 'evil', the US government argued for the existence of an underlying Islamist terrorist agenda by focusing on geographic proximities and superficial similarities such as suicide attacks and aeroplane hijackings that were somehow related to the Middle East and Islam (Hellmich 2012:14).

This polarised language actively sought to elide the middle ground between (agreement with) 'us' and 'the terrorists', to suppress debate about the efficacy of the ways in which the 'war on terror' was about to be fought, and even where the causes for 9/11 might be found (at the very least, 'there' not 'here': see Gregory 2004: 22). But it also effected what Gayatri Chakravorty Spivak calls an 'epistemic violence' in its 'asymmetrical obliteration of the trace of [the] Other': that is, all non-white, non-Western, non-terrorists were erased in the enunciation of Bush's 'us' versus 'them' binary (1988: 280–1). As a number of writers have argued, these particular manifestations of imaginative geographies and the rhetorical manoeuvres that undergird them have continued to inscribe difference and efface context in the political, cultural and media discourses around the war on terror in the years since Said's reflections.[4] In the process, they have constructed a hierarchy of grievability which claims the centre ground for the suffering and death of white Western bodies (for example, those that perished at the site of the 9/11 attacks, or soldiers' deaths in action), while the suffering and death of those people geographically, culturally or ethnically distant from that category is rhetorically elided (Butler 2009). This hierarchy of grievability, sedimented in the mediatisation of the war on terror in Western media, has material, realworld consequences. For example, the persistence of the idea that any non-white, non-Western person encountered in a theatre of war might turn out to be an enemy combatant, which gained currency in the media depiction of US and allied soldiers' experiences in Afghanistan and Iraq, has proliferated into a range of contexts. US President Barack Obama's 2012 re-categorisation of all military age men in combat zones as 'militants' erased the possibility of civilian existence in these territories – and removed the necessity and capacity to record levels of civilian deaths, a point we will shortly return to (Becker and Shane 2012; Greenwald 2012). More recently a similar presumption of guilt has shaped a trend for non-white, non-Western persons to be removed from flights as a result of the unfounded suspicions of white, Western fellow passengers that they might be terrorists (Evans 2016; Rampell 2016).

IMAGINED GEOGRAPHIES OF WAR

Media representations are implicated in the imaginative geographies that underpin these developments, and in this regard it is not insignificant that both military and media technologies construct similar viewing positions that seem to make these particular imaginative geographies more likely. More than a century of rapid technologisation has, as Paul Virilio noted (1989), exponentially accelerated the optical and geographic reach of both military and moving image technologies. Those individuals whose economic and geographic circumstances permit them to acquire a multiplicity of images of conflict, from social media, internet or television news, and fictional and documentary representations, might be forgiven for experiencing this proliferation of audio-visual access as immediate, unprecedented, perhaps even comprehensive. However, the asymmetry of this viewing position, the 'customary privilege to inspect the rest of the world', produces a pseudo-colonialist perspective rather than a guarantee of holistic knowledge and understanding (Gregory 2004: 21).

A more accurate characterisation of the ways in which images have functioned in the post-9/11 period would be that of Derek Gregory and Allan Pred, for whom the ubiquity of conflict images has precipitated what they call the '"image wars" of the twenty-first century', in which the borders 'between news and entertainment . . . and between different modes and genres of photographic representation' are increasingly blurred (2007: 2), and where, as we have suggested, asserted truth claims and style-based reality effects (such as shaky handheld camerawork or the mimicking of archival footage) can supersede empirically verifiable information or its corresponding absence. Images have long been put to propagandist ends in war and conflict, and in recent years, as James Der Derian so presciently pointed out, the insistent imaging of conflict locations, alleged combatants and military targets by military technologies from the air has been mobilised by the Western 'military-industrial-media-entertainment network' to produce a narrative of distanced, accurate, 'virtuous' warfare that produces minimal casualties (2001: xi, xv). This has been matched by a long-standing tendency by

Western media of under-reporting – either wittingly or unwittingly – the civilian casualties of wars perpetrated by Western powers, through embedded journalism or other forms of military or state information control, as John Pilger has revealed (2010). As far as it is possible to estimate, the actual extent of civilian casualties remains strikingly at odds with media reports and the layperson's impression of the scale of the human consequences of post-9/11 military action. At the same time that politicians and military media representatives continue to talk in the media of active management of collateral damage, estimates of civilian deaths directly resulting from post-9/11 military action continue to rise. Spring 2015 estimates by the Watson Institute of International and Public Affairs at Brown University put these deaths in Afghanistan at 26,000, in Iraq at 165,000 and in Pakistan at 21,500,[5] while Joachim Guilliard et al. point out that the numbers might be much higher, since such estimates do not include deaths 'from indirect fallouts of the war, such as lack of basic health care, hunger or contaminated drinking water', which tend to 'exceed the number of those directly killed' (2015: 16).

Moving images offer the possibility of breaching geographical and imagined distances. Drawing on the work of Jacques Rancière and Immanuel Kant, Michael Shapiro has argued that cinema, in its experiential intensity, and its circulation within and beyond the movie theatre, can function as a productive site at which sedimented perspectives can be transcended, and 'the worlds of pain, suffering, and grievance' produced by war and conflict can be made available 'for reflection and renegotiation' (2009: 155). Films on aspects of the war on terror that might fit Shapiro's category include, variously, James Longley's *Iraq in Fragments* (2006), Rick Rowley's *Dirty Wars* (2013) and Abderrahmane Sissako's *Timbuktu* (2014), since each works hard to bring to the screen experiences that have been marginalised in Western media accounts, and to find cinematic forms that can do justice to these experiences. However, cinema can also perpetuate colonialist, imperialist and Orientalist imaginative geographies, or participate in cultural or governmental revisionism, a tendency that seems most sharply drawn in US narrative cinema on the war on terror. For example, narrative films such as *The Hurt Locker* (Kathryn Bigelow, 2008), *Stop-Loss* (Kimberley Pierce, 2008) and *American Sniper* persistently construct a highly partial, paranoid, imagined 'Iraq' defined by checkpoints, IEDs and ambushes, in which it is difficult to discern Iraqis in terms other than as 'militants', and military personnel are positioned as victims. Such trends are representative, for Terence McSweeney, of a wider tendency in American cinema to 'erase, forget or disremember' troubling aspects of the US's recent history in 'a process of selective amnesia, in which film and the media play a central role by influencing which issues are focused on, which stories remain untold and which characters are presented as worthy or unworthy of a voice' (2014: 45). This is a problem not just because of cinema's capacity to persuade, but because US cinema's global reach is significant: it has the largest box office market share of any country, garnering US$10.19 billion of box office revenue in 2015 (only China has anything like this market share, $7.18 in the same period).[6] At the time of writing, it is the US that has supplied the most watched movie about post-9/11 military intervention, the Iraq war-set *American Sniper*, which at the time of writing is the highest-grossing US movie of 2014, and the highest grossing war movie of all time.[7]

As a historically significant site for the manifestation of national and cultural narratives about military action, as well as a powerful medium through which audiences are invited to understand actions, locations, peoples and histories about which they may have very limited personal experience, cinema – and particular the cinema of North America and its military allies – demands ongoing scrutiny. At a time when Western spectators are physically removed from the theatres of conflict, experiencing the war on terror in highly mediated ways that fail utterly to approximate the lived experience of war and its consequences on the ground, there is an urgent need to reflect critically on the epistemology of war that holds sway, to map the erasures that this epistemology enacts, and to examine the role of cinema and its media contexts in perpetuating these erasures. As Judith Butler asks,

> What is formed and framed through the technological grasp and circulation of the visual and discursive dimensions of war? This grasping and circulation is already an interpretive maneuver, a way of giving an account of whose life is a life, and whose life is effectively transformed into an instrument, a target, or a number, or is effaced with only a trace remaining or none at all. (2010: ix–x)

This volume answers Butler's call through a productive and necessary interdisciplinary intersection of film studies, cultural studies, and politics and international relations. Examining Western cinema's role in the epistemology of contemporary war from different disciplinary perspectives, and addressing a variety of film texts and contexts, the authors collected here reveal that which is hidden, removed and left out of sight in the formation of Western understandings of the war on terror, its players and consequences.

Cora Goldstein begins the discussion in Chapter 2 with an examination of the portrayal of American use of air power, analysing Hollywood war films from the 1950s to 2015 in order to trace the evolution of discourses about honour and courage, justice and collateral damage across this period. Goldstein identifies a distinct change in the manner in which American war films allow the spectator to imagine the killing of civilians in war. In war films from the 1940s and 1950s mass civilian death was implied, but never made visually evident: even some of the most devastating destruction caused by the aerial bombing of both Germany and Japan remains unexplored, rendered cinematically insignificant in comparison to the horrors unleashed by the Nazi regime. In the post-9/11 movies, distinct moments of violence against civilians, when shown, are seen up close. The violence and killing of non-traditional combatants is targeted, concrete, bounded, explainable and just. The devastation of towns, cities and their residents – the collective damage that could have turned locals into fierce (and morally justified) defenders of their homes – emerges, at best, as a backdrop of rubble and trash. What these different ways of depicting air war casualties have in common is that in all cases, the suffering, dying and death of civilians remains out of sight, while the legitimacy of the national war discourse remains unquestioned.

Continuing the focus on the US air war, in Chapter 3 Agnieszka Piotrowska looks at the contested deployment of drones in the war on terror. She offers a comparative analysis of two films which examine the ethical dilemma of the drone pilot through contrasting aesthetic means: the mainstream narrative film, *Good Kill* (Andrew Niccol, 2014), and Omer Fast's experimental film *5,000 Feet Is the Best* (2011), which was exhibited in art gallery settings. Both films attempt to draw the viewers' attention to the psychological damage suffered by the drone operator as well as the bodily vulnerability of those innocents who are destroyed by drones. However, as Piotrowska shows, it is the experimental film that seems to find more productive ways to pose questions about the bodily consequences of drone warfare, both for the pilot and for those he or she targets. The art gallery context for Fast's exhibition of his work frees him up from the aesthetic and narrative strictures of mainstream film production and reception. The chapter thus permits reflection on the extent to which the context of production can affect cinema's power to persuade or to question, a point returned to later in the book in Lisa Purse's chapter on *Zero Dark Thirty*.

Robert Burgoyne in Chapter 4 continues the focus on bodies in war, and on how they are framed. Burgoyne turns his attention to the depiction of the soldier's body, in order to elucidate how the long tradition of photographing soldiers at war has been inflected in relation to recent wars. Moving beyond the focus on film, his case studies are Harun Farocki's series of video installations, *Images of War (at a Distance)* (2011–12), which shows various technologised situations for Iraq-based soldier training and debriefing, and the documentary *Restrepo* (2010), along with the accompanying book of photographs entitled *Infidel* (2010), by the photographer Tim Hetherington and the writer Sebastian Junger, which focuses on the experiences of a platoon of soldiers based in the Korengal Valley of Afghanistan. Through his examination of these artists' work, Burgoyne identifies two competing cultural framings of war that circulate in the twenty-first century: a conception of a bodiless, 'virtual' or 'surgical' war on the one hand (Der Derian 2001), and on the other an evolving artistic and critical interest in that which has previously been hidden behind claims of surgical strikes and minimal collateral damage: the 'corpography' of war, the bodily experience and consequences of war (Gregory 2014).

In Chapter 5 Thomas Gregory considers what the focus on the US soldier's experience risks leaving out of the picture, in his analysis of Dan Krauss's award-winning 2013 documentary, *The Kill Team*. The film seeks to tell the story of the killing of three civilians in the Maywand District of Afghanistan by a group of US soldiers. Despite the fact that the soldiers took photographs documenting the violence they inflicted on the Afghan victims, and despite the fact that each of the victims had families who were devastated by the murders, the film's screen time is dominated by the soldiers and the soldiers' relatives, their legal battles and their emotional responses. Gregory's essay thus highlights a striking manifestation of Butler's hierarchy of grievability, and shines a light on the erasures it can enact. Read alongside a number of other essays in this volume, Gregory's case study shows that the privileging of the experiences of US soldiers at the expense of non-US dead stands out as a perennial feature of US film, but Gregory also argues that scholars across disciplines have a responsibility to foreground these erasures in cultural representation.

James Harvey's essay (Chapter 6) makes the case that mainstream film-making can still be a site for the problematisation of polarised ideas around war and its consequences. One of a number of essays here that explore the forms an ethical cinema might take, Harvey examines Paul Thomas Anderson's *The Master* (2012), about the travails of a psychologically troubled soldier, Freddie Quell, returning from

World War II, and his slide into a cult. The film is visually preoccupied with Freddie's face, and specifically, its unreadability, constructing Freddie as an unknowable soldier, and offering his face as the site at which ideas of motivation, mission, psychological trauma and justified action connected to war can be opened up for contemplation rather than closed down. Here the erasure of meaning has a productive, generative function, but Harvey also shows that this emphasis on unknowability locates the film alongside a number of other cultural responses to the post-9/11 era which are concerned with the opacity of images, rather than their alleged certainty.

Jessica Auchter approaches questions of imagery and meaning from a different angle in Chapter 7, considering how images of dead bodies have circulated in Western media and culture during the war on terror. Rather than focus on the soldier bodies that are addressed in the preceding chapters, Auchter's essay seeks to understand the terms under which dead enemy bodies are shown or hidden. Using the deaths of Muammar Qaddafi and Osama bin Laden as case studies, Auchter explores the relationship between technologies of visualisation and erasure, and the political narratives that circulate around dead enemy bodies and which affect their materialisation or obfuscation. In the process, Auchter reveals the 'rules' of bodily display that apply to dead bodies in the contemporary era, and the complex political, cultural and visual schemas within which these displays are suppressed or foregrounded.

Lisa Purse returns to issues of opacity, erasure and the visualising of dead bodies in Chapter 8's discussion of *Zero Dark Thirty* (Kathryn Bigelow, 2012), the fictionalised account of the CIA's hunt for Osama bin Laden and his eventual assassination by US forces in Pakistan. Purse argues that the film displays a structural ambivalence that permits audiences with contrasting views about the subject matter to see their views reflected, a strategy rooted in the unreadable face of the central protagonist, CIA investigator Maya (Jessica Chastain). In an analysis that ranges across the torture scenes that open the film and the shots of Maya in an aircraft after the mission culminated that close the film, Purse argues that the enigma of Maya's unreadable face directs attention away from the erasures the film enacts, in its select presentation of the historical record, and in its framing of the people and places involved in the hunt for bin Laden. Only at certain moments does a different mode of address emerge, one that seems to invite a pause for reflection on the situations the film describes. But these are fleeting, and fail to add up to a legible strategy that can counter the erasures that elsewhere structure *Zero Dark Thirty*. As a result, the essay complements Harvey and Piotrowska's earlier reflections on the issue of what forms cinema must take if it is to encourage a questioning attitude to the war on terror in its viewers.

Janet Harris re-poses this question in the context of documentary film-making for broadcast television in Chapter 9. Writing from a film producer's perspective about the coverage of British military operations in Iraq, Harris offers a comparative analysis of the coverage of the same battle in two different British television documentary series, *Andy McNab's Tour of Duty* (ITV4, 2008, ep. 2) directed by Tom Peppiatt, and *Soldier, Husband, Daughter, Dad* (BBC1, 2005, ep. 7), directed by Harris for the BBC. Harris reveals the different commercial and institutional pressures that shape broadcast television documentary-making of this kind, and the techniques used and decisions made to keep the viewer watching. What becomes clear is the extent to which these pressures and techniques erased the Iraqi experience of the war in favour of more easily understandable narratives focused on the British military perspective – a tendency that chimes with the emphasis on the soldier's experience in the US context. Moreover, broadcast television has sought to emphasise the emotional and sensory dimensions of that military experience, with little appetite for examining what was happening politically in Iraq. As a result, a complete televisual account of the British military operation in Iraq is not possible, and television documentary becomes complicit in a more general blindness to forms of conflict resolution that are alternatives to military action.

Shohini Chaudhuri closes the collection with an essay that crystallises the dominant tendencies in cinematic representation that the volume seeks to map, and the violence that these representational moves do to the visibility and agency of particular peoples affected by the war on terror and its connected military campaigns. Making clear the damaging logic of erasure of the dominant representational regimes of US and European cultures, Chaudhuri also offers a vision of what might be possible as an alternative, indeed an antidote, to this regime. To do this she analyses a film not about the war on terror, but about decolonisation struggles in Africa in the 1960s, 1970s and 1980s, Swedish film-maker Göran Hugo Olsson's *Concerning Violence: Nine Scenes from the Anti-imperialistic Self-defense* (2014). Chaudhuri's essay shows that the most productive strategies to combat erasure in media representations might well be founded in an explicit acknowledgment of the colonialist, Orientalist ideas that undergird those erasures. In a different context, *Concerning Violence* shows the way, and offers hope that cinema can begin to unpick what Chaudhuri calls the 'amnesiac histories of recent wars' and the radicalising rhetoric that circulates around them.

NOTES

1. The interested reader might begin with Bordwell 1987; Wilson 1988; Lapsley and Westlake 1988: 67–104.
2. Samuel P. Huntington's 'clash of civilizations' thesis, elaborated in a 1993 essay, was widely cited after 9/11, as David Holloway points out (Holloway 2008: 7).
3. For example, on 12 September 2001 the US *New York Post* and *USA Today* both led with the headline 'Act of War'; the UK *Daily Telegraph*'s headline was 'War on America', and the *Guardian*'s 'A declaration of war'. A selection of US and UK headlines is available at <http://www.telegraph.co.uk/news/worldnews/september-11-attacks/8745304/911-Newspaper-front-pages-the-day-after-September-11.html> (last accessed 1 May 2016).
4. See, for example, Butler 2009; Kellner 2010 and 2012; Khatib 2006; Alsultany 2012; and Chaudhuri 2014.
5. Available at <http://watson.brown.edu/costsofwar/costs/human/civilians> (last accessed 1 May 2016).
6. Box office data provided by Statista, and available at <http://www.statista.com/statistics/252730/leading-film-markets-worldwide--gross-box-office-revenue/> (last accessed 1 May 2016).
7. Warner Bros press release available at <http://www.timewarner.com/newsroom/press-releases/2015/03/08/american-sniper-is-the-highest-grossing-film-of-2014> (last accessed 1 May 2016).

BIBLIOGRAPHY

Alsultany, E. (2012), *Arabs and Muslims in the Media*, London: New York University Press.
Bell, G. (1907), *The Desert and the Sown*, London: William Heinemann.
Becker, J. and S. Shane (2012), 'Secret "kill list" proves a test of Obama's principles and will', *New York Times*, 29 May. Available at <http://www.nytimes.com/2012/05/29/world/obamas-leadership-in-war-on-al-qaeda.html?pagewanted=1&_r=1> (last accessed 1 May 2016).
Bordwell, D. (1987), *Narration and the Fiction Film*, London: Routledge.
Bush, G. W. (2002), State of the Union Address (29 January). Available at <http://edition.cnn.com/2002/ALLPOLITICS/01/29/bush.speech.txt/> (last accessed 1 May 2016).
Butler, J. (2009), *Frames of War: When Is Life Grievable?* London: Verso.
Chaudhuri, S. (2014), *Cinema of the Dark Side: Atrocity and the Ethics of Film Spectatorship*, Edinburgh: Edinburgh University Press.
Cole, J. (2006), 'A treatment for radical ignorance about Islamic radicalism', *Chronicle of Higher Education*. Available at <http://new.hnn.us/article/22355#sthash.baPDRdQT.dpuf> (last accessed 1 May 2016).
Der Derian, J. (2001), *Virtuous War: Mapping the Military-Industrial-Media-Entertainment Network*, Boulder, CO: Westview Press.
Dillon, M. and J. Reid (2009), *The Liberal Way of War: Killing to Make Life Live*, London: Routledge.

Evans, M. (2016), 'Man escorted from easyJet flight after passenger said she did not feel safe', *The Telegraph*, 6 April. Available at <http://www.telegraph.co.uk/news/2016/04/06/man-escorted-from-easyjet-flight-after-passenger-said-she-did-no/> (last accessed 1 June 2016).

Fisk, R. (2001), 'Locked in an Orwellian eternal war', *The Independent*, 19 February. Available at *ZMagazine* <http://www.zmag.org/crisescureevts/Iraq/fiskiraq.htm> (last accessed 1 May 2016).

Goldstein, J. (2011), *Winning the War on War*, New York: Penguin.

Greenwald, G. (2012), '"Militants": media propaganda', *Salon*, 29 May. Available at <http://www.salon.com/2012/05/29/militants_media_propaganda/> (last accessed 1 May 2016).

Gregory, D. (2004), *The Colonial Present*, Oxford: Blackwell.

Gregory, D. (2014), 'Corpographies: making sense of modern war', *Geographical Imaginations: War, Space, Security* (21 December): 30–9. Available at <https://geographicalimaginations.files.wordpress.com/2012/07/gregory-corpographies.pdf> (last accessed 1 May 2016).

Gregory, D. and A. Pred (2007), *Violent Geographies: Fear, Terror, and Political Violence* Abingdon: Routledge.

Guilliard, J., R. M. Gould, L. Henken, K. Mellenthing, H. von Sponeck; T. K. Takaro and J. Wagner (2015), *Body Count: Casualty Figures after 10 Years of the "War on Terror" – Iraq, Afghanistan, Pakistan* (March), trans. Ali Fatollah-Nejad, Berlin: IPPNW (International Physicians for the Prevention of Nuclear War). Available at <http://www.ippnw.de/commonFiles/pdfs/Frieden/Body_Count_first_international_edition_2015_final.pdf> (last accessed 1 May 2016).

Hellmich, C. (2012), 'Here come the Salafis: the framing of al-Qaeda's ideology within terrorism research', in C. Hellmich and A. Behnke (eds), *Knowing Al-Qaeda: The Epistemology of Terrorism*, London: Ashgate, pp. 11–28.

Holloway, D. (2008), *9/11 and the War on Terror*, Edinburgh: Edinburgh University Press.

Huntington, S. P. (1993), 'The clash of civilizations?' *Foreign Affairs* (Summer), pp. 22–49.

Jabri, V. (2010), *War and the Transformation of Global Politics*, London: Palgrave Macmillan.

Kellner, D. (2010), *Cinema Wars: Hollywood Film and Politics in the Bush–Cheney Era*, Chichester: Wiley Blackwell.

Kellner, D. (2012), *Media Spectacle and Insurrection, 2011: From the Arab Uprisings to Occupy Everywhere*, London: Bloomsbury.

Khatib, L. (2006), *Filming the Modern Middle East: Politics in the Cinemas of Hollywood and the Arab World*, London: I. B. Tauris.

Lapsley, R. and M. Westlake (1988), *Film Theory: An Introduction*, Manchester: Manchester University Press.

McSorley, K. (2012), 'Helmetcams, militarized sensation, and "somatic war"', *Journal of War and Culture Studies*, 5.1, pp. 47–58.

McSweeney, T. (2014), *The 'War on Terror' and American Film: 9/11 Frames Per Second*, Edinburgh: Edinburgh University Press.

Morley, D. (1999), 'Bounded realms: household, family, community, and nation', in H. Naficy (ed.), *Home, Exile, Homeland: Film, Media, and the Politics of Place*, New York: Routledge, pp. 151–68.

Pilger, J. (2010), 'Why are wars not being reported honestly?' *The Guardian*, 10 December. Available at <http://www.theguardian.com/media/2010/dec/10/war-media-propaganda-iraq-lies> (last accessed 1 May 2016).

Pinker, S. (2012), *The Better Angels of Our Nature: Why Violence Has Declined*, New York: Penguin.

Rampell, C. (2016), 'Ivy League economist ethnically profiled, interrogated for doing math on American Airlines flight', *The Washington Post*, 7 May. Available at <https://www.washingtonpost.com/news/rampage/wp/2016/05/07/ivy-league-economist-interrogated-for-doing-math-on-american-airlines-flight/> (last accessed 1 May 2016).

Said, E. (2003 [1977]), *Orientalism*, London: Penguin.

Shapiro, M. J. (1997), *Violent Cartographies: Mapping Cultures of War*, Minneapolis: University of Minnesota Press.

Shapiro, M. J. (2009), *Cinematic Geopolitics*, Abingdon: Routledge.

Spivak, G. C. (1988), 'Can the subaltern speak?', in C. Nelson and L. Grossberg (eds), *Marxism and the Interpretation of Culture*, London: Macmillan, pp. 271–313.

Sylvester, C. (2014), 'Terror wars: Boston, Iraq', *Critical Studies on Terrorism*, 7:1, pp. 11–23.

Virilio, P. (1989), *War and Cinema: The Logistics of Perception*, trans. Patrick Camiller, London: Verso.

Wilson, G. M. (1988), *Narration in Light: Studies in Cinematic Point of View*, Baltimore, MD: The Johns Hopkins University Press.

CHAPTER 2

Good Kill? US Soldiers and the Killing of Civilians in American Film

Cora Sol Goldstein

In this chapter, I explore the way in which Hollywood films have portrayed the killing of civilians during wartime. My focus is on how American feature films have depicted American combatants killing an enemy that is not a conventional soldier. I focus on two sets of war films to explore the representation of civilian killing: films about World War II (both from the wartime period, and recent), and films about the post-9/11 wars in Afghanistan and Iraq. My contention is that the way in which the American killing of civilians in wartime has been dealt with has changed substantially.

There have been more than 1,300 movies made that take place in the context of World War II, and most of these are American. During the 1941–55 period, American combat films concentrated on the depiction of air war. In these films bombings were repeatedly shown, but victims – even when their existence was implied or even commented upon – were not seen. Moreover, bombings were repeatedly justified as necessary for the war effort. More modern World War II films, however, usually focus not on bombers and bombings, but rather on infantry warfare. In these films American soldiers are killing – and being killed – by enemy soldiers. The killing of civilians through allied bombs disappears from the conceptualisation of World War II. It would seem that our contemporary horror at the idea of mass killing in war shapes the way we imagine and portray World War II. This has important repercussions culturally and politically. It allows the continued reification of World

War II as the epitome of a just war, and makes contemporary wars seem excessively violent and even criminal.

In this context the wars of the post-1945 period seem violent in a new way. Films produced after 9/11 that take place during the wars in Iraq or Afghanistan do sometimes show American soldiers considering the decision to kill, and sometimes even killing, non-traditional combatants. In these cases the victim is often portrayed as an enemy fighter that looks like a civilian but is actually dangerous. These scenes of killing, nonetheless, are made immediate and personal. Directors are not relying on the viewer to imagine mass death, but rather personalising and detailing a specific moment of violence. By personalising killing we are operating with a new scale – it is the death of an individual that we are confronted with, not the killing of hundreds or thousands. Killing is seen from a micro-level, and it is not the result of heavy firepower or indiscriminate bombings, but of punctual, precise and measured action in response to a specific threat.

IMAGINING WORLD WAR II: 1940S–1950S

It is interesting that a war in which the American military was responsible for the deaths of thousands of civilians is remembered as the quintessential just war. It is not that the killing of civilians during World War II has been glorified in post-World War II US, but rather that the magnitude of German and Japanese civilian deaths during the war has simply not been highlighted. The extent and the depravity of the Nazi crimes against humanity, and the unconditional defeat of the Third Reich, have made this silence possible. Nazi criminality, particularly the German extermination campaign against the European Jews, has become, *ex post facto*, sufficient justification for any American military policy during the war itself.

Yet there is no doubt that World War II was a hugely destructive war in which none of the belligerents abided by the present-day rules held in the West on the treatment of civilian populations. Aerial warfare was of course fundamental in World War II. The potency of the weapons, and the death and devastation that resulted from their use, is staggering. In 1937 German and Italian planes bombed Durango and later Guernica. In 1940 the Luftwaffe bombed London for seventy-six consecutive nights, killing more than 20,000 people. The Germans also targeted other British industrial and port cities, such as Birmingham, Liverpool, Southampton, Manchester, Bristol, Belfast, Cardiff and Coventry. The

Luftwaffe conducted heavy and sustained bombing campaigns against the Soviet Union, Poland and the Netherlands (Overy 2013).

The American and British bombing campaign killed somewhere between 300,000 and 600,000 civilians in Germany alone. In 1941 the US Army Air Forces (USAAF) focused on hitting military targets through precision bombing raids. By 1942 the Royal Air Force (RAF) Bomber Command was conducting aerial bombings on German cities. The combination was meant to cripple the German war industry, destroy German morale and inflict revenge. By the end of the war the Americans and the British jointly targeted German cities through aerial bombing. The bombings were often on city centres and included military targets, simultaneously inflicting mass damage on the civilian population of the region. Kassel was subjected to an ongoing bombing campaign that lasted from 1942 to 1945. In Hamburg, during the last week of July 1943, Allied bombs killed more than 40,000 civilians and practically levelled the entire city. In January 1945 the USAAF dropped some 40,000 tons of bombs on Berlin, Cologne and Hamm, and the RAF bombed Bochum, Munich and Stuttgart. Towards the end of the war, in February 1945, more than 1,200 RAF and USAAF bombers attacked Dresden in four raids, dropping 3,900 tons of bombs, and killing some 25,000 people, almost all civilians. By the end of World War II hundreds of thousands of German civilians had been killed by Allied bombs in Germany (Bessel 2009).

Japan met a similar fate. In fact, American incendiary bombs destroyed dozens of cities across Japan. On 10 March 1945, 334 American B-29s dropped 2,000 tons of napalm and incendiaries on Tokyo, in a strike code-named 'Operation Meetinghouse'. Operation Meetinghouse was the most destructive aerial bombing in the history of warfare, killing more than 100,000 civilians, razing nearly half the city and destroying 280,000 buildings. During the following week US planes dropped explosives on Nagoya, Osaka and Kobe. On 6 August 1945 the B-29 Enola Gay, with its crew of thirteen men, released the first nuclear bomb ever used, over Hiroshima. The initial explosion killed some 80,000 civilians, and thousands more died from radiation poisoning. Days later a second B-29 bomber dropped the plutonium bomb 'Fat Man', weighing nearly 10,000 pounds, over Nagasaki, killing 70,000 people (Dower 2000).

This reality does not form part of the way World War II is remembered and memorialised through Hollywood film. During the war itself cinema became a central component of the US government's propaganda arsenal. The Roosevelt administration called on Hollywood to produce movies that would contribute to the American war effort.

These movies were meant to entertain, inspire, politicise and educate both American troops and the home front. The belief was that film was a powerful mechanism of indoctrination, and that movies could have an important ideological impact on viewers. By 1940 there were several government outfits involved in manufacturing an image of the war for public consumption. A year later President Roosevelt merged the information-control agencies into the Office of War Information (OWI), and this office spearheaded a collaboration between the government and Hollywood through two agencies, the Bureau of Motion Pictures and the Bureau of Censorship. The OWI gave Hollywood political directives, prescreened movies and monitored content. For their part, many Hollywood directors and movie stars were eager to collaborate with the war effort. Incentive films, training films and recreational films focused on patriotism and the need to defeat America's enemies. While the government commissioned Frank Capra's seven-part *Why We Fight* series (1942–5), Hollywood dealt with many of the same themes through feature film. The ninety million Americans who went to the movie theatres each week were a ready audience (Doherty 1999: 1–15).

Aviators became the romantic heroes of World War II. The American combat films from the World War II period were most often about the air force. This fact reflected the prevailing belief that air war was the key to victory. Moreover, bombing was so very dangerous for the crews involved that stories of air war presented high drama. Hollywood studios produced dozens of films on pilots and bombers, such as *Cavalcade of Aviation* (Thomas Mead and Joseph O'Brien, 1941), *Flight Lieutenant* (Sidney Salkow, 1942), *Thunder Birds* (William A. Wellman, 1942), *Eagle Squadron* (Arthur Lubin, 1942), *Flying Tigers* (David Miller, 1942), *Bombardier* (Richard Wallace and Lambert Hillyer, 1943), *Air Force* (Howard Hawks, 1943), *The Memphis Belle* (William Wyler, 1944), *The Fighting Seabees* (Edward Ludwig, 1944), *Passage to Marseille* (Michael Curtiz, 1944), *Winged Victory* (George Cukor, 1944) and *Thirty Seconds Over Tokyo* (Mervyn LeRoy, 1944). These films portrayed the technological splendor of aeroplanes, the resolute bravery of aviators and the power of bombs. The airmen in these films are portrayed as strong yet vulnerable – they are committed and ready for sacrifice, yet their missions are risky and their fates uncertain. The heroes are soldier–citizens, working together and learning about the supreme importance of discipline and collaboration. The bomber pilot, while often the heroic centre of the film, is not a rogue figure, but rather a thoughtful and intelligent man who ponders the moral consequences of aerial warfare, always reaching the conclusion that bombing, although destructive, will shorten the war, save American lives and help the US defeat its enemies.

In spite of the fact that the American bombing campaigns killed thousands of civilians, the US government, with the collaboration of Hollywood, was able to create the image of a 'clean' war for the home front. The bombings themselves, the spectator is told through dialogue and shown through images, target military installations, and not civilians. Moreover, the American bombs seem to reach the target with impressive precision. Movies made during the war depicted the bravery of pilots and aircrews, and the magnificent power of bombs and aeroplanes, but not the devastation and mayhem that followed a bombing raid.

After 1945 the government's political commitment to movies set in the World War II context disappeared, but Hollywood continued to make combat films set in the period. In fact, from 1948 to 1954, as the second Red Scare swept America and the House Un-American Activities Committee investigated Hollywood for traces of subversive pro-Communist activity, the studios produced many feature films about World War II. The war proved to be a good background for stories of danger, adventure, romance and melodrama, and always promised a happy ending of victory, moral certainty and American strength. In fact, 1949 was a pivotal year for World War II combat films, with movies such as *Battleground* (William A. Wellman), *Command Decision* (Sam Wood), *Home of the Brave* (Mark Robson), *Task Force* (Delmer Davies), *Fighter Squadron* (Raoul Walsh), *Tokyo Joe* (Stuart Heisler), *Twelve O'Clock High* (Henry King) and *Sands of Iwo Jima* (Allan Dwan), being released. The Korean War, 1950–3, did not divert Hollywood's attention away from World War II films, and these continued to be made throughout the conflict.

In 1952 a Hollywood film confronted the American use of nuclear bombs. *Above and Beyond* (Melvin Frank and Norman Panama) was the first American feature film focused on the bombing of Hiroshima. It does address the issue of mass civilian killing, although it does not show the effects of a nuclear bomb on the human targets. The film is the dramatised story of Operation Silverplate, and focuses on Colonel Paul W. Tibbets, Jr, the pilot of the Enola Gay. His superior, deciding if Tibbets (played by Robert Taylor) is the man for the job, asks him a loaded question:

If you pressed that little buzzer you might stop the war tomorrow. You would save half a million American lives, and probably as many of the enemy's. But by pressing that buzzer you would have to kill 100,000 people in one play. What would you do?

Tibbets makes up his mind quickly but thoughtfully, concluding that he would press the buzzer. Tibbets, whose personal life is increasingly destroyed by the burden of preparing for the secret mission, is nonetheless committed to the project. The justification for dropping the atomic bomb is stated clearly: 'It is a chance to end this war without the invasion of Japan.' But it is acknowledged that there is a high price to be paid – the bomb will kill thousands of civilians.

Without hubris, Tibbets repeatedly shows that he is fully aware of the repercussions of bombing. When a nuclear scientist hesitates at the thought of the bomb creating 'three square miles of total destruction', adding that it is 'not a very pretty thought', Tibbets responds:

> I was flying B17s overseas. Before every mission I'd walk through the bomb bay on my way to the cockpit and I could reach out and touch the bombs. Every time, I knew that even though our targets were industrial, there'd be people down there who'd get killed by these bombs, and I'd feel uncomfortable. But I flew the airplanes and dropped the bombs. Sure I felt uncomfortable just now. I wouldn't think much of myself if I didn't.

In a dramatic shouting match with his wife, who is losing confidence in him, Tibbets again justifies bombing without glorifying it:

> Let's clear up a little piece of morality right now. It is not bombs alone that are horrible, it's war. War is what is wrong, not just its weapons. Sure we are at war, innocent people are dying, that is horrible. But to lose this war to the gang we are fighting would be the worst thing imaginable for our kids. Don't you ever forget it!

This monologue takes for a given a truism that, if anything, has become more believable with time: the Allies had to win the war to prevent the Axis from doing so. In a letter to his mother the night before he is to fly a B-29 and drop the atomic bomb, Tibbets confesses that he is frightened. His fear is not just of his own mortality, or of killing thousands of civilians, but of the bomb *not* being powerful enough to end the war:

> I'm scared. There is a good chance that I will die tomorrow. I've faced that before, often, it's never easy. But I'm not sure that's it. Maybe I'm scared of making a mistake. One little slip can ruin a mission. Maybe that's it, but I don't think so. Maybe I'm scared of dropping one bomb that can kill thousands of people. It's a

hard thing to live with, but it's part of my job, and I've got to do it. Mostly I'm scared for my sons, and for their world. I'm scared what can happen if this thing we are unleashing tomorrow doesn't stop this war.

Tibbets is aware of the power of the bomb, and has some moral misgivings about killing thousands of civilians. Yet he repeatedly expresses the firm belief that it is the bomb that can end the war, and therefore it is necessary. Winning the war is the ultimate goal, and all sacrifice is worth it in order to advance that goal. At the end of the film, after a remarkably risky mission over Hiroshima, a journalist asks Tibbets how he feels about dropping a bomb that killed 80,000 people. He does not answer, but the viewer sees him receiving a medal. It is clear that the end – winning the war – is supposed to justify the means – the mass killing of civilians. The effects of the atomic bomb on the ground are not shown.

IMAGINING WORLD WAR II: 1960S–2015

The US dropped some eight million tons of munitions on Vietnam, more than it used on Germany and Japan combined. Although most American films about Vietnam have not focused on the air war, many have showed combat as brutal, and critiqued the effects of fighting on veterans. Films such as *Taxi Driver* (Martin Scorsese, 1976), *The Boys in Company C* (Sidney J. Furie, 1978), *The Deer Hunter* (Michael Cimino, 1978), *Coming Home* (Hal Ashby, 1978), *Apocalypse Now* (Francis Ford Coppola, 1979) and *Platoon* (Oliver Stone, 1986), illustrate the critical nature of films exploring the Vietnam War and its repercussions.

Interestingly, the critical treatment of the Vietnam War in film did little to change the portrayal of World War II in American movies. Movies about World War II continued to be made, and these were no less cleansed and purified than their predecessors. While Vietnam was shown as a hellhole, and American intentions and actions there questioned and attacked, World War II films from the 1970s and 1980s, such as *Operation: Daybreak* (Lewis Gilbert, 1975), *Midway* (Jack Smight, 1976), *Hanover Street* (Peter Hyams, 1979) and *Code Name: Emerald* (Jonathan Sanger, 1982), portrayed World War II as necessary and ultimately just. World War II continued to be an appealing context to explore adventure, romance and drama, while at the same time maintaining a sense of moral and political certainty and righteousness.

World War II films continued to be produced in the period between 1990 and 2001, and several were box office hits. Steven Spielberg directed two World War II epics, *Schindler's List* (1993), a Holocaust narrative that garnered US$96 million at the box office, and *Saving Private Ryan* (1998), a classic combat film that follows a group of US soldiers, that made $216 million. *Pearl Harbor* (Michael Bay, 2001), the story of two friends who go off to join the air force, received negative reviews from the critics, yet made $198 million domestically.

Even after 9/11, as critical 'sand films' dealing with the wars in Afghanistan and Iraq were developing, Hollywood film-makers continued to explore World War II. Films like *Windtalkers* (John Woo, 2002), *Hart's War* (Gregory Hoblit, 2002), *Saints and Soldiers* (Ryan Little, 2003), *In Enemy Hands* (Tony Giglio, 2004), *Straight into Darkness* (Jeff Burr, 2004), *Flags of Our Fathers* (Clint Eastwood, 2006), *Letters from Iwo Jima* (Clint Eastwood, 2006), *Defiance* (Edward Zwick, 2008), *Everyman's War* (Thad T. Smith, 2009), *Spoils of War* (Jean Liberté, 2009), *Inglourious Basterds* (Quentin Tarantino, 2009), *Red Tails* (Anthony Hemingway, 2012), *Company of Heroes* (Don Michael Paul, 2013), *Unbroken* (Angelina Jolie, 2014), *Fury* (David Ayer, 2014), *The Monuments Men* (George Clooney, 2014) and *Saints and Soldiers: The Void* (Ryan Little, 2014), show that World War II is still present in the American cinematic imagination. A few of these films did rather well in the box office: *The Monuments Men* made $78 million, *Unbroken* $90 million, and *Inglourious Basterds* $120 million.

Some of the more recent World War II films are quite graphic and gory, and they certainly show the war differently than did combat films made during the 1940s and 1950s. *Saving Private Ryan*, praised for its relentless realism, exemplifies this. There is no doubt that the movie is violent and brutal, and that the audience sees gruesome scenes and witnesses bodies in different states of dismemberment. The results are visually shocking. No combat film from the World War II period looked anything like *Saving Private Ryan*. Decorum and censorship criteria limited what film-makers showed in the 1940s. The depiction of violence in film, and in particular in combat film, has changed in remarkable ways.

Nonetheless, a crucial theme is missing from the increasingly graphic and bloody portrayals of World War II, namely the killing of civilians through bombing. By emphasising the story of the infantry, Hollywood movies now focus on man-to-man fighting between trained combatants. Similarly, portrayals of marines, POWs, intelligence operations, submarines, resistance and secret operations, while dramatic and interesting for the viewer, do not make visible either bombing or violence against civilians. When American soldiers are shown interacting with German or Japanese civilians, they are imagined as being sympathetic towards the non-combatants.

Pearl Harbor is somewhat of an outlier, since it deals with pilots in the World War II context. Yet in the film, bombing is imagined as victimless. *Pearl Harbor* is a dramatisation of the Doolittle Raid, and the aim of the bombing campaign was to destroy military and industrial targets. Alec Baldwin, playing Lieutenant Colonel James Doolittle, explains this in the film: 'Our mission is to hit . . . aircrafts and tank factories.' When the audience views bombs dropping, they are seen crashing against industrial warehouses and factories. *Pearl Harbor* is an ode to childhood, friendship and flying. In the film, bombing is shown as clean and victimless. It is also portrayed as the path to certain victory.

There have been no modern American feature films made about the bombing of Tokyo, or Berlin, or Hiroshima, or Nagasaki. Therefore, it has been possible to make the issue of large civilian casualties disappear from the cinematic record, and from the way viewers imagine World War II. A war that is increasingly distant has been visually reconfigured and purified.

IMAGINING THE 'SAND WARS': 2001–14

There is no doubt that the limits of tolerance towards the killing of civilians in wartime have evolved radically since World War II. That war was maximally destructive and brutal, and violence was often indiscriminate. The violence against civilians continued in the wars of the 1950s and 1960s. Approximately 1.5 million civilians were killed during the Korean War, and some two million in Vietnam. The Vietnam War was a limited war, in which the US did not deploy all of its military might. Yet American strategists did not pay much attention to collateral damage, or to its prevention. The American armed forces and the CIA intentionally killed civilians, destroyed villages, kidnapped and assassinated political opponents, carried out a defoliation campaign and bombed Hanoi.

After Vietnam, however, the precepts of *jus in bello* (acceptable wartime conduct) developed into a legal and philosophical doctrine in the West (Walzer 2006). The indiscriminate killing of civilians is now seen as a violation of the rules of war, and therefore it is inconceivable to carry out military operations that target civilians or that will necessarily cause extensive collateral damage. Just War theory has shaped the way in which the US fights its wars. Since public pressure, international opinion and lawfare demand that wars be fought following the exacting precepts of *jus in bello*, the US military has taken significant steps to reduce the violence against civilian populations.

The US military attempted to adhere to the principles of *jus in bello* in Afghanistan and Iraq, seeking to avoid indiscriminate violence against civilian populations. In order to minimise civilian casualties, both the Bush and the Obama administrations embraced the use of small units of special operations forces and used smart weapons to launch precision strikes against military targets. In this context, drones have become the symbol of the new American technological approach to war. In theory, drones allow the targeted killings of the enemy and the decapitation of its leadership, while sparing civilians. Yet the invasions of Afghanistan and Iraq killed civilians, and there has been collateral damage throughout the wars. Much of the fighting has taken place in densely populated areas, and fighters have often been interspersed with civilians (Goldstein 2012).

Hollywood film-makers have turned to the wars with interest. On 11 November 2001, exactly two months after the terrorist attacks in New York and Washington, Karl Rove, President Bush's top political strategist, met with forty-seven studio chiefs and producers to discuss the role that Hollywood could play in the war effort. Rove emphasised that this was not an attempt to control Hollywood or to impose a rigid propaganda line. Rather, he suggested that Hollywood could work in concert with the administration's broader communications strategy. It is not certain, however, what, if anything concrete, came out of this arrangement, beyond the creation of the 'The Hollywood 9/11 Committee', that made a few public service announcements. Whatever the Bush administration may have wanted, Rove was not able to establish anything similar to the collaborative model established between the federal government and Hollywood during World War II. The control and dissemination of information is much more complicated now than it was in the 1940s.

Much like the post-Vietnam war films, many of the movies set in Afghanistan and Iraq are highly critical. There is no doubt that the military occupations of Afghanistan and Iraq do not fit comfortably within a narrative of American war prowess. The post-9/11 combat movies tend to show the failures of the American government, the excesses of the military and the breakdown of men after combat duties. Three main themes, in fact, can be discerned in the war films dealing directly with the wars in Afghanistan and Iraq. The first subset of movies show a military elite performing difficult and dangerous feats – from detonating bombs to hunting down terrorists. Films like *The Hurt Locker* (Kathryn

Bigelow, 2008), *Zero Dark Thirty* (Kathryn Bigelow, 2012), *Lone Survivor* (Peter Berg, 2013) and *American Sniper* (Clint Eastwood, 2014), exemplify this. The second group of films, such as *Redacted* (Brian De Palma, 2007), *Rendition* (Gavin Hood, 2007), *Lions for Lambs* (Robert Redford, 2007) and *Green Zone* (Paul Greengrass, 2010), are critical of the US government, alleging lies, conspiracies and even crimes. The third group focuses on the struggles facing combatants as they return to civilian life. There is an embedded social and political critique in these films as well, since it is implied that war unhinges combatants, and that society does not respond competently to their struggle. Movies like *Home of the Brave* (Irwin Winkler, 2006), *In the Valley of Elah* (Paul Haggis, 2007), *Stop-Loss* (Kimberley Pierce, 2008) and *Brothers* (Jim Sheridan, 2009), treat the problem of readjustment to civilian life.

Most of these 'sand films' proved to be box office flops in the US, even though they had famous actors in them. *In the Valley of Elah* (starring Tommy Lee Jones), an anti-war film marketed as a thriller, made $6 million. *Stop-Loss* (starring Ryan Philippe), about redeployment and its brutal consequences, garnered $10 million. *Redacted*, a devastating portrayal of American soldiers committing war crimes, made less than $1 million. *Rendition* (starring Jake Gyllenhaal and Reece Witherspoon), an indictment of American anti-terrorist practices, made $9 million. *Lions for Lambs* (with Tom Cruise), a statement against the Bush administration's claims for war, made $15 million. *The Messenger* (Oren Moverman, 2009; starring Woody Harrelson), a military drama, made $1 million. Even *The Hurt Locker*, the movie that won the Oscar for Best Picture in 2009, fared poorly at the box office, making only $17 million. Although the film was received very well by the critics, it was the lowest-grossing movie to ever win Best Picture. To put the box office numbers in some perspective, in 2009 many movies did very well: *A Christmas Carol* (Robert Zemeckis) garnered $137 million; *Harry Potter and the Half-Blood Prince* (David Yates), $300 million; *Transformers: Revenge of the Fallen* (Michael Bay), $402 million, and *Avatar* (James Cameron), $749 million. It is evident that most war movies set in the post-9/11 context have not attracted the American public.

Three movies set in the context of the post-9/11 wars, however, did do well at the box office: *Zero Dark Thirty* made $95 million, *Lone Survivor* $125 million, and *American Sniper* $350 million. The first two are high-action manhunts based on real events. In the first, introduced in the preview as 'the greatest manhunt in history', a group of Navy SEALs tracks down and finds Osama bin Laden; and in the second, a Navy SEAL team sets out to capture and kill Taliban leader Ahmad Shah. *American Sniper*, also based on a true story, depicts the wartime experience of the deadliest marksman in the American military. These films have obvious good guys and bad guys, show a highly trained American military elite performing very challenging duties and propose a narrative in which the American troops are fighting against a highly dangerous enemy.

How do *Zero Dark Thirty*, *Lone Survivor* and *American Sniper* deal with the issue of American military troops killing, or contemplating killing, local civilians? The films about the wars in Afghanistan and Iraq for the most part play out during the lengthy post-invasion period, when American troops tried to 'pacify' the regions. They are not about the initial bombing campaigns, but rather about counter-insurgency operations. In *Redacted*, a poignant anti-war statement, a couple of inexperienced American soldiers are shown sexually harassing women, raping a teenage girl and later killing her family. The message is that the brutality of war has pushed these men to the brink, and made them commit heinous crimes. But this film is an anomaly, and was not widely seen. In most of the post-9/11 combat movies in which an American soldier is viewed killing, or pondering the possibility of killing, a woman or a child, the victim is shown to be a dangerous criminal, not an unarmed civilian. It is only possible to kill the victim and remain decent if the victim is really a perpetrator, and would cause harm to American troops in a direct way. A short analysis of the three 'sand films' that have done well at the box office in the past couple of years, illustrates this point.

Zero Dark Thirty (2012) is a three-hour movie, but it is only in the last twenty minutes, the climax of the film, that the viewer sees American soldiers interacting with civilians. The movie is focused on how the operation to kill bin Laden was prepared. Eventually an elite Navy SEAL team raids bin Laden's compound in Pakistan during the night, and is able to locate and kill bin Laden. As they do so, they are confronted with other men (armed), women and children. These people are in nightgowns and obviously taken by surprise by the American raid. The SEAL team kills the men they encounter (all terrorists whose name the Americans know), and one woman. She is, however, an obvious danger: she picks up the gun that her husband, just shot by the SEALs, had been intending to use against them. The Americans spare the other women and do not harm the children. In fact, they guide the children away from the violence so that they do not have to see the carnage. The only people shot by the SEALs are armed, with the exception of bin Laden, who is killed as soon as he opens the door. His guilt and criminality, of course, are the premise of the film. Therefore, the violence exerted by the SEAL team is shown as proportional, measured and just.

Lone Survivor (2013) deals with the ethical dilemma of killing civilians quite directly. In this film, a team of Navy SEALs are told that they must track a senior Taliban commander 'who has killed twenty marines last week', and will continue to do so unless stopped. The target's culpability is, therefore, made apparent. Four marines are sent on this mission, and they are faced with an army of enemies. Although determined and brave, the American soldiers are clearly outnumbered. The special operations team is surprised during a stakeout in the mountains of Afghanistan by a group of goat herders. One of these goat herders is a boy around the age of ten. The Americans are confronted with the decision whether to kill the goat herders in order to protect their secret mission. The four soldiers are evidently conflicted and confused, and wary of the idea of killing civilians. One claims that the group of Afghans should be killed, explaining that even the child represents the enemy, and must be eliminated. He chooses to see the young boy not as a child, but as a dangerous enemy soldier: 'That is not a kid. That is a soldier. Death, look at death. Look at that soldier.' The other Americans, however, are reticent. One argues that killing civilians will cause uproar at home: 'CNN will be up our ass.' Yet another takes the moral high ground, and explains that the rules of engagement prohibit them from killing the goat herders: 'We cannot do it man. They are *unarmed* prisoners.' Ultimately unable to kill the group of unarmed men and the child, the SEALs let the Afghans loose, and compromise their mission. The film offers a neat morality tale. It is precisely the boy who was spared, who helps the main American character, Marcus, later in the film. The boy and his father tend to Marcus's wounds, feed him and protect him. When a Taliban fighter is trying to strangle Marcus, it is the boy who gives the American a knife with which to defend himself. At the end of film, in fact, the child hugs Marcus, and Marcus kisses his forehead. *Lone Survivor* promotes the idea that American soldiers are wary of killing civilians. When confronted with the possibility, they recoil, even if this threatens their own safety and the possibility of carrying out their mission.

American Sniper (2014) ups the ante, and the film begins with the protagonist deciding if he should kill a woman and a boy around the age of ten. In the movie, Clint Eastwood's dramatisation of Chris Kyle's best-selling autobiography, the actions of the sniper are studied from his perspective. Kyle, played by Bradley Cooper, faces a dramatic decision. From his rifle scope, perched on a rooftop, he sees a woman and a young boy emerging out of a ruined building and moving in the direction of an American marine convoy patrolling the area. Kyle is immediately drawn to them, and remarks: 'Her arms aren't swinging. She is carrying something.' He speaks on his radio and tries to get confirmation, but is only told that it is his decision as to whether to shoot. His spotter, shocked and worried, tells him: 'They'll fry you if you're wrong. They'll send you to Leavenworth.' The viewer watches the scene as if from Kyle's perspective, and it unfolds in an instant. We clearly see the woman taking a grenade from under her clothing, and handing it to the child. A Russian-made anti-tank grenade is about to be used against American soldiers. Kyle shoots the boy before he can throw the explosive, and when the woman reaches to pick up the fallen grenade, he kills her as well. Kyle is sweaty, shaken, and obviously rattled by what he has done, but it is evident to the viewer that Kyle made a difficult decision against proper targets. Although non-traditional combatants, the mother and child are shown to be dangerous warriors – there is no doubt that they meant to harm the American military. Much like in the World War II movies of the 1940s and 1950s, then, the act of violence is justified because it is seen as necessary to save American lives. The targets of Kyle's shots are always shown to be evil and dangerous. There is no collateral damage done, but rather moments of shocking – but justified – punctual violence.

Movies like *Zero Dark Thirty*, *Lone Survivor* and *American Sniper*, however graphic and violent they may be, show the American soldier abiding by a familiar moral code. Insurgents are hunted and killed, but innocent civilians are spared and protected. Our celluloid soldiers may be tormented by their actions in the aftermath of war, but they are highly moral and play by the rules of modern war accepted in the West. Even in the midst of wars imagined as technological, the contemplation of the possibility of killing a non-traditional combatant is made to appear personal, and very human. This is rather comforting for the viewer. Whatever we may think about the wars in the Middle East and Central Asia, it is reassuring to imagine that the American soldier preserves a certain comprehensible code of morality even in battle.

In this sense, *Good Kill* (Andrew Niccol, 2014), the first American feature film made about drone warfare, is original, since it centres on the issue of collateral damage. Unlike *American Sniper*, which came out six months prior, the movie was not a popular or critical success, and made less than $320,000 at the box office. Yet from a political perspective, *Good Kill* is interesting. The movie, said to be based on actual events, follows Ethan Hawke as Major Thomas Egan, an experienced F-16 fighter pilot who has become a drone operator. Therefore, *Good Kill* does not take place in Afghanistan, Iraq or Yemen, but rather in the outskirts of Las Vegas.

In *Good Kill* the spectator sees the process of bombing from the viewpoint of a drone crew. In a trailer in a USAAF base in the Nevada desert, the drone crew sits at video screens monitoring and controlling the Reaper and, when given orders, launching strikes. The destructive capacity of drones is made evident in the film, both through dialogue and images. Once the missiles strike we see an explosion of flames, referred to as 'hellfire', and after the blaze ceases, the viewer sees the bodies of the victims on the video screens of the drone operators. As Egan's superior, Lieutenant Colonel Jack Johns tells the recruits, 'It ain't a bunch of pixels you are blowing up. It's flesh and blood. You pull the trigger here, and somebody's going to blow away.' The process of killing through bombing is depicted as a brutal one, that shatters human bodies into pieces. As a drone operator remarks, 'I count six [dead bodies] . . . good luck finding out what bits go in what casket.'

Good Kill shows that drone strikes kill civilians, including unarmed women and children. In a particularly dramatic moment, the drone crew is preparing to blow up an explosive plant with armed men guarding it. Yet two young children unexpectedly appear on the scene, playing with an old wheel. 'Airman' Vera Suarez asks if the mission should be aborted. Her superior answers 'negative', and the drone strike is launched. In the aftermath of the explosion, the drone crew and the audience see dead figures plastered on the ground, and the wheel lying untouched. As the film progresses, and the CIA takes over control of the drone missions, the number of strikes increases, as does the amount of collateral damage. The CIA instructs the drone crew to hit targets even when civilians are observed in the area. This is shocking to witness, because in post-9/11 American war movies American soldiers are rarely seen killing non-combatants. In *Redacted*, an exception to this pattern, the soldiers killing and raping are violating military and legal codes. In *Good Kill* civilians are killed, but not out of malice or error. The drone crew is following explicit orders.

Yet again in *Good Kill* the protagonists seem to abide by a familiar ethical code. They are increasingly shocked and horrified by their duties, and question the morality of killing non-combatants. In fact, they are distraught by bombing targets when this causes the death of unarmed civilians. Unlike the celluloid aviators of World War II movies, exemplified by Colonel Tibbets in *Above and Beyond*, Egan and Suarez do not see their actions as justified. Towards the end of the film, in fact, both refuse to follow orders and orchestrate a strike that would kill, among others, a woman and a child. It is not that Egan is a pacifist, or that he does not believe in the post-9/11 wars. Throughout the movie Egan craves to return to combat and fly F-16s. He rejects neither war nor combat, but rather drone warfare, which he considers to be unheroic and criminal. Collateral damage is imagined as the consequence not of war, but of drone technology.

CONCLUSION

Hollywood combat films allow us to imagine war. Approximately 10 per cent of Americans fought in World War II, and less than 1 per cent have fought in the post-9/11 wars. In all cases the wars were fought far from the American home front. Our experience with these wars – our way of imagining what these wars are like – is heavily dependent on what we are shown through the media.

There has been a change in the manner in which American war films allow us to imagine the killing of civilians in war. In war films from the 1940s and 1950s mass civilian death was implied, but never made visually evident. The spectator had to imagine the results of bombing, for instance. Given the context, this makes sense. During World War II Hollywood collaborated actively with the US government, and created an image of the war that could appeal to the public. The war was certainly purified for the viewer. In the years since the end of World War II Hollywood films about the war have become much more graphic, yet the destruction caused by the aerial bombing of both Germany and Japan has remained unexplored. The Nazi crimes against humanity were so grave, and the Holocaust so monstrous, that any attempt to discuss American (and British) aerial bombardment seems revisionist and dangerous. Movies about World War II, still popular, focus on infantry fighting and on the bravery of American soldiers.

In the post-9/11 movies, distinct moments of violence against civilians, when shown, are seen up close. The targeted killing of an individual is easier to show visually and to dramatise, than is a mass bombing. In *American Sniper*, for instance, the viewer is focused on Kyle's amazing ability to hit targets. It is these moments that are examined, not the devastation of Fallujah, a place that emerges as a backdrop of rubble and trash. The scenario of urban destruction is a given that is not discussed – the violence that created it, and its implications for the people of the city – not brought up. The violence that is highlighted, on the other hand, is targeted, concrete, bounded, explainable and just. Killing, even when the victim is a non-traditional combatant, is depicted as necessary, controlled, calculated and precise.

BIBLIOGRAPHY

Basinger, J. (1986), *The World War II Combat Film: Anatomy of a Genre*, New York: Columbia University Press.

Basinger, J. (1998), 'Translating war: the combat film genre and *Saving Private Ryan*', *Perspectives*, October, pp. 1, 43–7.

Bessel, R. (2009), *Germany 1945: From War to Peace*, New York: HarperCollins.

Blackmore, T. (2012a), 'Eyeless in America: Hollywood and Indiewood's Iraq war film', *Bulletin of Science, Technology, and Society*, 32.4, pp. 294–316.

Blackmore, T. (2012b), 'Eyeless in America, the sequel: Hollywood and Indiewood's Iraq war film', *Bulletin of Science, Technology, and Society*, 32.4, pp. 317–30.

Biguenet, J. (2014), 'The profound contradiction of Saving Private Ryan', *The Atlantic*, 5 June. Available at <http://www.theatlantic.com/entertainment/archive/2014/06/the-false-patriotism-of-saving-private-ryan/371539/> (last accessed 6 June 2015).

Crawford, N. (2013), *Accountability for Killing: Moral Responsibility for Collateral Damage in America's Post 9/11 Wars*, Oxford: Oxford University Press.

Doherty, T. (1999), *Projection of War: Hollywood, American Culture, and World War II*, New York: Columbia University Press.

Dower, J. (1986), *War Without Mercy: Race and Power in the Pacific War*, New York: Pantheon Books, 1986.

Dower, J. (2000), *Embracing Defeat: Japan in the Wake of World War II*, New York: W. W. Norton & Company.

Dower, J. (2011), *Cultures of War: Pearl Harbor, Hiroshima, 9-11, Iraq*, New York: W. W. Norton & Company.

Fedman, D. and C. Karacas (2012), 'A cartographic fade to black: mapping the destruction of urban Japan during World War II', *Journal of Historical Geography*, 38.3, July, pp. 306–28.

Fisher, D. (2011), *Morality and War: Can War be Just in the Twenty-first Century?* Oxford: Oxford University Press.

Friedrich, J. (2008), *The Fire: The Bombing of Germany, 1940–1945*, New York: Columbia University Press.

Goldstein, C. (2012), 'Just war theory and democratization by force', *Military Review*, September–October, pp. 2–9.

Gregory, D. (2011), 'From a view to a kill: drones and late modern war', *Theory, Culture & Society*, 28.7–8, pp. 188–215.

LaRocca, D. (ed.) (2014), *The Philosophy of War Films*, Lexington: The University Press of Kentucky.

Lyman, R. (2001), 'A nation challenged: the entertainment industry; Hollywood discusses role in war effort', *The New York Times*, 12 November. Available at <http://www.nytimes.com/2001/11/12/us/nation-challenged-entertainment-industry-hollywood-discusses-role-war-effort.html> (last accessed 1 May 2016).

Manjikian, M. (2014), 'Becoming unmanned: the gendering of lethal autonomous warfare', *International Feminist Journal of Politics*, 16.1, pp. 48–65.

Olsen, J. (2012), *A History of Air Warfare*, New York: Potomac.

Overy, R. (2013), *The Bombing War: Europe 1939–1945*, London: Allen Lane.

Overy, R. (2014), *The Bombers and the Bombed: Allied Air War Over Europe 1940–1945*, New York: Viking Books.

Primoratz, I. (ed.) (2010), *Terror from the Sky: The Bombing of German Cities in World War II*, New York: Berghahn Books.

Prince, S. (2009), *Firestorm: American Film in the Age of Terrorism*, New York: Columbia University Press.

Pulver, A. (2014), 'Why are we so obsessed with films about the Second World War?' *The Guardian*, 17 July. Available at <http://www.theguardian.com/film/2014/jul/17/why-so-obsessed-second-world-war-films> (last accessed 6 June 2015).

Sebald, W. G. (2004), *On the Natural History of Destruction*, New York: Random House.

Sherry, M. (1989), *The Rise of American Air Power*, Yale: Yale University Press.

Singer, P. W. (2009), *Wired for War: The Robotics Revolution and Conflict in the 21st Century*, New York: Penguin.

Tanaka, Y. and M. Young (eds) (2010), *Bombing Civilians: A Twentieth-Century History*, New York: New Press.

Tirman, J. (2011), *The Deaths of Others: The Fate of Civilians in America's Wars*, Oxford: Oxford University Press.

Thomsen, M. (2011), 'Shooting gallery: why aren't there any civilians in military video games?' *Slate*, 12 September. Available at <http://www.slate.com/articles/technology/gaming/2011/09/shooting_gallery.html> (last accessed 6 June 2015).

Walzer, M. (2006), *Just and Unjust Wars: A Moral Argument with Historical Illustrations*, New York: Basic Books.

CHAPTER 3

'5,000 feet is the best': Drone Warfare, Targets and Paul Virilio's 'Accident'

Agnieszka Piotrowska

5,000 feet is the best. I love it when we're sitting at 5,000 feet. You have more description, plus at 5,000 feet I mean, I can tell you what kind of shoes you're wearing from a mile away . . . There are very clear cameras on board. . . . I mean if someone sits down, let's say, on a cold surface for a while and then gets up, you'll still see the heat from that person for a long time. It kind of looks like a white blossom, just shining up into heaven. It's quite beautiful.

INTRODUCTION

The above are the words of the drone operator recorded in Omer Fast's short experimental drama documentary entitled *5,000 Feet Is the Best* (2011) which premiered first at Venice Biennale in 2011.[1] The words demonstrate the operator's extraordinary disavowal of the purpose of his mission – which is to kill. They also demonstrate the operator's apparent seduction by the beauty of the technology deployed – without giving it much thought what that beauty is connected to – namely death.

In the week of 7 November 2015 UK and US newspapers reported triumphantly that the ISIS 'madman Jihadi John' had been killed by a drone attack in Syria. 'It looks like we smoked that son of a bitch', asserted the *New York Post* (Steinbuch and Schram 2011), in a tone that even some of the *Post*'s readers would have found uncomfortable.

Two days later the massacre in Paris took place – 130 innocent people were killed by ISIS terrorists. The juxtaposition of the two incidents – not directly linked but nonetheless connected – throws into sharp focus the issues at stake: the questionable morality of the use of a drone vis-à-vis the absolute immoral horror of innocent civilians slaughtered deliberately by Islamist fundamentalists in the heart of Europe. How does one even begin to process in an artistic way the horror of the times we live in?

In this chapter I will look at two films which attempt to do just that. I will examine the filmic construction of *5,000 Feet Is the Best* versus *Good Kill,* a feature film (Andrew Niccol, 2014, starring Ethan Hawke)[2] as texts dealing with ethical dilemmas evoked by contemporary political war engagements, which deal specifically with drone warfare. In particular, I will discuss the films' narrative structure and the characters of the drone operators they present. Whilst both films consider innocent civilian deaths caused by drones, any kind of agency on the part of the victims in the films is in some way erased, despite the films' attention to the ethics of this warfare.

In this context, I will build on the work of Paul Virilio (2005) as well as Judith Butler (2004) and Edward Said (2003 [1979]) to illuminate the extent to which certain lives and traumas now might 'matter less' in the era of the contemporary technologised 'accident'. I will also draw on Emmanuel Levinas (1969) and Jacques Lacan (2006) to explore the psychoanalytical framework with which to think about *5,000 Feet Is the Best* and the ways in which film form can provoke an ethical response. What are the tools deployed to achieve such a response in the two films? The two texts come from very different cinematic and cultural traditions: one is an experimental piece of work to be exhibited at galleries and small screenings and the other has ambitions to be a mainstream Hollywood movie. Could one argue that one of these films is more successful than the other in terms of evoking an ethical disturbance and, if so, why? This chapter offers some responses to these questions.

Both films make a crucial point: people who shouldn't be dying do die in the middle of a most mundane daily task they are performing – and they die not just because of somebody's error but also because of the all-embracing and unacknowledgeable fear of terrorists, whose elimination appears to justify all means. What Catherine Malabou (2012) calls the 'ontological accident' is here not merely the psychological trauma suffered by the perpetrators, not even the innocent lives lost, but rather the persistent impact of the acceptance of moral nihilism affecting the way we perceive the world and what is deemed acceptable in it.[3] This

acceptance is part and parcel of the contemporary neo-liberal surveillance culture of which drones are but one element. In addition I argue
that *5,000 Feet Is the Best* evokes Emmanuel Levinas's ethical para-
digms of the 'infinite responsibility for the Other'. To my mind the film's
fragmented, uneasy construction and the film-maker's use of fiction is an
ethical gesture in itself. I will briefly point to the 'un-representativeness'
of trauma theorised by Lacanian psychoanalysis and the techniques the
film-maker deploys to evoke that trauma. Finally, I will draw on Judith
Butler's notion of grievable lives (2009: 33) to explore a further erasure
the films elaborate: that of women.

GAMES AND THE DRONE FILM

One could argue that the two films under discussion share the ethical viewpoint and the subjectivity of the respective main character, the
drone operator, whose state of mind is disturbed by his involvement
in drone warfare. The two films offer a version of a 'mind game' as
means of involving the spectator in a profound way. It is worth evoking
here Thomas Elsaesser's definition of the 'mind-game film' that seeks
to describe those mainstream Hollywood movies in which the narrative hides a narratological secret (2009: 13). Elsaesser sets out some of
the conditions of the 'mind-game film', including the main character
not being quite aware of what s/he is involved in: Fincher's *The Game*
(1997) or *Fight Club* (1991) or even Sam Mendes's *American Beauty*
(1999) are just such examples. This creates unexpected turns in the narrative and plot twists which surprise the audience. A mind-game film
therefore, according to Elsaesser, comprises movies that are 'playing
games, with the audience's (and the characters') perception of reality'.
Here I argue that Fast plays games with the spectator by dislodging
the narratives and the expectations of the viewer. I will expand on the
notion directly.

   Good Kill is not fully a mind-game film in Elsaesser's definition –
Major Egan, the main character, is a man in pain but his actions are
rational and the consequences predictable. He appears disengaged from
human relationships, particularly those with his wife and family. He is
damaged, as are all those working with him. However, he is immersed
in what might appear to be a mind-game film conceit: a morally skewed
universe with which he is out of step. He is not so much suffering from
a post-traumatic stress disorder as he is overcome by a moral disturbance which then translates itself into a full-blown mental breakdown.
It is the necessity of accepting the killing of another human as a daily
job in between organising barbecues and taking children to school that

begins to strike the drone pilot as obscene. The film presents the absurdity of the situation: the drone operator is in fact more 'normal' than everybody else surrounding him, since at least he has some moral difficulties in accepting the daily murder as routine.

Without explicit moralising, *Good Kill* brings about the chilling realisation that despite everything we know about routine murder, it is reminiscent of Hannah Arendt's 'banality of evil' (1963). In her reports commenting on the Eichmann trial in Jerusalem she famously makes the same point throughout her writings: the evil is committed not by monsters but by ordinary people just 'doing their jobs'. Major Egan suffers but he is in a system which not only accepts the murder of civilians – their erasure – as an inevitable fact of war, but appears to also erase any moral doubts or suffering connected to that fact. Somebody has to do it, allegedly to keep us safe. In the film Major Egan has no support from his wife or colleagues: he questions a number of procedures with his superiors but is not able to change anything. He has to leave his job – but his ordinary humanity is lost.

The theme of challenged masculinity runs through a number of American films post-9/11, notably *The Hurt Locker* (Kathryn Bigelow, 2008) and *American Sniper* (Clint Eastwood, 2014), where the same scenario is repeated: a warrior cannot do anything but be a warrior: in everyday circumstances his masculinity fails. In *Good Kill* and *5,000 Feet Is the Best* the additional challenge is the daily routine, the loneliness and claustrophobia of the drone operator. These are juxtaposed visually with vast aerial shots of Nevada – in *5,000 Feet Is the Best* Fast takes this exercise further, switching the positions of the civilians and casting an ordinary American family in the position of the victim. Masculinity is undermined in both films – in *5,000 Feet Is the Best* the film-maker undermines the status quo of the spectator too.

Omer Fast's short experimental piece of work, whilst covering the very same emotional and actual landscape as *Good Kill* (the two films are shot near Las Vegas and in the Nevada desert), is bolder in its ambition: it does not tell us what to think, it shifts our comfort zone so that nothing is certain anymore. I argue that this might be due to its 'puzzle-like' structure and style in which the viewer is disoriented, dislodged out of the ordinary and drawn into the world of the drone. In this connection I will discuss Elsaesser's notion of 'productive pathology' (2009: 26), reformulating it somewhat to interrogate the effect the film might have on the viewer.

Elsaesser's concept of 'productive pathology' suggests that an unstable protagonist in a Hollywood movie offers a pathway to circumventing the accepted and expected ways of seeing the world, thus propelling the narrative of a movie into new directions. I suggest here instead that if the film itself offers this destabilising view of the world, one could argue that 'productive pathology' might take place within the worldview of the spectator, thus offering a chance to dislodge more than the film's plot: it could dislodge a particular spectator's rigid view of the world.

To my mind *5,000 Feet Is the Best* is indeed a mind-game film of a certain kind – despite not quite fulfilling the criteria above. For a start, it is not a feature film – it is an experimental documentary with elements of fiction. Experimental film usually operates within alternative narrative structures – or indeed no structures (Bordwell 2013: 206). But this film does more than that: it creates difficult emotions in the spectator that relate directly to the politics of our contemporary world. The film's stylistic devices of repetition, interruption and doubling do fit in with Elsaesser's final criterion, when he points out that 'one overriding common feature of mind-game films is a delight in disorienting or misleading spectators (besides carefully hidden or altogether withheld information, there are the frequent plot twists and trick endings)' (2009: 18).

In Fast's film the split protagonist is more complex than Major Egan in Niccol's film – the latter is straightforwardly a good and uncomplicated person who begins to feel an overwhelming guilt about the work he and his colleagues are doing through drone flights in Afghanistan and then Yemen. In *5,000 Feet Is the Best* the actual pilot presents a less than simple picture – he is traumatised, but a part of him also enjoys the sense of immense power which he has over the living and the dead. This certain state of productive pathology or paranoid schizo-awareness is created in the spectator as a response to the narrative and audiovisual disturbances of the film. I suggest that Fast creates circumstances in which the spectator becomes so involved in the film that indeed s/he is almost a character in it. So why is this even worth mentioning? Because I suggest it is productive in a way that a straightforward narrative, even with a good heart at its core, does not deliver. By dislodging our assumptions and expectations, Fast pushes us into an uncomfortable position in which new solutions may not be found but are at least looked for.

Elsaesser's notion of the 'creative potential' of conspiracy theories adds a pertinent dimension to consideration of how *5,000 Feet Is the Best* seems to work on the spectator:

> Paranoia, one can argue, is also the appropriate – or even 'productive' – pathology of our contemporary network society. Being able to discover new connections, where ordinary people

operate only by analogy or antithesis; being able to rely on bodily 'intuition' as much as on ocular perception; or being able to think 'laterally' and respond hyper-sensitively to changes in the environment may turn out to be assets and not just an affliction. The 'creative potential' of conspiracy theories lies in the way they help deal with impersonal bureaucratic systems, based on protocols and routines, and practicing mysterious forms of inclusion and exclusion, rather than implementing transparent laws and explicit prohibitions . . . Paranoia and conspiracy theories, by shifting perspectives and generating horizons with higher degrees of complexity, can lead to new kinds of knowledge. (2009: 26)

The notion of a suspended state of mind, that is, not quite knowing what is going on, on the part of the spectator, with switches in points of view, repetitions of scenes with a different emphasis or ending, doubling of the main narrator and shifts between the 'real' and the 'fictional', does create a condition of profound instability which might indeed lead to new forms of knowledge. One of the questions one begins to want to think through is a particular ethical unease produced by watching and killing at a distance in this film – quite different to that evoked, for example, in *American Sniper*, where the distance between the sniper and the potential target is that much smaller, thus feeding into the more traditional notion of the bodily risk experienced by the warrior. The superior technology which makes the work of the sniper possible at all is nonetheless enhanced by his embodied, proximate courage, associated in *American Sniper* with 'traditional' masculinity. The two latter elements are not discernible in the drone warfare as depicted by Fast. What is therefore the ethical landscape Fast's film presents?

DRONES – NO RISK AND NO VALOUR

Good Kill and *5,000 Feet Is the Best* despair over the new era, the era of the drone. Drones, both their technology and their distancing of the one who kills from the one who is killed, are a troubling example of the changing face of warfare post-2009.[4] Over the twentieth century the embodied encounter with the enemy has gradually given way to a more distant affair. Historically a victory in combat could have been measured in terms of personal courage, of engaging one's own fragile body in a fight with the war enemy. Your conquest or failure would be a result of your valour as well as the technology available. One could argue that there is still an element of it even in contemporary warfare: when you shoot somebody with a gun you still must aim and therefore be not far away usually.[5] When you fly a bomber, you risk your own life in the proceedings. This risking of one's own life justifies the struggle, and is somehow a part of a longing for war to be still (in the service of) a 'just cause'. The preparedness to die and sacrifice one's own life on the altar of the cause lends the violence inherent in any war some nobility, however illusory that nobility may be.

The drone is a harbinger of a different encounter – a direct embodied encounter and the element of bodily contact on the part of the participants in warfare is replaced by a distant voyeuristic moment in which one group of people, unbeknown to them, is observed closely and then murdered, whilst the other does the observing and killing with no risk whatever to their bodies. The drone encounter, if one can call it that, appears to be a direct heir of the processes of spying, the surveillance systems, machinery and culture – not in any way connected to traditional warfare of 'knights' who fight an honourable battle to the death.[6]

The power relationship is translated from a risky bodily encounter, in which the opponents have an illusion of an equal just struggle, to a destructive, insidious power game that foregrounds the ability of watching unnoticed. This 'watching' takes place to gather information in order then to see and to kill – as if by magic, as if the killer had a magic cloak of invisibility. The perpetrator is unseen but he sees everything and his/her power is absolute.

TECHNOLOGY AND ACCIDENT

In a sense the two films are, therefore, about technology, and war technology more specifically, not quite delivering what they were designed to deliver. Drones were designed to be more precise and strategic than conventional warfare. They were deployed in Afghanistan, Iraq and Pakistan post-2000 and in particular post-2008. President Obama hoped they would diminish the number of civilian casualties. Instead, drones have become the harbingers of civilian destruction.[7] A report from the International Human Rights and Conflict Resolution Clinic (Stanford Law School) and Global Justice Clinic (NYU School of Law), *Living Under Drones: Death, Injury, and Trauma to Civilians from US Drone Practices in Pakistan* says the following:

> Drones hover twenty-four hours a day over communities in northwest Pakistan, striking homes, vehicles, and public spaces without warning. Their presence terrorizes men, women, and children, giving rise to anxiety and psychological trauma among civilian communities. (Cavallaro et al. 2012, vii)

Drones thus create serious accidents outside their stated mission. This is what Fast's film is about more perhaps than Niccol's film – though both also begin to interrogate a kind of ethical accident that is made possible by technology.

It is here that Paul Virilio's notion of the accident is productive. Virilio presents this idea first in his 2005 book *L'accident originel*. The date matters: 2005, that is, before the drone expansion and its accidents, but after 9/11 and the launch of the 'war on terror'. Virilio links 'the accident' – and more specifically a technological accident – to the notion of an 'attack'. The philosopher proposes that the twentieth century swamped us with mass-produced accidents one after the other 'from the sinking of the *Titanic* in 1912 up to the Chernobyl meltdown in 1986' (Virilio 2007: 5). He sees them as attacks on the very texture of what human beings are or could be. These attacks/accidents are linked to humanity's advancement through technology but they also have stalled our ethical progress as the value of human life has become less important. These reflections are significant to consider: what is the price our culture has to pay for our technology-based progress? Does the advancement justify the victims/losses on the way? Are there any remedies we can apply to attempt to stall the seemingly inevitable link between technology and destruction – physical and moral? These are the questions that Virilio poses directly and indirectly, before he moves on to the equally crucial notion of ethical responsibility. It is here that he demands we stall and think as the questions of responsibility for our actions have not been either asked properly or addressed. This reflection leads us directly to Emmanuel Levinas.

For Virilio the 'imperative responsibility' (not 'infinite responsibility' like that of Levinas but clearly resonating with the latter) lies in the exposure of these 'accidents' so that we, as consumers of technology which inadvertently produces the accidents, can be aware of the danger – and hence can make a conscious effort to resist the relentless and on occasions criminal march of technology without responsibility. The two films in their different ways are example of the imperative responsibility and also the Levinasian 'infinite responsibility for the Other'.[8] Their mission is to draw our attention to what is going on, and what is done in our names in various remote part of the world. Which side of the debate are we going to align ourselves with? Niccol in his film – which has mainstream ambitions and is made by an American director and producer – offers a pro-drone argument in the guise of Major Egan's superior officer's speech, in which he suggests that either you accept the drone or you accept terrorists. This is clearly a false dichotomy; nonetheless the notion of fear that that argument deploys is something with which we are familiar on a daily basis: this is how politicians speak to us. Fast's film is not engaged with this kind of a choice; it gives us no opportunity to consider any other alignments, only the one against the drone.

In this, Fast's film is indeed truly Virilian and Levinasian: the existence of evil does not excuse or alleviate our choice of using some other evil to resolve anything. Moreover, the whole circumstance is complicated further by these wars being waged by and against the Other – the exotic Other whose embodiment, culture and customs are different from those in the West. It is beyond the scope of this paper to discuss the implications of this in great detail but there are shades of Orientalism here as discussed by Said (1978) in which the exotic Other narrated by the Western scholar, politician or journalist has so few points of convergence with a Western subject as to become almost sub-human. This is reiterated in Judith Butler's discussions of grievable lives in *Frames of War* – again building directly on Said's ideas. There is something disconcerting in the representations of the Other in Niccol's film: the people on the ground, those who are being the subject of drone interrogations are often curious, doing mysterious or bad things that we cannot condone. Fast refuses to engage in these representations and his message is simpler: we must refute both the terror of the terrorists and the terror of the drone if our hope is to somehow emerge on the side of the survivor and not the monster of the 'mind-game film'.

REPETITIONS AND FICTIONS: AN ETHICAL DECISION BY THE FILM-MAKER?

It is therefore Fast's film which really embodies the Levinasian 'infinite responsibility for the Other' without any reservations – the Other being the victim of the drone accidents but also us, the viewers. Through the content embodied in its experimental form, it is the film's striking key objective to catapult the viewer out of her/his indifferent state of apathy to a more activist and active stance. Fast achieves this through the juxtaposition of different kinds of images and contrasting film-making techniques, including the central strategy of repetition. To illustrate this, let me offer a more detailed analysis of the film.

First, the film consists of an actual interview with a drone operator, which is blurred and brief, then a fictionalised one, which is characterised by a repetition of a dialogue, and finally there are a number of re-enactments. Fast repeats three times a fictionalised beginning of an interview between the interviewer (who is Fast's avatar) and the actor–drone operator. Every time, the interviewee avoids answering a direct

Figure 3.1: a drone's eye view in Omer Fast's *5,000 Feet Is the Best* (2011).

question about the drones, and instead talks about matters seemingly not connected to the interview, which nonetheless touch upon the key issues of the film, namely those of truth and lies, Otherness, ethnicity and money. It is only the third repetition of the interview which produces a narrative of the 'accident', namely, a casual chain which culminates in the innocent family being blown up by the drone's attack (see Figure 3.1). It is that sequence which is the core of Fast's film and I will return to it.

What of these repetitions? Why this narrative device? A psychoanalytic framework helps to elucidate the logic of Fast's film. 'Repetition' – the second fundamental concept of psychoanalysis and the one that Lacan refers to in his Seminar XI (1981) – is well established by Freud, but also reformulated by Lacan and linked to 'repression' and trauma. Lacan focuses on Freud's famous dictum that we repeat what we cannot remember, an impulse that is connected to the notion of 'deferred action', *'après coup'*, and Freud's *'Nachträglichkeit'* (afterwardness). It is crucial to understand that the idea of 'deferred action' only becomes significant or traumatic retrospectively (Parker 2011: 115). The British psychoanalyst Ian Parker stresses that the traumatic point cannot be simply dissolved into another narrative of the self, and that the core of the trauma is something which touches 'the real' and hence cannot be symbolised fully in language. This I would suggest is what takes place in Fast's film. The drone pilot cannot symbolise the trauma of being an executioner of innocent people. The fictionalised interview repeats the film-maker's attempt to get to the kernel of that trauma – but the words point to something else too. The interviewer says to the actor–drone operator 'you are not a real pilot', and repeats three times 'you are not a real journalist', reflexively pointing to the fact that the actor is playing the pilot, and may also be standing in for the film-maker in some way. The exchange points to the instability of the film's signifiers, which begin to stand for different meanings: Fast is not a journalist, he is interested in 'truth' not 'fact'. As the film is fictionalised, his attempt succeeds – and I suggest that it might not have done so in a purely documentary situation, simply because the reality of the film-maker versus his/her subject is impossible to undermine: the positions are fixed, one knows, the other one tries to find out. They can only become 'un-fixed' when the text no longer has a clear relationship to recorded reality – as in a fiction film. It is the fundamental relationship to knowledge which is being destabilised in Fast's film: nobody knows much. Fast attempts to communicate to us this ethical disquiet and stresses over and over again his fundamental lack of trust in the knowledge produced by Western media.[9]

However, perhaps something else is going on with this repetition and the doubling of the persona of the pilot. It unsettles the viewer on the one hand and on the other reminds us, without ever actually verbalising it, that the act of seeing and looking and enjoying the voyeuristic situation repeats itself on so many levels: everybody in the film is involved in the act of looking but not quite seeing while at the same time being deeply desirous of the seeing. The operator – the pilot – looks at the world from his game-like station. We too are like drone operators watching Fast's film's images, but unlike the pilot, our agency is limited in this instance to seeing. On the other hand, the mind-game nature of the film demands our active attention: to work things out but also, it seems to me, to demand for this agency to be taken elsewhere, outside the moment of seeing, to the world out there – in order to attempt to change it. But the repetitiveness of the broken narrative disturbs us also in a different way – it feels peculiar, out of the ordinary, uncanny.

THE UNCANNY

Nicholas Royle's monograph on *The Uncanny* (2003) explores the uncanny phenomenon, starting first of all with Freud's seminal article of the same name but taking his investigation in different directions. Royle reminds us that 'the uncanny seems to be about strange repetitiveness' (2003: 356). It has to do with the return of something repressed, something no longer familiar, 'the return of the dead, the constant recurrence of the same thing' (ibid.). Royle recalls that a compulsion to repeat leads Freud to his theory of the death drive, the drive which is both the most destructive force in our psyche, and in the world, but also the powerful creative drive which sometimes can make things happen – as we act forcefully in order to create spaces which we hope might still exist after we are gone (ibid.: 360). The repetitiveness and doubling is thus, for Royle, also a part of the 'uncanny', a sense of impending doom and death. There is both the notion of the double in Freud's essay but also, through an interpretation of E. T. A. Hoffmann's short story *The Sandman* (1816), an exploration of a fear of 'being robbed of one's eyes'. It is the seeing double but not seeing at all which Royle finds fascinating and which is relevant to Fast's film and our perception of it.

In *5,000 Feet Is the Best* the juxtaposition of the fictional and actual drone operator creates an uncanny tension between the two versions of the same man attempting to get at the testimony, which will form an account that the interviewer and the viewer can hear and understand. They are each other's doppelganger – and the viewer's perception is thrown, confused, dislodged by these repetitions of actions and situations: the subject of the interview, both the actual one and the fictionalised one is, after all, death, killing, dying. The repetitions and the use of the doppelganger is at the heart of the film's 'productive pathology' – it is this very device which upsets the viewer to the point of questioning what our position really is vis-à-vis these atrocities which take place daily on our behalf and in our names.

I have written elsewhere about doubles in a documentary context and their disturbing effect on the subject/viewer of the film (Piotrowska 2014). Many writers and thinkers have addressed the issue of the double and its anxiety- (and indeed paranoia-) generating quality. Mladen Dolar's work (1991) points out the destabilising quality of the presence of the double, citing the Lacanian object cause of desire – *l'objet petit a* – the often misunderstood 'object lack' which triggers desire but is not desire. The pertinent passage is worth citing in full. If, as Lacan, maintains, one can only have access to the Real on the condition of the loss, the 'falling out' of the object a, then:

> the double is that mirror image in which the object a is included. The imaginary starts to coincide with the real, provoking a shattering anxiety. The double is the same as me plus the object a, that invisible part of being added to my image. In order for the mirror image to contain the object a, a wink or a nod is enough. Lacan uses the gaze as the best presentation of that missing object; in the mirror, one can see one's eyes, but not the gaze, which is

the part that is lost. But imagine that one could see one's mirror image close its eyes: that would make the object gaze appear in the mirror. This is what happens with the double, and the anxiety that the double produces is the surest sign of the appearance of the object. (Dolar 1991: 13)

In *5,000 Feet Is the Best* we experience that loss – the loss of knowing exactly what is right and wrong. We witness the doubles which complement each other in an uncanny way but also perhaps represent the parts of us, the spectators, that we would rather forget: the desire to be good and to belong, the knowledge of what is bad and what is good mingled with the sense of yearning for the power over life and death. This clearly can produce a 'shattering anxiety' in a spectator – and hopefully, more than that, a 'productive pathology' too, and a desire to change things.

THE ETHICAL GESTURE OF THE FICTIONALISED

In the documentary encounter, Fast talks to the actual drone pilot in a blurred, out-of-focus interview, but according to the film-maker the pilot would not say much in any event:

He was very resistant, he often broke the interview, talked about technical aspects but not much else, and when he thought things were getting too hot, he had a cigarette break and then we would talk more – I decided to use the material off camera.[10]

The fact that Fast felt uncomfortable about getting him to say more is reminiscent of the famous controversy between Lanzmann and Bomba in the iconic film *Shoah* (1985). There Bomba, a former barber from Treblinka who, in order to survive, had to collaborate with the Nazis, shaving female inmates' heads before sending them to the gas chamber, becomes emotional and refuses to go on with his testimony, only to be told by the film-maker: 'I apologise but you know we have to do it. You must go on. . . .' For Lanzmann, the absolute obligation of the witness is to give testimony even if that testimony is too painful for the witness to bear. In the now famous and ongoing debates about this moment, Shoshana Felman (1992) supported Lanzmann's decision based on the Levinasian notion of the 'infinite responsibility for the Other' as the responsibility vis-à-vis the audience, posterity and history. In Levinas it is the face of the other which is the immediate trigger for the 'infinite responsibility for the Other': in Lanzmann's film it is Bomba's face, clearly full of pain. Not everybody agrees where the lines of responsibility lie. Dominic LaCapra (2004) and Brian Winston (2012) accuse Lanzmann of being brutally unethical vis-à-vis the subject of his film, Bomba. One could argue, as I have done elsewhere (Piotrowska, 2014), that in the embodied encounter between the film-maker and the subject of her/his film it is *the face* of the *immediate* Other which ought to evoke the 'infinite responsibility' – and not the more abstract face of history and posterity.

To my mind, it is the Levinasian approach that is adopted by Fast in his film. He does not ever push his interviewee beyond the latter's comfort zone: his face, presented as a blurred image to the viewer, is clearly very visible to the film-maker and demands recognition and respect, which overrides a demand for the truth and testimony. Fast thus creates fictionalised and fictional accounts based on his unrecorded and informal conversations with the drone operator, as well as his own ideas of what may have happened and what may have been felt, reminding us perhaps of Cathy Caruth's statements regarding testimony, namely that it is not just the issue of what we can learn but what is ethical to tell (1996: 25), or Derrida's assertion when commenting on Blanchot's *The Instant of My Death* (2000: 15–20) that a true testimony has to be fictionalised if it is going to attempt to get at the kernel of the trauma at all.

Fast's decision to abandon the documentary mode of representation therefore frees him to create a text which is both powerful and truthful, painful and ethical. The technique of creating a film made up of broken sequences mirrors the representation of a fragmented body but also of a split self, a 'split subject' as Lacan would have it. We are all split subjects but the actual pilot's supposed tranquil and detached account of the beauty of the drone's action as juxtaposed with the fictional pilot's tormented and failed attempts to come up with a narrative that gets close to his own trauma, offers an idea of what it might feel like to be the operator of an accident which turns into an 'attack' (paraphrasing Virilio) on his own humanity.

In the retelling of the nightmare of this accident, Fast uses a device of transposing the situation from Afghanistan onto a fictional white American family. It is a simple device which once and for all demolishes the notion that there is something exotic and different about the Other, whether in Afghanistan or the West Bank – the plight of a family would be exactly the same if they were American. It is in that move that Fast emerges from the frameworks of Said's *Orientalism* and creates something new – the move which never quite takes place in *Good Kill*. It takes a viewer a beat to realise that the narrative is unusual – another

Figure 3.2: the family encounter armed men on the road in *5,000 Feet Is the Best* (2007).

'mind-game' moment which forces us to make connection thus far not made, even though once named, they might seem obvious. The commentary mentions a 'provisional authority' and the geographical references are not right – we realise quite quickly that the director wants us to imagine the horror of the drone 'accident' as if it were taking place in a Western suburb, and happening to a Western white family. The whole situation is reversed as it were – the white family is controlled and stopped in a different environment, by soldiers and militia of a non-Caucasian ethnicity (see Figure 3.2). The end-point of this narrative reversal is motivated by the father of the family driving off in the wrong direction, not wanting to wake up his wife – the good husband that he is, another slightly ironic comment on the utter failure of masculinity in modern times.

THE CRISIS OF GENDER AND BELONGING

War is a patriarchal masculine gesture: Judith Butler uses the expression of 'missiles being ejaculated' (2010: 90). On the other hand, as touched upon previously, it is a gesture which also castrates the men who get too involved in it so intensely so they cannot fulfil the 'manly' duties ascribed to them in times of peace. In *Good Kill* one of Major Egan's symptoms is that he cannot make love to his beautiful wife any more – we recall similar domestic dramas in *The Hurt Locker* and

American Sniper. Why a man's capacity for sexual intercourse with his wife is considered a key element of maleness is perhaps a question for another time: there is something disturbing in the connection of a maleness which penetrates the enemy and a 'necessary form' of sexual maleness which involves an ability to perform and penetrate one's wife (and if this requirement is not fulfilled, the warrior's female partners might well leave – they threaten to do so in *The Hurt Locker* and *American Sniper*. In *Good Kill* the wife does leave). If this crisis of masculinity takes centre stage in these films, women have not been represented as anything but victims in the vast majority of war cinema and television. There are some exceptions, like Maya in *Zero Dark Thirty* (2012) or Carrie in *Homeland* (2011–15), both of whom are determined, effective, full of agency, but also almost insane, almost on the brink of a total collapse. I have disputed the perception of Maya as 'autistic' elsewhere (Piotrowska, 2015), but the fact is that in our culture war does not sit easily with perceptions of what woman can – or perhaps ought to – do in society. The two characters mentioned above have given up their right to be a mother or a wife in these films. The assumption is that it is necessary to give up one's femininity as defined by patriarchy to be any good in a war situation.

In *Good Kill* there are three female characters – all of them powerless in the face of patriarchal systems of hierarchy. Major Egan's wife appears the least sympathetic of the three. She is demanding without making any effort to understand her husband's plight, the film suggests she might be unfaithful and she leaves at the end – even after the drone pilot really tries to share his suffering with her. The second woman is the woman in Afghanistan who gets repeatedly raped by a Taliban man, a narrative move that positions her as a passive victim in relation to whom the drone team, situated at a huge distance away, are distraught and powerless. This storyline functions in a rather facile way, falling into familiar stereotypes of the exotic Other, the stereotypes warned against by Edward Said a long time ago, and here simply reproduced yet again, for our benefit, for the benefit of the viewer's sense of justice in which the bad person is punished in the end. In the context of thousands of innocent people dying as a result of drone accidents or simply a callous decision, this narrative device appears naïve at best and manipulative at worst. The final woman presented in the film is the team member, a fellow drone operator: here a clear effort is made to invest her with more agency: she talks back to the bosses, calls what they are doing an act of terrorism. She is more sympathetic to the suffering of the main drone operator and offers a kind of juxtaposition to the non-understanding wife. She is also non-white. One could argue that this is too a feeble an attempt perhaps at redressing the power inequality mentioned above, between the feminine exotic Other and the all powerful white man but at least she does have some agency. I found the suggestion that there has to be some romantic or sexual tension between Major Egan and his female colleague disappointing: it would have been more interesting to have them simply remain colleagues and friends.

In Fast's film, perhaps surprisingly, the woman's voice is not heard either and the story told constructs a predominantly male domain: the militia at the roadblock are men, the three guerrilla soldiers who stopped the family are men, the father, the actual drone pilot, the actor drone pilot and his interviewer, an accidental hotel guest, another guest who is a conman, and then the one who is conned: they are all men – so at least thirteen men that we see. There is a woman who is part of a con story told in one of the fictional drone pilot's detours and another, significantly the wife and mother, who is completely deprived of agency in Fast's film, deeply asleep when the decisions are being made concerning her life and that of her family. The narrator clarifies that the mother of the family does have 'the road map' but she is asleep. In her sane and appropriate 'womanness' (as a wife and a mother) she might know what to do, but unfortunately she is not conscious of the events as they unfold, and so the father gets lost without her presence or influence, and the mother's unconscious absence has fatal effects on her family. It is not clear whether Fast uses the image of a sleeping woman simply to make a point about impotent and confused masculinity (the father doesn't wake her up as he is a caring husband), but in the end the impression is that everybody is utterly powerless. Similarly, in *Good Kill* disembodied voices issue instructions the basis of which are a mystery: they draw from technology, making decisions on our behalf. We come full circle to Virilio's triumphant march of technology that brings with it accidents that threaten our very humanity.

CONCLUDING REMARKS

Both films under discussion attempt to draw our attention to the psychological damage suffered by the drone operator as well as the bodily human vulnerability of those innocents who are destroyed by drones. The two films go about the presentation of this dual trauma in different ways: *Good Kill* uses more traditional ways of storytelling, Fast deploys a number of experimental and psychoanalytical techniques in order to produce a different kind of experience in the spectator – the 'productive pathology' of the mind-game film which might make us question the political status quo which surrounds us. In addition, to my mind Fast's refusal to 'represent' the actual suffering, leaving it to us to imagine it, is more effective than the detailed, laborious and rather too literal, too 'on the nose' portrayal of the way the drone operation works in *Good Kill*.

Fast's move to present the 'accident' family as an American family dismantles the notion of the exotic Other who suffers somewhere we cannot see or imagine. It refuses to buy into the comfortable and false notions of this Other promoted by the East and West divide as described in Said, and which still persists in much media and political discourse today.[11] Instead, that device in the film of swapping the roles and the power positions of the characters (so the family affected is American not Middle Eastern or Asian or non-white in some other way) changes the structure of the possible narrative. This speaks to Judith Butler's notion of 'grievable lives', on which Butler points out that lives and bodies in non-Western cultures appear to have a different value to Western politicians and the media (and to us therefore) from atrocities and deaths in the so called 'first world' (2008). This differentiating between the importance of different lives and deaths is ethically reprehensible. One cannot put a different value on a life based on its ethnicity – that value has to be constant. Butler has been thinking and writing about this issue for many years and in different volumes, and indeed sees this Western stance on the Other as profoundly immoral. The quote below is from her earlier work *Undoing Gender* (2004), and encapsulates perfectly the issues at stake:

> It is one thing to argue that first, on the level of discourse, certain lives are not considered lives at all, they cannot be humanized, that they fit no dominant frame for the human, and that their dehumanisation occurs first, at this level, and that this level then gives rise to a physical violence that in some sense delivers the message of dehumanization that is already at work in the culture. It is another thing to say that discourse itself effects violence through *omission*. If 200,000 Iraqi children were killed during the Gulf War and its aftermath, do we have an image, a frame for any of those lives, singly or collectively? Is there a story we might find about those deaths in the media? Are there names attached to those children? (Butler 2004: 34)

In other words, the invisibility of the Other in the media and in the perceptions of Western culture, despite the actual high visibility of people's lives through the drone, makes the technological Virilian 'accident' more bearable. Omer Fast, through his simple and effective device of making the victims who would otherwise always be the exotic Other, more like us, the Same, brings the horror of these accidents closer to home. His successful attempt of creating a moment of 'productive pathology' as we watch the film might contribute to a lasting change of attitudes. Through that device the bodies of the Other become vulnerable, just like ours are, and that vulnerability and its recognition, Butler insists, is the first step towards accepting the humanity of the Other, and hence towards offering resistance to the acceptance of 'the accident'.

NOTES

1. 'The film is based on two meetings with a Predator drone sensor operator, which were recorded in a hotel in Las Vegas in September 2010. On camera the drone operator agreed to discuss the technical aspects of his job and his daily routine. Off camera and off the record he briefly described recurring incidents in which the unmanned plane fired at both militants and civilians – and the psychological difficulties he experienced as a result. Instead of looking for the appropriate news accounts or documentary footage to augment his redacted story, the film is deliberately miscast and misplaced: it follows an actor cast as the drone operator who grudgingly sits for an interview in a dark hotel. The interview is repeatedly interrupted by the actor's digressions, which take the viewer on meandering trips around Las Vegas. Told in quick flashbacks, the stories form a circular plot that nevertheless returns fitfully to the voice and blurred face of the drone operator – and to his unfinished story.' (Synopsis for *5,000 Feet Is the best* – <https://vimeo.com/34050994> (last accessed 5 August 2016)).

2. 'In the shadowy world of drone warfare, combat unfolds like a video game – only with real lives at stake. After six tours of duty Air Force pilot Tom Egan (Ethan Hawke) yearns to get back into the cockpit of a real plane, but he now fights the Taliban from an air-conditioned box in the Las Vegas desert. When he and his crew start taking orders directly from the CIA, and the stakes are raised, Egan's nerves – and his relationship with his wife (January Jones) begin to unravel.' (Plot synopsis for *Good Kill* – <http://www.ifcfilms.com/films/good-kill> (last accessed 5 August 2016)).

3. In Malabou's *The Ontology of the Accident* she defines the 'ontological accident' as an event which alters the brain and the perception of the subject and which cannot be reversed by any means, including psychoanalysis. She would include in these events occurrences such as a stroke or Alzheimers for example, but also war-related trauma.

4. Following President Obama's speeches on the efficiency of a drone – see a discussion of this in Coll 2014.

5. The counter-example would be *American Sniper*, which deals with the same moral issues as *Good Kill*, but where the telescope acts as the instrument of 'distant proximity'. However, there is an element of an actual risk taken by the sniper: he has to be physically closer than the drone operator.

6. The myth of a warrior who is both noble and potentially a virtuous ruler who might, on the way, be turned into a Prince Charming is one of the key archetypal images of Western culture. See, for example, Strawn and Bowen (2003), p. 55.

7. There are a number of articles and websites pointing this out, and the catastrophic ratio between reaching the targets and accidental civilian casualties, as in, for example, Ackerman's *Guardian* article, which states that instead of the targeted forty-one people the drones killed 1,147 people in this operation alone (2014).

8. Emmanuel Levinas is one of the most influential ethical thinkers of the late twentieth century, proposing his notion of the 'infinite responsibility for the Other'. That responsibility is set in motion by the Other whose arrival impacts on the 'I'. The 'I' therefore, the ego, is not the prime mover – the power of the decision-making is shifted from the 'I' to the Other. In other words, the freedom of the 'I' is constituted as receiving a challenge, an appeal from the Other and that appeal is then transformed into a demand which organises, or should do, the world we live in. Clearly these demands are almost impossible to carry out and yet we are asked to try and keep trying. Critchley in his study of the ethics of proximity *Infinitely Demanding* (2007) stresses that, despite the apparent and stated passivity, in truth the Levinasian subject is never passive as his 'ethical experience is activity, the activity of the subject . . .' (Critchley 2007: 14). Therefore, despite the responsibility for the Other being there a priori before anything else might take place. I have written about Levinas elsewhere (Piotrowska 2014).

9. The position of non-knowledge is the characteristic of the Lacanian school of thoughts – see, for example, Lacan, *Écrits* (1951: 12).

10. See 'From Reality', interview with Omer Fast (2015), Henie Onstad Kunstsenter, at 3.35 minute mark, <https://www.youtube.com/watch?v=6uHbDtThKXo> (last accessed 1 June 2015).

11. Said makes a number of points in his groundbreaking book. The Orient was Orientalised not only because it was discovered to be 'Oriental' in all those ways considered commonplace by an average nineteenth-century European, but also because it *could* be – that is, submit to being – *made* Oriental. There is very little consent to be found, for example, in the fact that Flaubert's encounter with an Egyptian courtesan produced a widely influential model of the Oriental woman; she never spoke of herself, she never represented her emotions, presence or history. He spoke for her and represented her. He was foreign, comparatively wealthy, male, and these were historical facts of domination that allowed him not only possess Kuchuk Hanem physically but to speak for her and tell his readers in what way she was 'typically Oriental'. My argument is that Flaubert's situation of strength in relation to Kuchuk Hanem was not an isolated instance. It fairly stands for the pattern of relative strength between East and West, and the discourse about Orient that it enabled (2003 [1979]: 6).

BIBLIOGRAPHY

Ackerman, S. (2014), '41 men targeted but 1,147 people killed: US drone strikes – the facts on the ground.' *The Guardian*, 24 November. Available at <http://www.theguardian.com/us-news/2014/nov/24/-sp-us-drone-strikes-kill-1147> (last accessed 10 November 2015).

Arendt, H. (1963), *Eichmann in Jerusalem*, London and New York: Penguin.

Blanchot, M. and J. Derrida (2000), *The Instant of My Death / Demeure: Fiction and Testimony*, trans. Elizabeth Rottenberg, Paolo Alto: Stanford University Press.

Bordwell, D. (2013), *Narration in the Fiction Film*, London and New York: Routledge.

Butler, J. (2004), *Undoing Gender*, London and New York: Routledge.

Butler, J. (2010 [2009]), *Frames of War*, London: Verso.

Caruth, C. (1996), *Unclaimed Experience: Trauma and the Possibility of History*, Washington, DC: The Johns Hopkins University Press.

Cavallaro, J., S. Sonnenberg and S. Knuckey (2012), *Living Under Drones: Death, Injury and Trauma to Civilians from US Drone Practices in Pakistan*. Stanford: International Human Rights and Conflict Resolution Clinic, Stanford Law School; NYU School of Law, Global Justice Clinic. Available at <https://law.stanford.edu/publications/living-under-drones-death-injury-and-trauma-to-civilians-from-us-drone-practices-in-pakistan/> (last accessed 11 June 2015).

Coll, S. (2014), 'The unblinking stare: the drone war in Pakistan', *The New Yorker*, 24 November. Available at <http://www.newyorker.com/magazine/2014/11/24/unblinking-stare> (last accessed 20 January 2016).

Critchley, S. (2007), *Infinitely Demanding: Ethics of Commitment, Politics of Resistance*, London and New York: Verso.

Dolar, M. (1991), 'I shall be with you on your wedding night: Lacan and the uncanny', *October* (Autumn), 58, pp. 5–23.

Elsaesser, T. (2009), 'The mind-game film', in W. Buckland (ed.), *Puzzle Films: Complex Storytelling in Contemporary Cinema*, London: Wiley Blackwell, pp. 13–33.

Felman, S. (1992), 'The return of the voice: Claude Lanzmann's *Shoah*', in S. Felman and D. Laub (eds), *Testimony: Crises of Witnessing in Literature, Psychoanalysis, and History*, London: Routledge, pp. 204–28.

Freud, S. (1951 [1919]), *The Standard Edition of the Complete Psychological Works of Sigmund Freud, Volume XVII (1917–1919): An Infantile Neurosis and Other Works*, London: Hogarth Press and the Institute of Psychoanalysis, pp. 217–56.

Hoffman, E. T. A. ([1816] 2011), *The Sandman*, London: Fantasy and Horror Classics.

Kafka, F. ([1915] 2014), *The Metamorphosis*, trans. Susan Bernofsky, London: W. W. Norton and Company.

Lacan, J. ([1951] [1966] 2006), *Écrits*, New York and London: W. W. Norton and Company.

Lacan, J. ([1973] 1998), *The Four Fundamental Concepts of Psychoanalysis*, trans. Alan Sheridan, New York and London: W. W. Norton and Company.

Lacan, J. ([1981] 1998), 'Seminar XI', in J.-A. Miller (ed.), *The Four Fundamental Concepts of Psychoanalysis*, trans. Alan Sheridan, New York and London: W. W. Norton and Company.

LaCapra, D. (2004), *History in Transit, Experience, Identity, Critical Theory*, Ithaca: Cornell University Press.

Levinas, E. (1969 [1961]), *Totality and Infinity*, trans. Alphonso Lingis, The Hague: Martinus Nijhoff.

Levinas, E. (1981), *Otherwise than Being or Beyond Essence*, trans. Alphonso Lingis, The Hague: Martinus Nijhoff.

Malabou, C. (2012), *The Ontology of the Accident*, London: Wiley Blackwell.

Parker, I. (2011), *Lacanian Psychoanalysis: Revolutions in Subjectivity*, London and New York: Routledge.

Piotrowska, A. (2014), *Psychoanalysis and Ethics in Documentary Film*. London and New York: Routledge.

Piotrowska, A. (2015), '*Zero Dark Thirty*: war autism or Lacanian ethical act', in A. Piotrowska (ed.) *Embodied Encounters: New Approaches to Psychoanalysis and Cinema*, London and New York: Routledge.

Royle, N. (2003), *The Uncanny*, Manchester: Manchester University Press.

Said, E. W. (2003 [1979]), *Orientalism*, New York: Vintage Books.

Steinbuch, Y. and J. Schram (2015), 'It looks like we smoked this son of a bitch', *New York Post*, 12 November. Available at <http://nypost.com/2015/11/12/us-airstrike-targets-jihadi-john/> (last accessed 15 August 2015).

Strawn, B. A. and N. R. Bowen (eds) (2003), *A God So Near: Essays on Old Testament Theology in Honor of Patrick D. Miller*, Winona Lake, IN: Eisenbrauns.

Virilio, P. (2007 [2005]), *The Original Accident*, London: Polity.

Winston, B. (2012), '"Ça va de soi": The visual representation of violence in the Holocaust documentary', in J. Ten Brink (ed.), *Killer Images*, London and New York: Columbia Press, pp. 97–119.

Zupančič, A. (2011 [2000]), *Ethics of the Real: Kant and Lacan*, London and New York: Verso.

Zupančič, A. (2008), *Why Psychoanalysis?* Uppsala: NSU Press.

CHAPTER 4

Post-heroic War/The Body at Risk

Robert Burgoyne

In this essay I explore two distinct cultural framings of war in the twenty-first century – an emerging theory centred on the doctrine of bodiless or 'post-heroic war', and an evolving artistic and critical interest in what one writer calls the 'corpography' of war (Luttwak 1995; Gregory 2015). Two projects serve as my examples: the video installation *Images of War (at a Distance)* (2011) by Harun Farocki, and the documentary *Restrepo* (2010), along with the accompanying book of photographs entitled *Infidel* (2010), by the photographer Tim Hetherington and the writer Sebastian Junger. The work of these three artists captures the competing cultural imaginaries that have formed around war today – the fascination with war conducted at a distance, so called 'wired war' or 'surgical war', calibrated for low risk and maximum potency, and its shadow double, the theatre of high drama and corporeal tragedy viewed close at hand in the work of Hetherington and Junger. Both projects have attained high levels of cultural visibility. Viewed in isolation, each is fully coherent – and entirely inadequate. Seen together, they convey the contending constructions of war that have taken hold in Western culture today.

The polarised concepts of war presented in these works underscore the challenge of representing the pervasive violence of the current period, where new weapons and entirely new cultures of war, extending from the warped medievalism of ISIS to the remote weaponry of drone warfare, seem to confound the power of representation. Ranging from the sanguinary spectacles of terror seen in media events produced by ISIS to the nearly invisible, cybernetic weaponry of wired war, the new wars of the twenty-first century challenge us for a new symbolic treatment. The question Fredric Jameson posed in a 2008 essay, is war representable? (my paraphrase) has even greater salience today, as the proliferation of media images of conflict and carnage has exposed a corresponding narrative void, an absent metalanguage for war that could orient or map the contours of conflict in the contemporary moment (Jameson 2009: 1533). Marked by an extraordinary amplification of media imagery on the one hand, and by a radically diminished quality of narrative expression on the other, contemporary war, for all its stunning ubiquity, seems somehow to escape effective symbolic representation. The projects of Hetherington and Farocki, in this context, can be seen as an outline of the contradictory investments at the heart of the visual culture of war today, suggesting a framework for critical reflection.

Farocki's installation details the extensive use of computer game simulations and virtual combat scenarios in the training of US soldiers, illuminating one dimension of what the war theorist Christopher Coker has called the technological 'reenchantment of war' that has dominated military thinking in the late twentieth and twenty-first centuries (Coker 2004: 4). With an emphasis on optical surveillance, remote targeting and computerised weaponry, combat in contemporary war theory is conceived as decorporealised, bloodless, and 'hygienic', to use the word employed by war theorist James Der Derian (2009: xxxi). *Images of War (at a Distance)* illustrates the virtual training regimen that is now standard in the US military. Consisting of multiple screens of simulated combat scenarios, Farocki's installation depicts a series of computer-generated exercises designed to desensitise soldiers to the experience of battle through repeated screen challenges, in an effort to create a kind of muscle memory for actual combat. The work concludes with a video that depicts soldiers undergoing post-combat therapy, in which the actual, corporeal experience of battle, the traumatising and bloody performance of combat, is now translated back into simulated imagery via virtual reality headsets. The exhibition depicts a contemporary war culture that is blanketed in digital media from beginning to end.

In marked contrast, Junger and Hetherington's film *Restrepo*, and the accompanying book of photographs entitled *Infidel*, foreground the body of the soldier as a medium of sensory experience and as a body at risk. The film dramatises the limitations of so-called optical war in many current conflict zones, and highlights the 'edgework' of the modern soldier, as well as the intensified experience of touch and hearing that combat entails (McSorley 2012: 49). The visual and acoustic design of *Restrepo* effectively captures what the historian Derek Gregory calls the 'haptic geography' of combat, providing a first-person account of the way the body inhabits contested space (Gregory 2015: 3). The history and memory of battle, moreover, is inscribed directly on the bodies of the soldiers depicted in the film and the photographs, displayed vividly in their tattoos and in the practices of bodily scarification that are now part of the culture of modern combat. In contrast to the decorporealised training for war portrayed in the work of Farocki, *Restrepo* and *Infidel* emphasise the body of the soldier as a critical site of representation and meaning.

As different as they are, both projects are examples of contemporary artworks that explore the changing texture of war experience in the twenty-first century, depicting both the desensitising effects of hyper-mediated training as well as the overpowering sensory stimulation of combat engagement. At some level both the film and the installation attempt to bridge the remoteness of contemporary war. Viewed from a certain angle, both sets of projects appear to stand against the idea of 'disappearing war' that provides the theme and the impetus for this volume, offering, on the one hand, an exposé of the way digital media pervades twenty-first-century training for combat, and on the other, depicting what Santanu Das calls the 'touchscape' of modern war, the portfolio of bodily experiences that accompany war (Das 2008: 6). At one level the provocative assertion at the heart of this book – that war, for all its ubiquity in contemporary life, is somehow ghosted or rendered invisible by a media culture that bombards us with images of atrocity, insurgency and state violence on a daily basis – is to a certain extent contested in these ambitious works, which have garnered critical acclaim and a substantial share of public visibility. In the analysis that follows, I propose several variations on the theme of disappearing war, several ways that the paradox of war that is erased from view even as it saturates contemporary media, can be perceived in these two artistic projects.

HARUN FAROCKI: HYGIENIC WAR

Farocki's 2011–12 installation, *Images of War (at a Distance)* is a collection and presentation of four installations created in 2009 and 2010 entitled 'Serious Games, I–IV'. *Images of War* depicts the training of soldiers for the new wars of the twenty-first century, emphasising the elaborate use of virtual imagery to simulate combat, to create threatening environments and to programme responses and behaviour in a way that is meant to provide a premediated behavioural script for the actual conduct of war. Consisting of four large video panels, two of which are composed in what Farocki calls the soft montage of split screen, the videos represent one of the dominant training and post-combat regimens of the contemporary US military.

Figure 4.1: 'Serious Games I: Watson is Down' from Harun Farocki's *Images of War (at a Distance)* installation series (2009–10).

The first installation, 'Watson is Down',' consists of a split-screen rendering of soldiers training on computers to simulate the battle protocols and skill set of a tank crew attempting to navigate a hostile, computer animated landscape (see Figure 4.1). On one half of the screen we see the soldiers at their computers, on the other half, the computer-generated landscape through which the virtual tank is manoeuvring. 'Three Dead', the second video screen, depicts foot soldiers patrolling in a set in California designed to look like a village in Iraq, with actors dressed as Iraqis and sound piped in to simulate explosives and gunfire. The third screen, entitled 'Immersion', pictures soldiers re-enacting, through virtual reality headsets, the actual, physical, traumatic events of their war experience. As we watch the soldiers, we also see the virtual reality landscapes they are viewing, which are crafted to represent the locations where the traumatising experience occurred. Finally, we view a conventional-looking documentary entitled 'A Sun With No Shadows', as a military expert describes the way the virtual reality programmer selects certain cues to actively trigger memory responses in traumatised soldiers, circumventing the inner prohibition, the barriers to remembering that may have been erected. In a chilling commentary the psychologist says 'VRET offers a way to circumvent the natural avoidance tendency by directly delivering multi-sensory and context-relevant cues that evoke the trauma without demanding that the patient actively try to access his/her experience through effortful memory retrieval' (Brady 2015: 12).

The picture of contemporary war that emerges in Farocki's succinct presentation illustrates Der Derian's concept of 'hygienic' war – war without cost or cruelty. Going further than most theorists in suggesting the imaginary underpinnings and architecture of virtual war, Der Derian points out the close etymological relation of the words 'virtual' and 'virtuous', and claims that contemporary wired war might best be described as a dream of virtuous war. 'The United States diplomatic and military policies', he writes,

> are increasingly based on technological and representational forms of discipline, deterrence, and compellence that could best be described as virtuous war. At the heart of virtuous war is the technical capability and ethical imperative to threaten and, if necessary, actualize violence from a distance – with no or minimal casualties . . . Fought in the same manner as they are represented, by real-time surveillance and TV 'live-feeds', virtuous wars promote a vision of bloodless, humanitarian, hygienic wars. (Der Derian 2000: 772)

Written in 2000, in the aftermath of the first Gulf War and before the attacks of 9/11 and the wars in Iraq and Afghanistan, Der Derian's prescient essay has the value of describing not so much the conduct of actual war as it has occurred over the past decade and a half, but rather the emergence of a new cultural imaginary of war. Although the 'war at a distance' he describes as the present and the future modus of war has been countered by the bloody corporeal warfare of Iraq and Afghanistan, and by the rise of ISIS in the Middle East, the trend he describes in strategic thinking, in the training of soldiers, and above all, in the representation of war in contemporary culture has become one of the chief frameworks for imagining war in the twenty-first century.

The ongoing fascination with virtual war as a paradigm is illuminated in Farocki's videos. As we watch soldiers in *Images of War (at a Distance)* navigate the virtual battlefield, interact on a set with actors pretending to be Iraqis and recreate in video-game form the traumas of actual battle – in a 'landscape without shadows', as Farocki points out – it becomes clear that the imaginary reach of digital war supercedes its actual implementation and utility. As Der Derian writes about virtuous war, 'Call it a dream-state, a symbolic realm, or an unreality: virtuous war projects a mythos as well as an ethos, a fund of collective unconscious for an epoch's greatest aspirations and greatest insecurities' (Der Derian 2000: 774). Seen as a cultural dreamscape, a new mythology of war, virtual war conveys a powerful and seductive scenario in which the anguish of killing, the tragedy of loss, the consequences of war – and death itself – are commuted.

TIM HETHERINGTON AND SEBASTIAN JUNGER: THE BODY AND THE MEDIUM OF CULTURAL MEMORY

A very different iconography of contemporary war emerges in the photographs and films of Tim Hetherington and in the work of the writer Sebastian Junger, who collaborated with Hetherington in Afghanistan to produce *Restrepo* and the book *Infidel*. Against the disembodied depictions of violence that dominate the Farocki installation, the work of Hetherington and Junger centres on the somatic experiences of war, illuminating the way the embodied politics of war intersects with the history of war representation. Emphasising the body at risk, their work captures a range of genre associations, reaching back to the images of Edward Steichen and Alexander Gardner, and further, to the work of Goya and others.

In a series of dramatic, high contrast images, we view the extreme conditions of corporeal risk the soldiers experience in battle as well as the surprising, almost delicate imagery of soldiers sleeping. A tactile sense of physical life dominates the film and the photographs. The soldier's relation to the battle space, moreover, is portrayed as an immersive contest with the terrain, a life and death engagement with the mountain gravel, the low lying brush, and the invisible enemy fighters of the Korengal conflict zone. In the work of Hetherington and Junger, the soldiers' tactile, haptic experiences in the field in Afghanistan are placed in relief.

Gregory has written about the experience of war as a compendium of bodily experiences, a 'haptic geography' consisting of touch, hearing, smell and taste – senses that exceed and overwrite the limited knowledge of the battle zone provided by cartography and by sight:

> The remote orderings of military violence were never autonomous projections onto a pure plane; they also depended on the bodies of soldiers whose apprehension of the battle space was always more than visual. In part, this was a matter of affect, but it was also a matter of knowledge – of what I call a *corpography* rather than a cartography. (Gregory 2015)

Taking examples from literature, poetry and painting, Gregory provides a brief history of the sensory decoding that takes place in war – a history of the senses in the most extreme conditions of sense experience. He defines corpography in a way that I feel pertains directly to the work of Hetherington and Junger:

> By 'corpography' I mean a mode of apprehending, ordering and knowing the battle space through the body as an acutely physical field in which the senses of sound, smell, taste and touch were increasingly privileged (over the optical-visual register of cartography) to produce a somatic geography or a corpo-reality. (Gregory 2015)

Hetherington and Junger's work illustrates the particular sensual geography of the war in Afghanistan, a war that Gregory argues is defined not by the abstractions of remote targeting and cyber weaponry – although the weaponry of twenty-first-century war is widely deployed – but rather by the somatic experience of the battlefront. Contemporary warfare, he contends, is no less defined by corporeal experience than are the trench warfare of World War I, the desert warfare of World War II and the jungle war of Vietnam:

> Through the circulation of military imagery and its ghosting in video games, it is too easy to think of contemporary warfare as optical war hypostatised: a war fought on screens and through digital images . . . Yet for all their liquid violence, today's wars are still shaped and even confounded by the multiple, material environments through which they are fought and which they, in their turn, re-shape. (Gregory 2015)

The visual vocabulary of Hetherington and Junger's work, characterised by deep intimacy with life in the outpost, articulates in a concentrated way the physical exposure, the risk and the sense knowledge of space and terrain that the war in Afghanistan entails. It also conveys the sensuality of life in the outpost, rendered in a series of group shots and chiaroscuro portraits that recall the long history of visual representations of soldiers and war. Hetherington's still photographs, in particular, make explicit reference to the history of war photography – the work of Gardner, Steichen and Don McCullin among others – in a style that brings the new wars of the twenty-first century into dialogue with the past.

   In the double-voicing that imbues these images of embodiment – in the way the past communicates with the present in the poses, iconography and emotional life conveyed in this work – we can sense a historical intuition, an awareness of the historicity of the moment in which the images were made. The film *Restrepo* and the photographs collected in *Infidel* seem to thematise their own evanescence, conveying a powerful sense of the erasure of war, especially its imagery of loss and sacrifice, from the visual vocabulary of the West. Three pieces can be considered exemplary – the photograph 'Man Eden'; the image which I will call 'War Trauma', which won the 2007 World Press Photo award (both from *Infidel*); and the video *Sleeping Soldiers single screen*.

The first example, 'Man Eden', is a large, two-page photograph placed at the centre of the book. In this work we view a small group of shirtless men shovelling dirt into bags that will be used to reinforce their bunker (see Figure 4.2). The golden lighting, the muscled torsos and the poses of both relaxation and exertion communicate a sense of nonchalant grace and of physical pleasure in work. Task performance, ordinary behaviour, the camaraderie of life in the camp – the photograph 'Man Eden' recalls the well-known topos of life in the camp, first seen in war films in Edison's 1897 'War Actualities', and in an even earlier iteration in the American Civil War photography of Alexander Gardner and Matthew Brady. An impression of harmony and rustic enjoyment is evoked in this image, cross-hatched in a complex way by our awareness of what lies just outside the frame, the gun emplacements, the barbed wire, the invisible enemy soldiers. The central placement of the image in the book underlines its importance.

Figure 4.2: Tim Hetherington's 'Man Eden', from *Infidel* (2007).

Sebastian Junger has spoken of the 'truth of combat as a form of bonding', that war is the 'only chance men have to love each other unconditionally' (Junger 2013). In the photograph 'Man Eden', with its sense of intimate enclosure, this idea is powerfully expressed. Here, the bodies of the soldiers are portrayed in the iconographic language of male youth and beauty. Removed momentarily from the terror and mortal risk that surrounds them, the soldiers communicate the potential of youth, with the pathological experience of combat – its tearing of bodies and minds – bracketed out of frame. War enters the image only obliquely, in the physical togetherness of the men in the outpost, and in the echoes of earlier wars that reverberate in the image.

In its subtle evocation of the history of war photography and film, 'Man Eden' calls to mind an established tradition that can be traced to the beginnings of photography, a tradition now fading from view.[1] The images through which Western war has been understood and disseminated – most recently in the work of embedded photographers such as Hetherington – have, almost unnoticed, begun to disappear from media circulation. A deep invisibility now defines much of Western war, a phenomenon that can be traced both to the ascendance of remote, wired warfare, conducted at a distance, as well as the fact that most actual combat is today conducted by Special Operations units in top secret raids and skirmishes. As one writer describes it:

> The mythos of Special Operations has seized our nation's popular imagination, and has proved to be the one prism through which the public will engage with America's wars . . . The secrecy surrounding Special Ops keeps the heavy human costs of war off the front pages. But in doing so, it also keeps the non-military public wholly disconnected from the armed violence carried out in our name. It enables our state of perpetual warfare, and ensures that as little as we care and understand today, we'll care and understand even less tomorrow. (Gallagher 2016)

With so-called black units now conducting the majority of US combat operations, warfare has been removed almost entirely from the system of imagery by which we have come to know war and its costs. To paraphrase the words of Der Derian, war waged by the West has indeed become hygienic, fought through a combination of remote weapons and ground level actions by Special Ops units whose existence and operations are cloaked in secrecy, 'anonymous silhouettes to the country they serve'. (Gallagher 2016). In this regard, Hetherington's images of Battle Company seem almost like residual expressions, artifacts of an earlier period when the drama and carnage of war was photographed and circulated widely – the century and a half in which photography and film created 'a new public sphere of witnessing', and fashioned a relationship between the acts of violence of war and their larger cultural meaning (Lowry 2013).

In the second image I consider – a photograph of a shell-shocked soldier – Hetherington captures a young man in full combat gear a few moments after he has left the battleground. Leaning back, his hand to his face, the soldier radiates distress and exhaustion (see Figure 4.3). The blurred composition reinforces a sense of traumatic aftershock. Wide-eyed, looking vaguely toward the camera, the subject seems only partially aware of the photographer: the photo seems to ask us to imagine what he has just witnessed, to see past the image, to see through the soldier's eyes. The fraternal imagery of the earlier photo, 'Man Eden', has disappeared. What remains is a vision of isolation, a suggestion of psychological injury, and a gesture – one hand held to his face, covering one eye – that suggests an effort to blot from view the events he has just seen. This is the closing photograph in *Infidel*.

Figure 4.3: Tim Hetherington's photograph of a shell-shocked soldier, from *Infidel* (2007).

In an essay describing the imagery of the traumatised face in war films and photographs, Hermann Kappelhoff describes certain shots as 'formulas for pathos' (Kappelhoff 2012a: 4). The insistent focus on the face in the war film, he argues, especially the 'shell-shocked face', can be seen as part of an organised discourse of affective signals designed to create mirror experiences of fear, anxiety and loss in the spectator, emotions that can be readily mapped onto larger messages about nation and sacrifice. Reading a range of messages in the face of the traumatised soldier, Kappelhoff argues that the image of the shell-shocked face in war film and photography arouses in the spectator emotions of intense outrage and empathy for the young soldier, emotions that often quickly refocus into a sense of solidarity and identification:

> In this double-faced impression, the pathos formula gives expression to the fundamental dramatic conflict that structures the poetics of the Hollywood war movie genre. This is the difference between the meaningful death of the sacrifice *for* and the meaningless death of the individual *through* the actions of the nation, the difference between sacrifice and victim. (ibid.: 4)

In this reading, the image of the shell-shocked soldier catalyses a double-edged emotion in the viewer. Provoking an immediate response of anger and repudiation, the portrayal of shell shock is channelled into a sense of collective emotion, transformed into an emblem of sacrifice for nation. In the image of the shell-shocked face, Kappelhoff maintains, a portrait of solitary, psychological suffering is converted into an icon of national cohesion and purpose.

The photo of the traumatised soldier in Hetherington might be read, then, as a contemporary variant of this kind of pathos formula. Charged with emotion, it holds our attention in a way that suggests a latent cultural memory of earlier portrayals of war, reaching back beyond the particular historical frame of Afghanistan. The only photo of its kind in the collection, the photograph evokes an extensive figural history of the shell-shocked face in representations of war: Don McCullin's portrait of a traumatised soldier in Vietnam (1968), Picasso's *Guernica* (1937) and Goya's *Disasters of War* (1810–20) are not too far from view. With this image of battlefield trauma, Hetherington brings the war in Afghanistan into dialogue with the storied tradition of pictorial representations of war, foregrounding the immediate corporeal reality of combat, in which the body at risk becomes, once more, the centre of representation.[2]

When paired with the photo entitled 'Man Eden', however, the photograph of the shell-shocked soldier communicates a very different message. In these two images the contrast between the community of warriors and the isolation and psychological pain of the traumatised soldier comes to the fore. In a recent essay on the extraordinary rise in the number of cases of PTSD in the contemporary US, Junger concludes that the increase in cases, which is now epidemic despite the small number of soldiers engaged in active combat, is due in large part to the soldiers' withdrawal from a sense of community, their removal from the collective experience that defined the battle zone. The sense of shared risk and exposure is erased when they return from war, where isolation, incomprehension and social indifference are the dominant experiences. Moreover, the critical sense of a 'shared public meaning' for war, he argues, is entirely missing in present-day American culture, partially due to the geographic distance of recent wars, as well as to the absence of a clear mandate for war. The pathos formula of the shell-shocked face, described by Kappelhoff as a catalyst for a sense of shared sacrifice and communal cohesion, is here evacuated of its collective social meaning.

Hetherington's shell-shocked soldier photo – The World Press Photo prize winner of 2007 – also casts a new light on images of the past. In evoking the figural history of the shell-shocked face in painting and photography, the photo suggests both a tragic continuity with the past as well as a shift in cultural meaning. An emblematic image of war, Hetherington's photograph references the past in a way that comments on the new condition of soldiers in war, in particular, the experience of isolation that haunts the returning soldier. Hetherington's traumatised soldier, a work rich in genre associations, foregrounds psychological injury in a way that gives the history of war representation a new accent. In doing so, it inflects the past with the perspective of the present.

The video installation entitled *Sleeping Soldiers – single screen* (2009) presents another variation on the theme of the body at risk. Consisting of images of soldiers asleep, with the sounds and images of battle superimposed over their figures, *Sleeping Soldiers – single screen* goes beyond Farocki's soft montage of split screen to create a new type of ideational montage (see Figure 4.4). The use of subtle reverb on the soundtrack and lap dissolves connecting fragmentary visuals suggest the layered, associative imagery of dream. Shots of helicopters hovering overhead, the sounds of automatic weapons and scenes of soldiers running on the mountainside in a laboured attempt to seek cover in the bush are superimposed over the static figures of the young soldiers.

Figure 4.4: A still from Tim Hetherington's video installation *Sleeping Soldiers – single screen* (2009).

As the film exchanges one sleeping figure for another, the visuals and sounds of war unfold without interruption, as if the men were sharing the same dream.

Indirectly, the style and subject matter of Hetherington's video and his photographs of sleeping soldiers highlights the way specific historical conditions shape the imagery of war, creating a particular visual lexicon that comes to characterise certain conflicts. Although the theme of sleeping soldiers is a traditional topic in painting, and appears in a number of images in the World War II photographs of Edward Steichen and others, the photographs and the video, *Sleeping Soldiers*, acquire a new inflection and meaning in the early twenty-first century. The deep sense of intimacy, the closeness that allowed Hetherington to record soldiers in sleep, in moments of expressive physical exuberance, and close up in battle was possible only in the context of the brief period when photographers and journalists were embedded with troops, a period now past. The practice of embedded journalism brought new possibilities into view, while foreclosing others.

In *Sleeping Soldiers*, and indeed throughout Hetherington's work in the Korengal valley, the hardened, punitive masculinity we have come to associate with soldiers in contemporary cultural life is countered by images that emphasise the vulnerability and the youth of the men in war. The intimate relation that Hetherington establishes, however, also comes with certain limitations, foreclosing the possibility of explicit critique, and suggesting, at least for some writers, an uncritical embrace of the war in Afghanistan – an identification with the soldiers made possible by his and Junger's privileged insiders' perspective. One writer, in particular, has characterised *Restrepo* as a 'paramilitary film' (Lebow 2015). In my view, Hetherington and Junger's work underlines both the potential and the limitations of embedded journalism, which by definition presumes a collaborative relationship with the military. In an appreciative but critical essay, Duganne writes:

> Even though Hetherington's *Sleeping Soldiers* enlarges the visual scope of photojournalism beyond the formal tropes of instantaneity and immediacy as well as distance and reflection, in the end the installation does nothing to disrupt the combined effects that these representations of conflict have had on our visual understanding of the war in Afghanistan, including most importantly, the collusion of the US military with them . . . *Sleeping Soldiers* is the product of an embedding system that has likewise gone unchecked by the mainstream press. (Duganne 2015: 277)

CONCLUSION

This essay has focused on the cultural imaginary of war in the contemporary period, which is divided, I argue, between dream-like scenarios of wired war – war at a distance – and its mirror reversal, the persistent focus on contemporary war as an intensely somatic experience, linked to historical memories of earlier wars, and defined as a new layer in a long and deep emotional archeology of fraternity and loss. In the preceding pages I described several ways that the new wars, in a new century defined by war, are both spectacularly visible, as never before, and somehow erased from view, kept outside the frame, without narrative voice or social meaning. The two projects I consider here speak to this veiling of war in the very process of rendering it visually. Both works attempt to capture a transitional moment in the way war is represented and understood.

The artists I discuss in this essay present two alternatives, each of which is limited and partial, but which together provide a kind of map of the terrain. With their focus on the touchscape of modern war, Hetherington's films and photographs foreground the theme of the body as a medium of knowledge and imagination. In depicting the portfolio of embodied experiences in war – the adrenalised intensity of combat, the close fraternity among the soldiers, and the psychic and physical punishment of battle – Hetherington and Junger define and clarify a particularly charged zone of experience. In Farocki's *Images of War (at a Distance)*, by contrast, the spectacle of disembodied, virtuous war, war without visible risk or consequence, illuminates a fascination with power at a distance that reverberates in both popular and intellectual culture, with the work of video game artists on the one hand, and theorists such as Baudrillard and Virilio on the other, offering shared points of reference.

Rather than being seen as contradictory and incommensurate, the wartime images of embodiment in Hetherington and Junger and the invisible practices of wired war depicted in the work of Farocki may be better understood as the recto/verso of each other. On the one hand, images of the body at risk remind us of the existential character of war, even as the body is actively erased from the main theatres of conflict. The role of photography and film in creating a potent social awareness of the stakes and costs of war – provoking what one writer describes as a 'new public culture of witnessing' – has given war photography and film a defining role in the way we perceive and understand the history of twentieth- and twenty-first-century conflict (Lowry 2013). On the other hand, the myth of bodiless war, rendered powerfully as myth in the work of Farocki, speaks to a different cultural imaginary, one that is shaped by perceptions of ubiquitous violence and constant threat that can be contained only by satellite surveillance and networked weapons systems – an open-ended narrative cloaked in fantasies of omnipotence. Suspended somewhere between the two scenarios I have sketched above, contemporary war has to a large extent eluded the symbolic patterning that might provide a broad sense of social meaning and coherence. In these two radically different scenarios of war, however, we can see, in clarified form, the competing cultural imaginaries that now define the representation of war in the twenty-first century, and perhaps begin to engage with the changing character of war in contemporary life.

NOTES

1. For example, the imagery of horseplay and joking in camp before the onset of battle is part of the standard iconography of war representation, and has been seen in war films since Edison's 1897 'War Actualities', and, in an earlier iteration, in the American Civil War photography of Alexander Gardner and Matthew Brady.

2. For some writers the photo gives us a picture of war in Afghanistan that seems too familiar. As Erina Duganne reports, two judges on the World Press Photo jury in 2007 said later that Hetherington's photo was 'an amalgam of all the images of war and death that we have embedded in our memory', and that it was perfectly geared to the World Press Photo competition. For her, the mode of address of the photograph is politically suspect. She criticises it for 'casting the world in the same mold over and over again' (Duganne 2015: 272).

BIBLIOGRAPHY

Brady, S. (2015), 'The soldier cycle: Harun Farocki: *Images of War (at a Distance)*', *Performance Studies Reader Third Edition*. New York: Routledge. Available at <https://www.academia.edu/7468229/The_Soldier_Cycle_Harun_Farockis_Images_of_War_at_a_Distance_> (last accessed 18 January 2015).

Castner, B. (2014), 'Afghanistan: a stage without a play', *LA Review of Books*, 2 October. Available at <http://lareviewofbooks.org/essay/afghanistan-stage-without-play> (last accessed 15 May 2015).

Coker, C. (2004), *The Future of War: the Re-enchantment of War in the Twenty First Century*, Oxford: Blackwell.

Das, S. (2008), *Touch and Intimacy in First World War Literature*, Cambridge: Cambridge University Press.

Der Derian, J. (2000), 'Virtuous war/virtual theory', *International Affairs*, 76.4, October, pp. 771–88.

Der Derian, J. (2009), *Virtuous War*, New York: Routledge.

Duganne, E. (2015), 'Uneasy witnesses: Broomberg, Chanarin, and photojournalism's expanded field', in J. E. Hill and V. R. Schwartz (eds), *Getting the Picture: The Visual Culture of the News,* London: Bloomsbury, pp. 272–9.

Gallagher, M. (2016), 'Welcome to the age of the commando', *New York Times*, 30 January. Available at <http://nyti.ms/1SiJDvJ> (last accessed 9 February 2016).

Gregory, D. (2015), 'The natures of war', *Antipode*, 48.1. Available at <http://onlinelibrary.wiley.com/doi/10.1111/anti.12173/full> (last accessed 1 April 2016).

Hetherington, T. and S. Junger, (2010), *Infidel*, London: Chris Boot.

Hetherington, T. (2009), *Sleeping Soldiers* 3-screen video installation. Single screen version available at <https://vimeo.com/18395855> (last accessed 1 May 2016).

Jameson, F. (2009), 'War and representation', *PMLA*, 124.5 (October), pp. 1532–47.

Junger, S. (2010), *War*, New York: Hachette.

Junger, S. (2013), *Which Way is the Front Line from Here? The Life and Time of Tim Hetherington*, DVD.

Junger, S. (2015), 'How PTSD became a problem far beyond the battlefield', *Vanity Fair,* June 2015. Available at <http://www.vanityfair.com/news/2015/05/ptsd-war-home-sebastian-junger> (last accessed 1 June 2016).

Kappelhoff, H. (2012a), 'For love of country: World War II in Hollywood cinema at the turn of the century', unpublished manuscript (English translation supplied by the author).

Kappelhoff, H. (2012b), 'Sense of community: die filmische Komposition eines moralischen Gefühls' ['Sense of community: the filmic composition of a moral feeling'], in S. R. Fauth, K. Green Krejberg and J. Süselbeck (eds), *Repräsentationen des Krieges. Emotionalisierungsstrategien in der Literatur und in den audiovisuellen*

Medien vom 18. bis zum 21. Jahrhundert [*Representations of War: Emotionalising Strategies in Literature and Audio-visual Media from the Eighteenth to the Twenty-first Century*], Göttingen: Wallstein, pp. 43–57.

Lebow, A. (2015), 'The unwar film', in A. Lebow and A. Juhasz (eds), *A Companion to Contemporary Documentary Film*, Malden: Wiley Blackwell, pp. 454–74.

Lowry, R. (2013), 'Dead bodies and a standing president: Alexander Gardner's "terrible reality"', Presentation at the University of St Andrews, June.

Lowry, R. (2015), *The Photographer and the President: Abraham Lincoln, Alexander Gardner, and the Images that Made a Presidency*, New York: Rizzoli Ex Libris.

Luttwak, E. (1995), 'Toward post-heroic warfare', *Foreign Affairs*, May/June. Available at <https://www.foreignaffairs.com/articles/chechnya/1995-05-01/toward-post-heroic-warfare> (last accessed 1 April 2016).

Luttwak, E. (2001), *Strategy: The Logic of War and Peace*, Cambridge, MA: Harvard University Press.

McDonald, K. (2012), 'Grammars of violence, modes of embodiment and frontiers of the subject', in K. McSorley (ed.), *War and the Body: Militarisation, Practice and Experience*, London: Routledge, pp.138–51.

McSorley, K. (2012), 'Helmetcams, militarized sensation, and "somatic war"', *Journal of War and Culture Studies*, 5.1, pp. 47–58.

Sharpe, R. (2010), 'Combat fatigue: Tim Hetherington's intimate portraits of US soldiers at rest reveal the other side of Afghanistan', *The Independent*, 11 September. Available at <http://www.independent.co.uk/arts-entertainment/art/features/combat-fatigue-tim-hetheringtons-intimate-portraits-of-us-soldiers-at-rest-reveal-the-other-side-of-2073877.html> (last accessed 1 April 2016).

CHAPTER 5

Disappearing Bodies: Visualising the Maywand District Murders

Thomas Gregory

The discipline of International Relations has always had a troubled relationship with the bodies that inhabit its world. The bodies that sweat, strain and toil to make consumer goods for the global market rarely feature in books about the international political economy. The weak, malnourished and dehydrated bodies of refugees fleeing war zones around the world rarely figure in discussions about immigration. And the broken, bloody and bruised bodies of those targeted in war are often invisible in discussions about military conflict. In her recent book *Bodies of Violence: Theorizing Embodied Subjects in International Relations*, Lauren Wilcox argues that the body rarely figures in discussions about war in spite of its central role, leaving the discipline ill-equipped to deal with the dead and injured bodies that are piling up around us. The corporeal dimension of international politics has been neglected for so long that Wilcox is concerned that it has become almost 'unrecognisable even as the modes of violence that use, target and construct bodies . . . have proliferated' (2015: 1). Likewise, Christine Sylvester (2012) has warned that the discipline's obsessive interest with states and state systems means that people's embodied experiences of war are often erased from view. Thirty years after Elaine Scarry first penned the phrase, it is still possible to read pages upon pages of military history without ever encountering a basic acknowledgement that the primary purpose of 'the events described is to alter (to burn, to blast, to shell, to cut) human tissue' (1985: 65).

If the discipline of International Relations is marked by its silences around the body at war, then cinema can be seen as one of the few places where the embodied effects of war can be seen in full view.

Few can forget seeing the bullet-riddled bodies, unclaimed limbs and puddles of blood on Omaha Beach during the frenetic opening scenes of Steven Spielberg's *Saving Private Ryan* (1998). The volatile bodies of suicide bombers wearing explosive vests and the armoured bodies of those sent to defuse them are essential to the story told by Kathryn Bigelow in *The Hurt Locker* (2009); and in *Lebanon* (2009) we see both the hot, sweaty and constricted bodies of the Israeli soldiers cloistered inside the tank and the bodies of those civilians visible through their gun sight. There are, of course, many films where the pain and suffering caused by war is kept hidden from view or celebrated with stylistic representations that mask the full horror. Nevertheless, it seems that film is uniquely placed to capture the death and destruction caused by war, along with the embodied experiences of those living and dying on the front lines.

This chapter is concerned with the appearance of the body in cinematic representations of war, but it pays particular attention to those bodies that manage to disappear from view even when they seem to form a central part of the narrative. The case study that forms the basis of this work is not a fictional account of war but an award-winning documentary entitled *The Kill Team* (2013), which was written, directed and produced by the journalist Dan Krauss. The documentary claims to provide an unflinching portrait of a group of American soldiers who executed at least three Afghan civilians, posed for photographs alongside their corpses and then removed body parts from their victims to keep as souvenirs. In the press notes, for example, the film-makers promise to 'take us inside a story that was largely impenetrable to the media'. But what is remarkable about the film is just how little attention is focused on the life and death of the victims. Drawing on Judith Butler's work on the politics of framing, this chapter will examine how the mangled, disfigured and mutilated corpses of these people were made visible. The argument is fairly straightforward: I will suggest that the decision to focus on the experiences of those who perpetrated these crimes came at the expense of those who were actually targeted. The pain and suffering that was inflicted on the bodies of these civilians – along with their names, their faces and their life stories – was quickly relegated to the margins of the debate.

DISAPPEARING VIOLENCE

I never wanted to kill anyone . . . ever

Spc. Adam Winfield

The Maywand District Murders, as they have become known, were a series of incidents that took place in the Afghan province of Kandahar, resulting in the deaths of at least three Afghan civilians and the imprisonment of seven American soldiers. The first attack took place on 15 January 2010 in the village of Lo Mohammad Kalay, where a fifteen-year-old boy was tending to his father's crops. Members of the Fifth Stryker Brigade had arrived in the village earlier that morning to investigate reports that Taliban insurgents were hiding in a maze of secret tunnels around the village, but what they discovered was not the network of enemy hideouts they had been expecting. Instead, they were greeted by a 'frustratingly familiar sight: destitute Afghan farmers living without electricity or running water; bearded men with poor teeth in tattered traditional clothes; young kids eager for candy and money' (Boal 2011). Undeterred, two soldiers – Specialist (Spc.) Jeremy Morlock and Private First Class (Pfc.) Andrew Holmes – peeled off from the rest of their unit to implement a plan they had devised back at base: to murder an innocent civilian but make it look like a legitimate combat kill (Boone 2011; Hujer 2010). Eventually they found the young boy, whose name was Gul Mudin, in a field on the outskirts of the village. Although he was unarmed and posed no threat to their safety, they detonated a grenade to create the illusion that they were under attack, before shooting him dead (Boal 2011).

After completing routine identification checks, which involved stripping the boy naked to search for tattoos and photographing his face on their portable biometric scanner, members of the unit started abusing his remains. His body was arranged into a series of poses, whilst soldiers took photographs of themselves with his corpse. In one image, Morlock can be seen squatting beside the body with his thumbs up (*Der Spiegel* 2011). In another image, the boy's body is held aloft by a scruff of hair like the carcass of a dead animal killed on a trophy hunt. Once they had finished taking pictures, the staff sergeant took a pair of medical shears from his pack and removed the boy's little finger, which he then presented to Holmes as a souvenir of his first 'combat kill' (Boal 2011). At least two more incidents involving the death of an innocent civilian, the planting of weapons to legitimise the kill and the desecration of the victim's body took place in the following months. In one of these attacks a deaf and intellectually disabled man was killed on a dark road close to their base after soldiers became suspicious of his activities (Boal 2011). In the second incident an elderly man was frogmarched from his home and executed in a neighbouring compound. In both instances body parts were removed from the victim and kept as human trophies, including teeth, fingers and parts of the skull (Boal 2011; Boone 2011).

One might expect a documentary about the murder and desecration of Afghan civilians to begin as such, but *The Kill Team* is primarily concerned with the actions of the perpetrators rather than the experiences of the victims. In an interview with *PBS*, director Dan Krauss argues that it was not the physical injuries of those targeted that interested him but the 'moral injuries' suffered by those who perpetrated these crimes. The aim of the film, he suggests, is to highlight the 'psychological wound that comes from having taken an action – or failed to prevent an action – that is a betrayal of one's core moral values' (Philips 2015). Rather than focusing on the disfigured corpses of the victims or the family members left behind, the film follows the legal battles that members of the unit face upon their return to the US. Krauss pays particular attention to the experiences of Spc. Adam Winfield, who was one of the youngest members in his battalion. In an interview, Krauss said that he was haunted by the tragic 'Shakespearean dimension' of his story: 'a young man who had attempted to act in the moral right and who instead found himself confronting a moral abyss' (quoted in Philips 2015).

We first encounter our protagonist in a prison cell at the United States Army Corrections Facility, where he is awaiting trial for premeditated murder. Dressed in his prison uniform, Winfield reflects on how it was that a man who 'loved wearing his uniform' and was a 'proud member of the Army' ended up inside a military penitentiary facing the possibility of life imprisonment (quoted in Krauss 2013). However, it soon becomes clear that the documentary is not interested in the crimes that he committed or the effects that they had on the families of those affected, and rather is preoccupied with the sense that he is being made a scapegoat by the military. During one of the first substantive scenes in the film, we find ourselves in a meeting room with Winfield and his parents as their attorney explains that the trial has been delayed because further evidence may have come to light, which he considers to be 'bullshit' (Montalvo quoted in Krauss 2013). But he warns the family that he has 'to walk a fairly close line on the morality of this because [Adam] is not entirely clean gloved' (quoted in Krauss 2013). His family clearly disagrees. Although he is implicated in the murder of at least one of the victims, his family maintain that he was forced to do it against his will by more senior colleagues (Goetz and Hujer 2011). As his mother Emma explains:

> It is a military justice system. Unlike the civilian world where there are impartial parties the people that are accusing Adam of these very crimes are, in essence, the same people who determine

who will hear the case, who will be the jury, who will hand down the decision for sentencing. They are the judge and jury, literally the judge and jury. (quoted in Krauss 2013)

The family's frustration with the military justice systems stems from the fact that Winfield did try to alert the authorities to the crimes that were being perpetrated by members of the Afghan Kill Team. Halfway through the film we are shown the transcript of a Facebook conversation between Winfield and his father Christopher, in which he admits that members of his unit have deliberately targeted Afghan civilians and then staged fake combat scenarios to mask their crimes. As Winfield explains:

> I couldn't take it anymore and I wanted to tell somebody what was going on. I didn't have access to MPs [military police] but if I told someone in the chain of command it would come right back because that's how things are in infantry units. We handle things in-house. (quoted in Krauss 2013)

When Winfield says that he is unsure how to proceed, his father offers to help out, promising to pass on the information to somebody back in the US without compromising his son's safety. After he left messages with a number of different agencies, it became increasingly clear that nobody wanted to hear what he had to say. Christopher tells the film-makers that he called Army CID in Virginia, the CID office in Fort Lewis, Senator Bill Nelson's office, the Army chaplain's office and the assistant chaplain's office, but no one ever returned his call (Krauss 2013). When he finally managed to get through to someone in the command centre at Fort Lewis, the officer told him that it was his son's word against the others so there was nothing he could do unless someone else confessed (Krauss 2013; see also Boal 2011; Goetz and Hujer 2011).

Rumours of his intervention eventually made their way back to base and his colleagues were not best pleased to hear that someone had snitched. As a result of his actions, Winfield was subjected to a campaign of intimidation and abuse. Following one trip to the Army chaplain, Winfield was hauled into the office of Staff Sergeant Calvin Gibbs – the man responsible for removing Mudin's little finger – and warned that his life was in danger (Krauss 2013). In his interview with film-makers, Morlock also admitted that he considered Winfield to be a 'liability' and had plotted with others to 'take him out' (quoted in Krauss 2013). Holmes also confessed to being part of conversations where plans were made to 'silence' Winfield, including one that involved dropping 'a tow bar on him so he'd go away' (quoted in Krauss 2013; McGreal 2011; Whitlock 2010).

It is clear that his attempts to alert the authorities to these murders had made him a target and his family clearly believe that he was a victim of circumstance rather than a willing executioner. As his father explains:

> Adam's a pawn in the big picture. He was stuck in the middle of nowhere. He had Taliban shooting at him on one side. He had his own guys threatening to kill him if he said anything on his other side. He had guns pointed at him in both directions. What do you do? (quoted in Krauss 2013)

The film also runs with this narrative, presenting Winfield as some sort of tragic hero who was being punished for trying to do the right thing. Although he was clearly responsible for some horrendous acts of violence, Winfield is portrayed as someone who risked his own life to expose these crimes, but was ignored by a military hierarchy unwilling or unable to accept that American soldiers could perpetrate such unspeakable acts of violence. He eventually pleaded guilty to the lesser charges of involuntary manslaughter and the use of an illegal controlled substance following a plea deal by his lawyer, and was sentenced to three years in prison. What is missing from this account is any discussion of the death and destruction that Winfield and his colleagues were responsible for causing. The pain and suffering experienced by the victims is almost incidental to the story. What matters are the experiences of this tragic young man, who was abandoned by those who were supposed to be looking after him and now is being punished for his attempts to make amends.

DISAPPEARING BODIES

> There are no good men left here
>
> Spc. Adam Winfield

The depiction of violence in *The Kill Team* raises some important questions about the disappearance of human suffering. Although the film promises to explain what happened on the dusty streets of Maywand, it is primarily concerned with the lives of those responsible rather than the deaths of those who were targeted. In one interview, the director suggested that the real purpose of the film was to raise questions about who was really responsible for the attacks on Afghan civilians. As Krauss explains:

> Ultimately, the anger the audience comes away with arises from the fact that Adam was put in that situation in the first place. He had some responsibility in what happened, but he should have never been there. That's the thing that really riles people, but their sympathy is also tempered by the fact that Adam had options – and this is something that he has a deep regret about. He's living with the idea that he could've done more, and that he should've done more. He has a huge amount of guilt that he didn't do enough to stop these guys (quoted in Kemmerle 2014).

The problem here is that the death and destruction caused by Winfield and his colleagues quickly disappears into the background. Although the mutilated corpses of the dead Afghans are clearly integral to the story, the film is not primarily concerned with them or their families.

The disappearance of the wounded body is reinforced during the second part of the documentary, which focuses on how it was that a group of seemingly ordinary men could commit such extraordinary acts of violence. Although we get a glimpse of the dead in photographs and hear details of their demise in the testimony of the perpetrators, the film is primarily concerned with the psychological state of those responsible rather than the experiences of the victims (see Figure 5.1). Indeed, it is not until the twentieth minute of the film that we see any evidence of the crimes that were committed. Considering that the film is only eighty-two minutes long, it is quite an achievement to cover so much of the story before actually revealing details of the violence that was enacted. It is also worth noting that none of the victims' families are interviewed at any point during the film, so we are given no insight into the damage these attacks had on the wider community. What matters are the reasons why these soldiers committed the crimes, not the effects they had on the people affected.

The film claims that there are three key reasons why this violence was allowed to occur: the boredom around base, the strategic decisions made by commanding officers and the lax disciplinary codes that allowed them to get away with so much for so long. The first argument suggests that the violence perpetrated by the Afghan Kill Team can be explained as a reaction to the glaring disconnect between the action and adventure these soldiers were promised and the boredom they encountered upon their arrival. In her work on the emotional burdens

Figure 5.1: Lawyer examines photographs of abuse in *The Kill Team* (2013).

of war, Victoria Basham has argued that more time is spent waiting for combat than actually fighting in it (2015: 129). In contrast to the frenetic images of conflict that we see in films and read about in novels, the reality of war is often much less exhilarating and it can be difficult for soldiers to deal with this fact. As Basham explains, 'boredom is both an enduring feature of war and something that soldiers in war must endure' (2015: 130–1). In *The Kill Team*, a number of the soldiers interviewed complained that they had been promised a 'warrior's paradise' only to discover that most of their time would be spent on routine foot patrols or lazing about base (quoted in Krauss 2013).

The interview with Pfc. Andrew Holmes illustrates this point rather well, as it exposes the stark contrast between their expectations and their actual experiences. Recalling his first live firefight, Holmes describes the excitement of having bullets 'flying right over our heads [and] hitting the trees right behind you' (quoted in Krauss 2013). Despite the obvious danger, he said that all he could think about was the music to '"Danger Zone" from *Top Gun*' (quoted in Krauss 2013). His colleague was even more explicit, telling film-makers that 'all the bullshit paid off right there, all the ruck marching and the dumb shit, it was all worth it' (Morlock quoted in Krauss 2013). This encounter with enemy troops turned out to be the exception rather than the norm. Much of the time spent in Afghanistan, Holmes argued, was as 'boring as fuck'. Once the initial buzz had dissipated, it 'was back to the grind, hating life, just sucking' (quoted in Krauss 2013). The suggestion here is that the murder and desecration of innocent civilians should be seen as an attempt by members of the Afghan Kill Team to overcome this boredom and satisfy their desire to become real warriors.

The second argument focuses on the soldiers' frustration with the strategic decisions that had been made by their superiors, which focused on winning the hearts and minds of ordinary people rather than defeating the enemy in open combat. The shift towards 'population-centric warfare', as it became known, was based on the idea an insurgency could not be defeated with guns and bullets but by gaining the support or tacit acquiescence of the local people (US Army 2006). Rather than killing insurgents or capturing territory, soldiers were now expected to fulfil an array of humanitarian roles, such as building schools, fixing hospitals and providing basic amenities (Kilcullen 2006). It has been suggested that this very public disavowal of kinetic force simply camouflaged the death and destruction that remained so essential to military operations (Gilmore 2011; Gregory 2008; Welland 2015a). However, it was not the concealment of violence that worried members of the Afghan Kill Team but the sense that their status as soldiers was being downgraded and undermined.

A number of soldiers interviewed in the film expressed their unease with the restrictions that had been placed on the use of force and the expectation that they should be assisting the Afghan people rather than killing them. This frustration was clearly apparent in comments made by Morlock when asked to describe a routine day out on patrol. As Morlock explains, 'we drive out to a village, find a local elder or mullah . . . and then you drive back' (quoted in Krauss 2013). He goes on, 'what the hell are we risking our fucking necks for, driving across the desert, waiting for our buddy to get blown up, just to go ask some old dude some questions?!' (quoted in Krauss 2013).

Some of the other interviewees were even more upset, suggesting the tighter rules of engagement were directly responsible for the attacks on civilians. As Pfc. Justin Stoner explains:

> You can't shoot someone because of this reason, you can't shoot someone because of that reason. They blow you up and you see them driving away. *It was nothing like everyone hyped it to be and part of that is probably why things happened.* (quoted in Krauss 2013, emphasis added)

The final reason that is given to explain the attacks on Afghan civilians was the lax disciplinary standards around the base, which allowed these young and impressionable recruits to lose sight of their moral compass. A number of references are made to the widespread use of drugs around base, with Winfield suggesting that plans to kill civilians were first discussed during their regular 'smoke sessions' (quoted in Krauss 2013). The film also makes some general points about the corrosive effects of war on an individual's capacity for moral reflection, suggesting the brutality of conflict inevitably leads to the erosion of normal moral standards. As Morlock explains, 'the constant pressure of having to kill and the risk of being killed yourself . . . it was impossible not to surrender to the insanity of it all' (quoted in Krauss 2013). The film does, however, single out one man in particular for criticism, with a number of the soldiers blaming Staff Sergeant Calvin Gibbs for leading them astray.

Although Gibbs is not interviewed in the film, it is clear from the other interviews that he made quite the impression when he arrived in Afghanistan. Holmes recalls one encounter with Gibbs in the gym when he asked him about the six skulls tattooed down the side of his leg. Although he didn't get a straight answer from Gibbs, a colleague was able to fill him in later on. 'They're the dudes he's killed', he was told (quoted in Krauss 2013). In addition to his imposing physique and morbid tattoos, Gibbs was also seen as a bit of a troublemaker, but those working under him saw this as a positive quality. Unlike squad leaders who 'followed the rules to a tee', one soldier argued that his indifference towards the rules gave them the confidence to go out on patrol in difficult areas. There was no question that he would give the order to return fire, even if it might violate the strict rules of engagement (Stoner quoted in Krauss 2013). However, the film suggests that his reputation as a troublemaker was responsible for leading others astray. Morlock, for example, claims conversations with Gibbs would often involve detailed discussions about how civilians could be killed without anyone getting caught (quoted in Krauss 2013). It was not long before these conversations turned into something more sinister.

Each of these arguments seeks to explain why these soldiers went on to commit such horrendous acts of violence. By drawing attention to the operational environment in which these soldiers were working, the mixed messages they were getting from their superiors and the detrimental impact war has on a soldier's ability to make sound moral judgements, the film certainly challenges the 'bad apple' narrative that was favoured by the military. But something is missing from the narrative. The emphasis that is placed on the psychology of the perpetrators ensures that the experiences of those who were targeted disappear from view. The violence that was inflicted on their bodies, the emotional turmoil experienced by their families and the difficulties faced by the communities recovering from these attacks is almost incidental to the narrative. This does not mean, of course, that the violence perpetrated by the Afghan Kill Team is entirely absent from view. We catch glimpses of their wounded bodies and we are told their names in passing, but the film is not interested in their voices, their concerns or their experiences. This is a film about the men who killed and mutilated them, not the victims themselves.

THE POLITICS OF GRIEF

> You're seeing guts and gore all the time and war and you're like: 'all right, whatever'. I mean I'm not going to make a fucking bone necklace but if you want one man then whatever, that's cool.
>
> Spc. Jeremy Morlock

The disappearance of the victims from the film's narrative shares a commonality with the official narrative that it tries so hard to disrupt. On the surface, it certainly seems that the film acts as an important antidote to the sanitised reports circulated by the Department of Defense. In a statement released shortly after details of the Maywand District Murders were first published in the German magazine *Der Spiegel*, the Pentagon sought to distance itself from the violence by locating responsibility with the individuals responsible. These attacks were, it argued, 'repugnant to us as human beings and contrary to the standards and values of the United States Army' (DoD 2011a). The rogue unit narrative was reiterated a few days later when a second batch of images was released by *Rolling Stone*, with the military seeking to blame a few bad apples rather than accept responsibility itself. As one official explained, 'we are troubled that any soldier would lose his moral compass' (DoD 2011b). The narrative gets a little more complicated, however, when you consider the results of an internal investigation, which accepted that lax disciplinary standards and mixed messages from above may have played a part. Extracts of the classified report, which has been seen by journalists at *Der Spiegel*, castigated senior officers for allowing soldiers to grow facial hair, wear short-sleeved tops and smoke drugs (Assmann, Goetz and Hujer 2011).

The report also blames Colonel Harry Tunnell, who was the commanding officer at Forward Operating Base Ramrod, for his 'inattentiveness to administrative matters' and for creating an 'environment in which misconduct could occur' (Assmann, Goetz and Hujer 2011). In particular, it suggests that Tunnell had failed to implement the military's preferred counter-insurgency doctrine properly because of his own personal preference for more traditional and more violent counter-guerrilla tactics. By continuing to emphasise the importance of kinetic operations and kill teams, it is suggested that the younger and more impressionable troops had become confused about their objectives (Assmann, Goetz and Hujer 2011). Although the film suggests that military officials were reluctant to consider wider questions of responsibility, it certainly seems that in private the military had recognised that these crimes were a product of the operational environment rather than a few dysfunctional individuals. Both the film and the official report seem very interested in the experiences of those who perpetrated the crimes and the reasons why they did so. Absent from these texts is any mention of the embodied effects of this violence on the victims or the grief experienced by their families.

The disappearance of certain bodies and the marginalisation of their experiences raises important questions about how these deaths were framed. In her recent work on the politics of grief, Judith Butler has suggested that there is a glaring disconnect between those deaths that are grievable and those that are not. For example, the loss of an American or British soldier is likely to provoke mass outpourings of grief, with thousands of people lining the streets to welcome home their body (2004: 34–5). By contrast, the death of an Afghan or Iraqi civilian is unlikely to generate the same level of concern (Gregory 2012). For Butler, this discrepancy arises from the fact that certain populations do not register as human beings in quite the same way as others because of their racial profile, sexual orientation or religious affiliation (2009: 31). As Butler explains:

> Specific lives cannot be apprehended as injured or lost if they are not first apprehended as living. If certain lives do not qualify as lives or are, from the start, not conceivable as lives within certain epistemological frames, then these lives are never lived nor lost in the full sense. (2009: 1)

This theoretical framework is particularly useful for thinking about the erasure of certain bodies and the disavowal of certain deaths in *The Kill Team* for two specific reasons. On the one hand, it draws attention to the normative violence that underpinned and enabled the attacks on Afghan civilians. On the other hand, it reveals how the film reproduces and reaffirms this exclusionary logic by privileging the experiences of the perpetrators over and above the experiences of the victims.

The discrepancy between those lives that matter and those that do not is clearly evident in derogatory language used by members of the Afghan Kill Team during the film. Reflecting on his thoughts immediately after killing and then mutilating the fifteen-year-old boy, Morlock confessed that 'he didn't register as a person, he was just there' (quoted in Krauss 2013). These sentiments are echoed by Winfield, who confirmed that Morlock and others would frequently make racist comments about the local population, referring to them as 'savages' and 'pieces of shit' (quoted in Krauss 2013). During his trial at Fort Lewis, Gibbs also admitted that he struggled to recognise his victims as human beings. When asked how he was able to inflict such terrible pain and suffering, Gibbs argued that it was no different to taking 'the antlers off a deer' (quoted in McGreal 2011). According to Morlock, the staff sergeant had a 'pure hatred for all Afghanis [sic] and constantly referred to them as savages' (quoted in Whitlock 2010). In the eyes of the Afghan Kill Team, the people they killed and the bodies they desecrated were not fellow human beings but savages who could be targeted without remorse (Gregory 2012). As Butler explains:

> Such populations are 'lose-able', or can be forfeited, precisely because they are framed as already lost or forfeited; they are cast as threats to humanity as we know it, rather than as living populations in needs of protection. (2009: 31)

Part of the problem is that the soldiers were unwilling or unable to differentiate between enemy combatants and the civilian population. As part of counter-insurgency operations, these soldiers were supposed to work with the local community to repair broken buildings and ensure that basic amenities were in place. But it is clear from the interviews that there was a great deal of resentment about these initiatives, particularly after one of their colleagues was killed by an improvised explosive device (Krauss 2013). Although they were supposed to be protecting the Afghan people and rebuilding their communities, most of those interviewed in the film said that they considered locals to be a threat. In response to one question about their relationship with local villagers, Holmes quipped that there were 'lots of friendly people here who want to kill us' (Krauss 2013). Likewise, Morlock complained that:

> We have been here for months and nobody is innocent because these guys know the Taliban. They are either working with them or they are not working with us, and we're here to help and they don't give us any. We're just getting blown up every time we go out there to, you know, just talk with them or build them a well. So fuck 'em! (quoted in Krauss 2013)

In their mind, the people they targeted were not innocent civilians but potential collaborators who were working with the Taliban to attack them and their colleagues. By constituting them as a threat and viewing them as a source of constant danger, the soldiers were unable to recognise Afghan civilians as fellow human beings. As a result, they considered their lives to be profoundly disposable, their deaths profoundly ungrievable.

The dehumanisation of the civilian population was not unique to members of the Afghan Kill Team but a problem that haunted military operations in Afghanistan and Iraq, as the violence witnessed at Abu Ghraib, Bagram airbase and numerous other sites would attest (Richter-Montpetit 2007; Puar 2007; Welland 2015a). The language used to justify the intervention presented Muslim countries as cruel, inhuman and savage, whilst the people that lived there were seen as threats to our very existence (Dalby 2003; Gregory 2004; Said 2001). In addition to the dehumanisation of people, Stephen Graham has shown how the language of occupation has worked to demonise entire cities and reinforce the view that residents should be treated with suspicion. Focusing on the two assaults on the Iraqi city of Fallujah in 2004, for example, he argues that the violence was legitimised on the basis that all 'military-age men' should be viewed as potential enemies irrespective of their actual status (2005: 4). The imaginative geographies that underpinned this assault constituted all those that remained as potential terrorists – leaving their bodies vulnerable, their deaths uncountable – on the basis that they were Iraqis living within a particular location (2005: 8). The view that civilians could be terrorists in disguise or insurgents in the making was a view shared by soldiers across the two conflict zones and reinforced by earlier iterations of the military's official doctrine.

The problem with *The Kill Team* is that it reinforces rather than undermines this hierarchy of grief. I am not suggesting for one moment that the film condones the violence that was inflicted or reinforces racist stereotypes about the Afghan population because this is clearly not the case. What it does do, however, is privilege the experiences of the perpetrators over and above the experiences of those who were targeted. At no point during the film are we asked to mourn the loss of these individuals or share in the grief that is experienced by their family members. Their names are hardly mentioned, their stories are never told and their voices are never heard. They appear only as an anonymous troupe of silent extras, whose fleeting appearance is remarkable only because it is so brief. The figure that we are asked to mourn is that of Adam Winfield, whose life has been ruined by the actions of the Afghan

Figure 5.2: Winfield and family after sentencing in *The Kill Team* (2013).

Kill Team (see Figure 5.2). Winfield is portrayed as the tragic hero of the piece, a young man who enrolled in the military because he wanted to make the world a better place. A young man who fell in with a bad crowd, who was encouraged to commit violent acts even though he knew it was wrong. A young man who tried to warn the authorities, but is now in prison because he did so.

The tragic loss of Winfield's future life is reinforced by the grief experienced by his family. In contrast to the victims, whose grieving families are nowhere to be seen, Winfield's parents are allowed to speak at length about the heartache they feel about his prison sentence and the anger they have for the military. In one scene we see Winfield's mum talking to him on the phone from their family home. Worried that he might give up, she tells him:

Adam, don't start losing faith now. I mean, I know you're there [in prison] day-to-day but, believe me, my heart breaks every day too. And maybe I am not confined, but *I am confined*. (quoted in Krauss 2013)

What matters to the film-maker is not the dismembered bodies of those targeted by the Afghan Kill Team or the families that they left behind, but the men who were responsible for committing these crimes and who are now serving jail sentences for their actions. By privileging the experiences of the perpetrators over the experiences of the victims, the film reinforces a hierarchy of grief that denies the Afghan people a politically qualified subject position and a recognisable human life. Their lives do not seem to matter quite as much as the lives of those who murdered them.

CONCLUSION

The purpose of this chapter has been to consider the visualisation of violence and the disappearance of the wounded body in *The Kill Team*. One might assume that the spectacular nature of the violence and the gruesome dismembering of the dead would ensure that the actions of the Afghan Kill Team be a central part of the film's narrative. However, the mutilated bodies of the victims and the emotional turmoil experienced by the families have only a fleeting role in the story. The purpose of the documentary is not to make this violence visible or to explore its effects on the local community but to shed some light on the lives of the perpetrators. The film's protagonist is not Gul Mudin, the fifteen-year-old boy murdered in his father's field, Marach Agha, the intellectually disabled man killed at the roadside, or Mullah Adahdad, the elderly gentlemen executed outside his house. Instead, the film focuses on the legal battles facing the soldiers upon their return to the US, the impact it has had on their families and the moral burden that they must shoulder for the rest of their lives. The victims and their families barely figure at all. They are a silent, uncredited and unacknowledged cast of background performers, whose stories quickly disappear from view. Their bodies are never made visible, their stories are never told and their experiences are clearly not considered relevant.

The erasure of civilian casualties from cinematic representations of war is not limited to this particular documentary, but is a problem that is reproduced across a variety of films, both in narrative cinema and documentary. As Cora Goldstein explains in Chapter 2, the hierarchies of grief that privilege the experiences of 'our' soldiers at the expense of 'their dead' has been a perennial feature of Hollywood film. The devastation caused by the strategic bombing campaigns on German cities is rarely evident in films set during World War II, which tend to focus on the heroic efforts of the pilots that dropped the bombs rather than the civilians suffering on the ground. Even the more graphic films, which depict the horrific injuries suffered by those fighting on the front lines in uncompromising detail, tend to focus on the pain and suffering of soldiers rather than civilians. Goldstein argues that the pain and suffering of civilians is slightly more visible in films about Afghanistan and Iraq but even then the suffering of others tends to disappear into the background. By focusing on the decisions of individual soldiers to target and kill individual civilians, epitomised in films such as *American Sniper* (2014) and *Zero Dark Thirty* (2012), we only see those deaths that are very clean, very calculated and very controlled. The thousands of others who were killed by heavy artillery fire, stray bullets and coalition airstrikes are never examined (see Chapter 2). Although the circumstances are very different, the suffering of civilians has been displaced by the decision to focus on the experiences of the soldiers and the violence they enacted. It is, as Christina Hellmich argues, 'the voice of the occupier that we get to hear, while the voice of the occupied is silenced' (2014: 474).

It is important to recognise that these silences and disappearances have implications beyond the specific story they are telling. The erasure of these 'foreign' bodies plays an important part in reproducing the hierarchy of grief that underpinned and enabled this violence. The fact that the film-makers did not feel it was important to show us the mutilated bodies of the victims until the twentieth minute of the film or dwell on the pain and suffering that was caused tells us a lot about the values attached to their lives. This does not mean that the solution would be to simply make these bodies reappear. Indeed, it has been suggested that these images may help to reinforce the dehumanisation of the Other, creating an ideological distinction between the body in pain and the body that inflicts pain (Gregory forthcoming). There is no guarantee that the mangled bodies of those targeted by members of the Afghan Kill Team will serve to reaffirm their humanity. It may even serve to reinforce their abjection (Dauphinee 2007). Nevertheless, this brief glimpse of the dead gives us an opportunity to think about the epistemological frames that seem to differentiate between those lives that matter and those that do not. More importantly, it gives us an opportunity to reflect on the pain and suffering that is inflicted on the bodies of others and the grief experienced by those left behind.

BIBLIOGRAPHY

Assmann, K., J. Goetz and M. Hujer (2011), 'Let's kill: report reveals discipline break-down in Kill Team Brigade', *Der Spiegel*, 4 April. Available at <http://www.spiegel.de/international/world/let-s-kill-report-reveals-discipline-breakdown-in-kill-team-brigade-a-754952.html> (last accessed 4 February 2015).

Basham, V. M. (2015), 'Waiting for war: soldiering, temporality and the gendered politics of boredom and joy in military spaces', in L. Åhäll and T. Gregory (eds) *Emotions, Politics and War*, Abingdon: Routledge, pp. 128–40.

Boal, M. (2011), 'The Kill Team: how US soldiers in Afghanistan murdered innocent civilians', *Rolling Stone*, 27 March. Available at <http://www.rollingstone.com/politics/news/the-kill-team-20110327> (last accessed 4 February 2015).

Boone, J. (2011), 'US Army "Kill Team" in Afghanistan posed for photos of murdered civilians', *The Guardian*, 21 May. Available at <http://www.theguardian.com/world/2011/mar/21/us-army-kill-team-afghanistan-posed-pictures-murdered-civilians> (last accessed 4 February 2015).

Butler, J. (2004), *Precarious Life: The Powers of Mourning and Violence*, London: Verso.

Butler, J. (2009), *Frames of War: When is Life Grievable?* London: Verso.

Dalby, S. (2003), 'Calling 911: geopolitics, security and America's new war', *Geopolitics*, 8.3, pp. 61–86.

Dauphinee, E. (2007), 'The politics of the body in pain: reading the ethics of imagery', *Security Dialogue*, 38.2, pp. 139–55.

Der Spiegel (2011), 'Murder in Afghanistan: court sentences "Kill Team" soldier to 24 years in prison', 24 March. Available at <http://www.spiegel.de/international/world/murder-in-afghanistan-court-sentences-kill-team-soldier-to-24-years-in-prison-a-752918.html> (last accessed 4 February 2015).

Gilmore, J. (2011), 'A kinder, gentler counterterrorism: counterinsurgency, human security and the war on terror', *Security Dialogue*, 42.1, pp. 21–37.

Goetz, J. and M. Hujer (2011), 'Adam's war: the good boy and the Kill Team', *Der Spiegel*, 31 March. Available at <http://www.spiegel.de/international/world/adam-s-war-the-good-boy-and-the-kill-team-a-754141.html> (last accessed 4 February 2015).

Goldstein, C. S. (2016), 'Good kill? US soldiers and the killing of civilians in American film', in C. Hellmich and L. Purse (eds), *Disappearing War: Interdisciplinary Perspectives on Cinema and Erasure in the Post-9/11 World*, Edinburgh: Edinburgh University Press, pp. 16–33.

Graham, S. (2005), 'Remember Fallujah: demonising place, constructing atrocity', *Environment and Planning D: Society and Space*, 23.1, pp. 1–10.

Gregory, D. (2004), *The Colonial Present: Afghanistan, Palestine, Iraq*, Oxford: Blackwell.

Gregory, D. (2008), 'The rush to the intimate: counterinsurgency and the cultural turn', *Radical Philosophy*, 150.8, pp. 8–23.

Gregory, T. (2012), 'Potential lives, impossible deaths: Afghanistan, civilian casualties and the politics of intelligibility', *International Feminist Journal of Politics*, 14.3, pp. 327–47.

Gregory, T. (2015), 'Dismembering the dead: violence, vulnerability and the body in war', *European Journal of International Relations*, 7 December.

Hellmich, C. (2014), 'Reply to Christine Sylvester, "Terrorwars: Boston, Iraq": an examination of differences between counter-terrorism and war as seen through the Iraqi experience of occupation', *Critical Studies on Terrorism*, 7.3, pp. 472–8.

Hujer, M. (2010), 'Did US soldiers target Afghan civilians? War crime allegations threaten to harm America's image', *Der Spiegel*, 13 September. Available at <http://www.spiegel.de/international/world/did-us-soldiers-target-afghan-civilians-war-crime-allegations-threaten-to-harm-america-s-image-a-717127.html> (last accessed 4 February 2015).

Kemmerle, K. (2014), 'Dan Krauss on "The Kill Team" and finding your film in the edit room', *Tribeca*, 25 July. Available at <https://tribecafilm.com/stories/dan-krauss-the-kill-team-interview> (last accessed 4 February 2015).

Kilcullen, D. (2006), 'Twenty-eight articles: fundamentals of company-level counterinsurgency', *Marine Corps Gazette* (Summer), pp. 29–35.

McGreal, C. (2011), 'Kill Team US platoon commander guilty of Afghan murders', *The Guardian*, 11 November. Available at <http://www.theguardian.com/world/2011/nov/11/kill-team-calvin-gibbs-convicted> (last accessed 4 February 2015).

Philips, C. (2015), 'Dan Krauss investigates the Kill Team', *PBS*, 15 January. Available at <http://www.pbs.org/independentlens/blog/dan-krauss-investigates-kill-team> (last accessed 4 February 2015).

Puar, J. (2007), *Terrorist Assemblages: Homonationalism in Queer Times*, Durham, NC: Duke University Press.

Richter-Montpetit, M. (2007), 'Empire, desire and violence: a queer transnational feminist reading of the prisoner "abuse" in Abu Ghraib and the question of "gender equality"', *International Feminist Journal of Politics*, 9.1, pp. 38–59.

Said, E. (2001), 'A clash of ignorance', *The Nation*, 4 October. Available at <http://www.thenation.com/article/clash-ignorance/> (last accessed 4 February 2015).

Scarry, E. (1985), *The Body in Pain: The Making and Unmaking of the World*, Oxford: Oxford University Press.

Sylvester, C. (2012), *War as Experience: Contributions from International Relations and Feminist Analysis*, Abingdon: Routledge.

US Army (2006), *FM3-24: The Counterinsurgency Field Manual*, Chicago: University of Chicago Press.

US Department of Defense (2011a), 'Statement by the army on photographs published by *Der Spiegel*', Release No. 228–11, 21 March. Available at <http://www.defense.gov/Releases/Release.aspx?ReleaseID=14353> (last accessed 4 February 2015).

US Department of Defense (2011b), 'Statement by the army on photographs published by *Rolling Stone*', Release No. 247–11, 28 March. Available at <http://www.defense.gov/releases/release.aspx?releaseid=14367> (last accessed 4 February 2015).

Whitlock, C. (2010), 'Members of Stryker Combat Brigade in Afghanistan accused of killing civilians for sport', *Washington Post*, 18 September. Available at <http://www.washingtonpost.com/wp-dyn/content/article/2010/09/18/AR2010091803935.html> (last accessed 4 February 2015).

Welland, J. (2015a), 'Liberal warriors and the violent colonial logics of "partnering and advising"', *International Feminist Journal of Politics*, 17.2, pp. 289–307.

Welland, J. (2015b), 'Compassionate soldiering and comfort', in L. Åhäll and T. Gregory (eds) *Emotions, Politics and War*, Abingdon: Routledge, pp. 115–27.

Wilcox, L. (2015), *Bodies of Violence: Theorizing Embodied Subjects in International Relations*, Oxford: Oxford University Press.

CHAPTER 6

The Unknowable Soldier: Ethical Erasure in *The Master*'s Facial Close-ups

James Harvey

The 'war on terror' was sold to a global public with a message of clarity and authority – in George W. Bush's words, 'you are either with us or against us.' However, it was soon clear how little knowledge was accessible, both to those in power and certainly to the spectators. This lack of knowledge was at odds with the saturation of images arriving each day thereafter from the Middle East. In Nicholas Mirzoeff's words, 'instead of moral and visual clarity, all is confusion' (Mirzoeff 2004: 18). In spite of this confusion, as Amy Gershkoff and Shana Kushner argue, the Bush administration's successful shaping of public opinion created a willingness to consent to conflict, based primarily on rhetoric and the deprivation of information (2005). Dense, almost opaque images of spectacular violence and suffering were attached to messages of defence and need, in ways both continuous and distinct from the twentieth century's visual culture of conflict. Drawing on Jean Baudrillard's infamous claim about terrorism's 'purest form of spectacle' (2003: 30), John Tulloch and Richard Warwick Blood note the way in which 'the semiotic/symbolic struggle of images spiralled on, entwined within the contemporary war of images' (2012: 115). The convoluted motivations, methods and outcomes of the post-9/11 socio-political landscape has spawned a culture of uncertainty and dread, replete with images whose import is not easily judged. Consequently, when conflict is depicted in contemporary media, our ability to judge things clearly is significantly clouded.

Describing this condition in the images of torture from Abu Ghraib, W. J. T. Mitchell suggests that 'it's as if the longer and more intensely one contemplates these kinds of images, the more opaque they become' (2011: 108). This opacity has certainly seeped into cinematic fictions produced in the US in recent years, evolving out of the pictorial realm and into the atmospheric. It is becoming clear that certain thematic, iconographic and aesthetic tendencies have developed in contemporary US cinema and when we relate these tendencies to the contemporary moment, we must surely argue that Mitchell's location of opacity has had an effect. These are films that embody a contemporary difficulty of making sense of things in the face of a war that is not only 'perpetual' (Vidal 2002) but also 'disappearing' (Mueller 2004: 1): textual indicators of the cultural impasse signified by contemporary conflicts. The apparently paradoxical effects of today's wars multiply the challenges of the historical debates regarding what is representable. A collision between ethical debates on art that deals with trauma and the cinematic response to the contemporary social confusion, this chapter shall ask: how does post-9/11 cinema construct an image that can embody, at once, the unknowability of the lived war experience and the confusion surrounding the historical circumstances of war?

In contemporary tales of paranoia like *Martha, Marcy, May, Marlene* (Sean Durkin, 2011) and *Take Shelter* (Jeff Nichols, 2011), an unsettling air of threat and looming chaos fuels the narratives. Both films couple psychical degeneration with unclear and non-present danger. We note a recurrent thematic and aesthetic turn away from clarity toward confusion, challenging the spectator and forcing us to ask, 'what is happening?' This challenge fits neither in the psychological rationality that David Bordwell associates with the dominant Hollywood formula (1985), nor the complex narratives Warren Buckland has written about under the name 'puzzle films' (2014). It is not that these films have a point to make in a straightforward or complex manner; rather they demand the engagement of a spectator in their meaning-making. The challenge of *Martha, Marcy, May, Marlene* and *Take Shelter*, and a film of especial interest for me here, *The Master* (Paul Thomas Anderson, 2012), occurs through the turn away from narrative to affect – from the uncovering of meaning to its erasure.

I wish to ask therefore: why is the erasure of clear meaning gaining ground in contemporary North American cinema? What drives this marked stylistic avoidance of representing things directly? This chapter shall consider one particular technique used for the clouding of the spectator's judgement: the erasure of discernible meaning in images of the human face. Approaching the face of Joaquin Phoenix's 'Freddie Quell' in *The Master*, I wish to argue that the film's strange expressivity of post-war trauma is an ethical challenge to the spectator. While recognising its significance for debates on representing the experience of (all) war, I shall argue that Quell's face is also of its time – that is, it is part of an ongoing discourse informing our comprehension of contemporary culture and post-9/11 North America. Quell's facade of unknowability broaches both the contemporary confusion about proliferating conflict zones and asymmetrical warfare. As such, it opens a space for discussing the ethics of spectatorship. Diverging from the standardised, formalist readings of the facial close-up (rarely differing from Béla Balázs to Bordwell) I shall contest the possibility of clearly attributing meaning. Focusing instead on the film's ethical challenge to the spectator, I shall argue that these images compel us to speculate upon the horrors of war, its effects on those involved and the possibility of portraying any of this through an image. I wish to claim that *The Master*'s unknowable soldier embodies a crucial ethics of representation for the contemporary war experience. At a time when mediatised forms of knowledge and 'expert' displays of acumen are inescapable, these close-ups potentialise an acceptance and embracing of the unknowable. The ethical erasure of clear meaning infers that it is only when our pretension to know is shown up for its ineptitude that a spectator can begin to engage with the unrepresentable experience of war.

THE FACE OF FREDDIE QUELL

The Master is hardly a 'war film'. Its central narrative concerns the entry of former soldier Quell into a Scientology-like cult called 'The Cause', led by Philip Seymour Hoffman's 'Lancaster Dodd' (dutifully referred to as 'Master' by his loyal followers). Much to the frustration of Dodd's family and despite his willingness to conform, Quell cannot be tamed. His essentially animalistic[1] character prevents him from finding peace and enlightenment in The Cause's journey to what Dodd calls 'our essential state of perfect'. While the bulk of the narrative weighs in on the cultural discourse framing the coming of Eisenhower-era values, the opening sequence's location in late-war Japan seems to frame his character and his motivations (or lack thereof). We initially see Quell as a sailor among his comrades. We do not see him in combat, but instead fooling around – the camaraderie of young men on the beaches of Japan. However, as suggested through his aggressive acts on the sand sculpture the sailors create on the beach, his libidinal energy far exceeds

Figure 6.1: Quell's difference is underlined through this dissonant dissolve in *The Master* (2012).

the offensive games of the others. The first time we see him in 'civilised' society, his strangeness is amplified. This is strikingly the case when offset against the Technicolor perfection of others, as is beautifully performed through the dissonant dissolve from the wartime face of Quell into the face of an anonymous woman he photographs some years later (see Figure 6.1).

While the film quickly departs from its wartime exposition, these opening scenes are an important lens through which the rest of the film must surely be viewed. Throughout, whenever Quell is framed in close-up, the spectator experiences a performance based on strange gestures, wherein meaning cannot be wholly discerned. From the opening sequence's anchoring of Quell's character in some sort of post-traumatic condition deriving from the effects of war, these images embody war's erasure of discernible meaning – the infamous 'fog of war' whereby soldiers' actions are themselves not wholly articulable. In this sequence then, I am approaching Quell's mysterious actions from the perspective of wartime trauma, its discordant effects on the individual and the consequentially discordant effects on his gesture and expression. Attaching this discordance to the preoccupation with wartime trauma and the contemporary confusion of the North American social, these strange close-ups construct an image that embodies, at once, the unknowability of the lived war experience and the confusion surrounding our historical circumstances. In order to explain how this framing of Quell's close-up occurs early on in the film, I shall now elaborate on an early sequence.

We are situated in a military building, as uniformed men are shown ascending a staircase. A voice-over explains the Navy's sympathy for the psychological trauma these men have experienced. We cut to a wide shot of the men seated at desks, as in school, looking on at the commander's explanation. We cut from one close-up of a blank face to another, to another, and so on and so forth. Quell is not pictured; instead, we are shown a number of anonymous military personnel, each interchangeable with the last, each marked by indifference to their environment, each apparently suffering post-traumatic stress disorder (PTSD). Montage works in an accumulative way here, each image amplifying the effects of the one preceding it. However, since each face is so vacant, it is vacancy itself that is being amplified. We cannot discern any meaning from these faces beyond the one applied to them through the attribution of PTSD heard on the soundtrack. The sense we are expected to make of this, then, is that the indiscernibility of each face is a result of things experienced during war. By attaching the effects of war to the erasure of discernible meaning in the expressions of soldiers, trauma itself is portrayed as indiscernible from outside: we cannot *know* trauma.

The cut taking us from this room to Quell sitting in therapy seems to make him representative of all these men (although we know this not to be quite true; from what we have seen minutes prior, Quell is quite singular from the rest of the group). What is implied throughout the opening sequence is made plain through the Rorschach tests he undergoes: from one image to another, he claims he sees nothing other than 'pussy' and 'cock'. What to the therapist appears (after just three questions) like a straightforward case of deeply repressed (possibly sexual) abuse appears less clear in a second interview that follows shortly after with a different therapist. Quell's face, framed in close-up throughout, is compelling and demanding. A play of dark and light is initiated by the contrast between the beige wall in the background and his shaded cheek; it is multiplied by the contours his grin carves into his face. These nasolabial lines (the creases made from smiling or frowning) intensify a person's expression. They are exemplary components of a face some call 'characterful' – a gold star for a performer. Each time Quell reacts to a comment, a nasolabial line spreads, drawing attention to the strain (both physiological and performative) this is putting upon his expressive capacities. Yet, when this appears to be leading to distress, he bursts into a laugh, thwarting our expectations. Thus, while Quell's face offers much expression, it also signals a major difficulty in our ability to define the meaning of that expression. This occurs a few times in a short space, demonstrating the way that performance and cinematography combine to erase meaning in the facial close-up. Such moments recur throughout the film and are suggestive, I am claiming, of an ethical response to the traumatic experience of war, which some theorists have termed 'unrepresentable'. Before considering similar close-ups in *The Master,* I shall first introduce some of the theoretical context for this argument. With reference to key contributions on the ethics of representing the horrors of war, I wish to ground the face of Freddie Quell in an aesthetic tendency defined long before 9/11. In spite of the historical difference, however, this tendency is peculiarly equipped to embody the challenges raised by a social climate where war is both 'perpetual' and 'disappearing'.

THE UNREPRESENTABLE

We do not struggle to think of examples of films dealing with the horrors of war. From *All Quiet on the Western Front* (Lewis Milestone, 1930) to *Katyn* (Andrzej Wajda, 2007), film-makers have not shied away from depicting the most brutal of conflicts. Yet some would say that by attempting to reconstruct events as they occurred, film – indeed, art in general – does a disservice to the magnitude of experience. The awful, inimitable nature of planned, mass killing arguably renders said event unrepresentable. However, the lines distinguishing representation from non-representation (and indeed misrepresentation) are rarely clear in advance. Instead, when philosophers have broached the subject, attention is primarily drawn to the aesthetic nuances demanded in difficult subject matter. One major intervention in this regard came from Jean-François Lyotard. Discussing representations outside our normal limits of perception, Lyotard makes recourse to the Kantian category of 'the sublime' in order to venture the idea of an 'aesthetic of the sublime': a 'failure of expression' giving rise to a tension between conception and imagination:

> [T]he impotence of imagination attests *a contrario* to an imagination striving to figure even that which cannot be figured, and that imagination thus aims to harmonize its object with that of reason – and that furthermore the inadequacy of the images is a negative sign of the immense power of ideas. (Lyotard 1991: 98)

For Lyotard, the inability to grasp, imagine and represent an abstract experience is simultaneously positive and negative. Avant-garde art apparently recognises this tension: from Cezanne's 'colouristic sensations' to Malevich's minimalism, a reduction of content is sought to broaden the experiential possibilities of the spectator (ibid.: 103). By forcing a spectator away from the notion of pre-defined content towards instead the openness of experience, the spectator encounters an 'ambivalent enjoyment' derived from the 'ontological dissociation' produced through the artwork's abstraction: 'the art object no longer bends itself to models but tries to present the fact that there is an unrepresentable' (ibid.: 101). Erasure becomes a key technique for signalling the requirement to go beyond our usual imaginative capacity. For Lyotard, this would surely be vital when we watch films that deal with the horrors of war. Beyond reconstruction of the event itself, an image must, in this sense, offer some sort of formal 'dissociation', acknowledging the 'inadequacy of images'.

Like Lyotard, Theodor Adorno issued a similar ethical imperative on representing the horrors of war. His famous statement – 'to write poetry after Auschwitz would be barbaric' (Adorno 1983: 34) – demanded an art that overcame both conventional narrative and poetic representations. In Adorno's argument, the classical approach of 'realistically' reconstructing history ultimately produces a reification of experience: 'even the most extreme consciousness of doom threatens to denigrate into idle chatter' (ibid.). We may note the reverberation of Adorno's prohibition on the *merely* poetic in a number of responses to films that attempt to show the unrepresentable. Perhaps the most famous case of this regards the divergent critical responses to Steven Spielberg's *Schindler's List* (1993), which demonstrate both the popularity and critical revulsion expressed at realist depictions of wartime atrocity.*

Appropriating Adorno's argument, Jean-Luc Godard uses his monumental *Histoire(s) du Cinéma* (1989–98) to explain how atrocities have apparently been (and continue to be) impossible to represent on film. Such horrors cannot simply be presented in a horrifying way, because horror has itself become too generic an affect to enable a suitable engagement with the magnitude and complexities of 'real' experience. Accordingly, *Histoire(s) du Cinéma* avoids the cliché rendering of atrocity, relying instead on a poetic use of video-editing, such as superimposition to reconfigure meaning in iconic cinematic images. Godard's one-time colleague, Jacques Rivette, also wrote explicitly about cinema's failures in tackling atrocity. Discussing Gillo Pontecorvo's *Kapò* (1960), Rivette describes how 'every traditional approach to "spectacle" partakes in voyeurism and pornography' (Rivette 1961: 54). The 'idle chatter' spoken of by Adorno is exemplified in Rivette's take on *Kapò*: the realist

---

*Discussed in detail by Lozhtisky (1997) and Walker (2005).

representation of atrocity has the ultimate effect of developing an audience that 'unknowingly becomes accustomed to the horror, which little by little is accepted by morality, and will quickly become part of the mental landscape of modern man' (ibid.). Through the aforementioned perspectives, it is clear that an ethical discourse has come together, proposing a cinematic approach to representing atrocity that is built on the necessity of foregrounding both the limits of the imagination and the distorting effects of the medium.

Such is the peculiarity of this ethical response to the horror of war, when cinema does achieve this complex nexus of ethics and aesthetics it signals an absolute break with the conventions of classical cinema. This is the claim of Gilles Deleuze in *Cinema 2: The Time Image* (1986). Writing in regard to Roberto Rossellini's war trilogy, Deleuze notes that the horror of war has produced a cinematic modernity based on an upturning of the narrative drive central to most films. Films like Rossellini's come to embody a new, revolutionary form of cinema: 'a cinema of the seer and no longer of the agent' (Deleuze 1986: 3). These films force us to dwell on the act of seeing over doing, on inactivity over activity, on duration over narration. Since, for Deleuze, the post-war period is taken as a break because it increased the number of unimaginable scenarios (ibid.: x), we can clearly see the motivation for anchoring his 'cinema of the seer' on the ethical aesthetics mentioned thus far.

Germany, Year Zero follows a young boy (played by the amateur actor Edmund Moeschke) around Berlin after World War II. He feels the burden of growing up in a post-war society, its savaged streets and people still plagued by remnants of Fascist ideology. In the climactic scenes, we watch him stray from his home and enter a blown-up building. It is from the top floor of this building that he will jump to his death; but for now, in the time between his entrance and his suicide, let us focus on Edmund's portrayal. It is, in the first place, not a surprise that Edmund ventures into this dangerous terrain. He is living in extreme poverty, forced to contravene the most desperate of measures set by the authorities in their attempts to enforce order, and has carried out the most misled of mercy killings on his sick father. After the parricide, Edmund's journeys around Berlin are a study in disorientation. His responses to others, his perception of spaces and the soundtrack that frames his movement, synthesise into a very strange final act. Once inside the building, he floats through the rubble, undeterred by the instability and danger of all that surrounds him. So apparently comfortable he appears, that he begins to play amongst the rubble, leaping to and around the light puddles pouring through the blown-out windows into the darkened space. The ambiguity

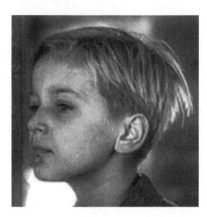

Figure 6.2: The opacity of Edmund Moeschke in *Germany, Year Zero* (1948).

of this scene accumulates, culminating in a close-up indicative neither of a boy helpless nor refreshed. In a shot reverse-shot, we see him look out through the window down at the passers-by. His expression is unchanged throughout: opaque and unrevealing of any source of interior meaning (see Figure 6.2). We see his family appear outside, searching the streets for him; we hear their yells from below as Edmund is again shown playing at the windowsill. Stylistically speaking, the build-up to the suicide revolves primarily around visuals of Edmund's face. In close-up, we view him looking at the destruction outside. He walks towards the frame, further magnifying his blank expression on the screen. He wipes his hand across his face, drawing greater attention to the facade, before finally closing his eyes and falling.

The force of the ambivalence here (in between feeling and numbness) confounds the spectator and defines the strength of this film in general. Jacques Rancière speaks of 'Edmund's silent face' (2006: 131), drawing attention to the challenge presented to us in our attempts to decipher meaning from his act. Edmund's face bears evidence of the effects of war, but the strangeness of the non-gesture cancels out this straightforward symbol of trauma. *The Master*'s use of the indiscernible close-up therefore has a traceable precedent almost seventy years prior, in post-war Italian neo-realism. From Rossellini's European modernism, through the American independent cinema of the Vietnam era, up to recent works by Elia Suleiman in Palestine and Pablo Larraín in Chile, the erasure of discernible meaning in the facial close-up has become a transnational expression of the inexpressible affects of war. It is in this sense that it signals such a striking cinematic response to a war that is both 'perpetual' and 'disappearing'. In the encounter between a face on the screen and the 'eye of the beholder', this conflicted (un)representation confronts us with a challenge to our perception. Further still, this perceptual challenge might even be considered an imperative, altering our ethical relationship to the image and its subject. I turn now to Emmanuel Levinas's writings on the face in order to elaborate on the ethical challenge presented through the close-ups of erasure.

ENCOUNTERING THE FACE

Like Deleuze's claim on Italian neo-realism, Levinas was writing in response to what he saw as a rupture in world history; World War II produced situations whereby one was forced to question – profoundly – humanity's relationship with the world and its people. Written in 1961, *Totalité et infini* expresses a dissatisfaction with existing responses to human responsibility emerging from the post-war era. He addresses the writings of Jean-Paul Sartre and Maurice Merleau-Ponty as well as the urtexts of phenomenology by Edmund Husserl and Martin Heidegger, claiming that these earlier writings always subsume the subjectivity of another into the reason of the self. In response, Levinas formulates an ethics of 'radical alterity': a way of acting based on the dual necessity of (1) separation between oneself and another and (2) responsibility to the survival of that distinct being. This ethical demand always arises in the determined moment whereby we see the face of another: 'the face speaks to me and thereby invites me to a relation incommensurate with a power exercised, be it enjoyment or knowledge' (Levinas 1999: 198).

Quell's face invites us into a relation incommensurate with any notion of enjoyment or knowledge. While Levinas wrote not solely about gestures like these but about all faces, we can, I think, understand *The Master*'s close-ups as foregrounding an ethical demand identical to Levinas's. Confronted with these images, we are being invited to recognise the fact that Freddie Quell has experienced something traumatic and beyond the realm of our own comprehension. Thus, in the early scenes, when Quell's face fills the frame, when his gestures confound our comprehension but compel our interaction, it becomes quite clear that the experience of war has resulted in a subject beyond the realms of reason. By contravening the limits of our understanding, a discourse is thus produced precisely through this lack of comprehension, infinitely posing the question, 'what does this mean?' This is precisely what Levinas privileged: 'Better than comprehension, discourse relates with what essentially remains transcendent' (ibid.: 195).

Levinas's argument is clear, emphatic and incredibly resonant with the argument I am making here. It also provides a useful lens through which to view the early film theory of Béla Balázs, whose writings have been instrumental to all subsequent perspectives on close-ups of the face in film and as such are unavoidable here. Balázs's *Visible Man* (1924) and *The Spirit of Film* (1931) are works that foreground the importance of the human face to cinema. There is, for Balázs, something primal in film's facial close-ups, something that reveals to us an essential quality all but dissolved in modernity. Much like Levinas, Balázs claims that the gestural possibilities (irrespective of what those gestures purport-edly represent) of the facial close-up (most adventurously explored in the silent period)[2] present the shared humanity of spectator and actor: the interplay of facial expressions represents 'a struggle between the type and personality, between inherited and acquired characteristics, between fate and the individual will, between the 'id' and the 'ego" (Balázs 2010: 31).

Unfortunately, the complexities of Balázs's perspective are far too often liquidised into a general foregrounding of the actor's psychology, so that the close-up is said to stand for little more than the so-called 'struggle' between things. Exemplified by the cognitive tradition of film studies,[3] the psychological approach to close-ups *tells us* what is being felt or thought; rare it is that one is challenged by the Levinasian discur-sive imperative. How does this approach deal with a face like Quell's? I wish to contend that *The Master* obliterates the cognitive aesthetic tendency of attributing inflexible rationalities to particular kinds of image. David Bordwell's essay, 'Intensified Continuity: Visual Style in Contemporary American Film' (2002) is an especially useful counter-point in this regard. For Bordwell, the close-up represents a 'stylistic tactic' (ibid.: 16) in the conventional aesthetic of contemporary Hol-lywood. Western audiences have apparently become accustomed to an intensified version of classical Hollywood's linearity of time and unity of space: we do not simply want things neat, clear and tidy; we want them more relatable and closer to our realities than ever before. The changing use of the close-up has, in turn, responded accordingly: 'actors are principally faces . . . Mouths, brows and eyes become the principal sources of information and emotion, and actors must scale the perfor-mances across varying degrees of intimate framings' (ibid.: 20).

While *The Master* is produced by a company becoming increasingly renowned for critical appraisals of American culture (in the same year as *The Master*, Annapurna Pictures also released the scathing and vio-lent social commentary, *Killing Them Softly* (Andrew Dominik, 2012)), it is nevertheless a US$32 million production featuring Hollywood

A-listers and an epic historical narrative. There is no reason not to consider the film in the light of Bordwell's framework for expensive works of contemporary American cinema. As such, we can see how Quell's face engages and disrupts Bordwell's cognitive appraisal. By highlighting what the predetermined response to these images is, the social and cultural significance is implicitly denied. The cognitive approach therefore renders the viewing of a film as distinct from the historical context. Rather than read into *The Master* a contemporary desire to tell a story in ever-increasingly relatable ways then, I instead locate it in a body of cinematic work dealing with recent traumatic events. Secondly, what Bordwell describes as the face's role as the 'principle source of information and emotion' is wholly undermined in *The Master*. Certainly the images of Quell to which I refer are emotional and representative of a kind of information, but neither the kind of emotion nor the content of information can be asserted outside of each spectator's particular encounter with his face.

When the cognitive rationality of appearance is threatened by a confounding image like Quell's face, one is forced to look for other forms of explanation. Rather than assert some totalising aesthetic principle, I wish to negotiate the thematic frame of the post-World War II narrative and post-'war on terror' production with the challenges posed by Quell's strange close-ups.

CONFRONTING FREDDIE

In its post-war, post-traumatic framing of Quell's incomprehensible expressivity, the first scene (which I discussed earlier) implies a causal relationship between the experience of war and the strangeness of the protagonist. As I have suggested, when presented with this strangeness we are confronted with an ethical imperative: forced into recognising the traumatic experience of war and its troubling of our perceptual capacities. Informed by the philosophical context I have outlined, I shall now turn to some more of Quell's close-ups in order to underline the prevalence of this technique in *The Master*, and to demonstrate how each scene furthers the film's complex approach to representation.

The second instance I shall discuss is how this happens during Quell's second private meeting with Dodd. Occurring shortly after Dodd's daughter's wedding ceremony, Quell has by this point been made truly welcome in the man's home. The two sit down to drink one of Quell's near-lethal-strength cocktails and discuss how he came to join their group. Dodd offers Quell 'processing' – a pseudo-scientific term for counselling through an intensive series of questions. As the questions begin ('what is your name?'), the camera cuts from a two-shot of the pair to a close-up of Quell positioned to the left of Dodd's face. We find ourselves placed implicitly and immediately in a dialogue with him. So, while it is clear that Dodd's questions are invoking an expressive reaction from Quell, our spectatorial position produces this dialogue constitutive of Levinas's encounter. As we will see, Quell's expressions are framed by the questions Dodd asks him. However, beyond a straightforward case of character psychology, I wish to claim that the visceral intensity of Phoenix's physiognomy exceeds the emotional representation some may associate with the scene. Our intimacy with this face confronts us, demanding we go beyond the surface of things and probe further into Quell's responses.

The image is darker than in the therapy session – half of Quell's face is cast in the shadow of the dark room. As we often find, his brow is furrowed, his eyebrows raised and his eyes locked assertively on the questioner. He answers his questions with a certainty that defies the usual elusiveness of his expression. His lip is cleft, so his words are spoken from out of the side of his mouth. This facial contortion is broached directly in one of Dodd's questions, when he asks 'do you get muscle spasms for no reason?' which prompts Quell to strain his jaw and neck, bending his appearance out of shape to a greater extent than usual. Quell's movement suggests an opening up – an inclination to be engaged by Dodd on this issue is expressed in such an action, suggesting that Dodd has perhaps managed to probe beneath his steely surface. Yet, when Dodd soon asks 'do your past failures bother you?', this opening up, which one may expect to persist or perhaps even increase at such a question, immediately switches to nonchalance: a shrug of the shoulders and an apathetic 'nope'. Dodd repeats the question three times with the effect of inducing three more 'no' answers.

As the interrogation continues, Dodd induces smiles, laughs and the semblance of intense thought from Quell. While it is as intense a physiognomy as one is likely to find in cinema history, this does little to confirm the spectator's comprehension and challenges our capacity for understanding. This soon changes however, when Quell demands that Dodd asks him more questions. He is set the task of answering the next series of questions without blinking, which frame what is to come as predictably strange. Quell appears confident – this is a game which he should like to win. Dodd's questions are brutal ('Do you ever think about how significant you are? Do you believe that God will save you from your ridiculousness?'), demanding a reaction – Quell resists, staring steadfastly back at the barrage of provocation. Asked about having sex with a member of his family, he answers 'yes' without hesitation.

This is a battle of wits between a man of logic and a man that thwarts logic – a tension that is underlined by the scene's shot reverse-shot technique, shunting back and forth at this time between the sensible face of Dodd and the intensity of Quell. The questions continue – 'Do you regret this? Have you killed anyone? Where is your mother?' Each question provokes an increasingly agitated response from Quell. Upon blinking, he exclaims ('fuck!') before smacking his cheek several times and readying himself for another round. Resolutely, he settles, returning to the sanguine expression from the start of the scene. When Dodd asks the same questions this second time, this calm expression remains for some time before lapsing again into frustration at the psychological demand of the questions and the physical demand of the game.

Dodd's questions supposedly reveal to us the root of Quell's problem: he is suffering from the war, from having accidentally killed a man, from sexual abuse in his family, from a dysfunctional upbringing by both his parents, and from his pining for a woman he left behind when he went to war. Therefore, too much is going on to permit for any single explanation. While Dodd's solution will be a painstaking initiation into his cult, the film itself is absolutely damning of such simplistic diagnoses or prescriptions. *The Master* wants us to experience precisely this feeling of not knowing clear-cut answers or reasons for things. When we see the experience of a profound trauma in close-up it is not so we can know it better – it is rather to pronounce its unknowability. These images foreground an erasure of interiority, making erasure an ethical imperative for representations of trauma. Drawing upon the ethical dialogues mentioned thus far, we can see how it is only when our pretension to know is shown up for its ineptitude that a spectator can begin to engage with the unrepresentable experience of war. Confronted with the face of a man that suffers, combined with the multitude of past agonies and present explanations, *The Master* constructs a space for deliberation on the participants of wars past and present.

Quell becomes a loyal servant to Dodd. Throughout the film, we see him aggressively enforce the silencing of those who would speak out against him. Yet his strangeness singles him out among the group, so he never appears entirely at home in this new social order. Nevertheless, while he does not fit, he sticks determinedly to Dodd's plan, turning down sex with Dodd's daughter and accepting the physical labours demanded by the cult's strange and rigorous training regime. Eventually, Quell comes to abandon The Cause. At a certain point in the film, we can spot the specific moment when his doubts surface. This occurs at the launch of Dodd's second sacred text. The close-up of Quell's face as he reacts to the event locates us again in a strange place. However, while previous close-ups are notable for their erasure of meaning alone, in this scene we may note the way his bodily movement thwarts his facial opacity and provides clues towards a clearer meaning.

The launch takes place in a large hall with a stage. As Dodd ascends the stage, his followers rise to their feet and applaud. A cut takes us from the middle of this crowd to Quell, standing, shot from a low angle, which places his face at the top of the frame and his neck in the centre. This is a strange shot, not used so far in the film (see Figure 6.3). We see Quell's head detached from his shoulders altogether; the frame begins halfway up his neck. The neck itself is in turn pronounced, more so even than the face, which suggests something significant about his bodily gesture here. His head is tilted back, but his eyes remain fixed on the figure on the stage. It is a stance identical to that of the soldier standing to attention for his commanding officer. The camera follows as he seats himself and refocuses on his face. His head remains tilted back, gazing abidingly up toward Dodd. When Dodd proclaims that he has unlocked the meaning of life and that it is laughter, the camera returns to Quell, whose firm gaze – mouth downturned, eyes wide, brow furrowed – is undone. His lids settle and his shoulders shift; his previously steadfast gaze loosens into an expression of apathy. We remain with him for some time before cutting away to a backstage area, where we find Quell pacing the floor, presumably searching for some way of deciphering what he has just heard (see Figure 6.4).

Figure 6.3: Gesture and expression begin to threaten Quell's usual opacity in *The Master* (2012).

Confronted with Dodd's paucity of explanation, this moment seems to show us Quell's disillusionment with Dodd, whose little substance has been made plain. We do not find this explanation in the face of Quell, but we can certainly see it in the change in bodily gesture here. The drooping of the shoulders turns this committed soldier back into a lost soul and provides access to his thus far impenetrable persona. This moment provides a subtle suggestion that, after the war, Quell was desperate for a master to show him the way. He thought he had found it in Dodd, but this scene of secular disillusionment erases those hopes.

Finally, in a scene of resolution, Quell returns to Dodd, having disappeared without warning. Dodd laments Quell's lack of commitment to The Cause and sings him 'Slow Boat to China' – a mournful song, which Hoffman manages to make sound pining and menacing in equal measure. When we take into account the scene's location at the end of the film, we might predict that this will be the moment that Quell finally opens up and allows us access to his innermost feelings. Indeed, the tear that trails his face for the entirety of the scene is suggestive of such empathic possibilities. However, like the wavering emotions and ambivalence of the therapy session, such clarity of expression is once again thwarted. As existing film theories (both from the cognitive school and in Carl Plantinga's theory of embodiment)[4] have suggested,

Figure 6.4: A return to opacity but, following the earlier expressiveness, meaning is more discernible, in *The Master* (2012).

our initial intimacy with the face potentialises an emotional response. Filling most of the screen, the face of Quell is seen initially to respond conventionally – he is clearly saddened by Dodd's song. This suggests that we might, at last, gain some access to Quell's psyche. As the scene goes on, however, the reaction alters: this sad response is substituted by laughter, entirely at odds with the apparent emotion of the scene. The laugh appears forced, as if representative of an inability to express the appropriate feeling. As he dips his head south of the frame, his crying is held back altogether. When he raises his head again he appears calm and composed, especially in contrast with the troubled face of Dodd. In these late scenes, the erasure of clear meaning is persisted with. Both scenes appear to provide chances for the spectator to situate Quell's expression within an extremely legible narrative of disappointment and withdrawal from Dodd's group, before eventually confounding further the possibility of clarity. We are ultimately left on very unclear terms, never sure of what to make of Quell and his experience.

CONCLUSION

I have argued that the close-up images of Freddie Quell's face force the spectator to confront the scarring effects of war and the impossibility of experiencing authentically those effects, second-hand, through the expressive capacities of performance. Instead, we encounter a range of strange gestural performances, from the opaque to the bizarre. The erasure of clearly discernible meaning produces a dialogue between the spectator and the image. We are surely compelled to figure out what goes on beneath the image and what the surface itself represents; but we come to realise that this figuring-out can only go so far before we must accept its unknowability. Thus, when meaning is erased from the close-up of a face, we are forced into a position of radical alterity. It is from this ethical location that *The Master* allows us to broach a personal response to war. By carving into the face of an expressive but estranging protagonist the trace of an experience that is unknowable to the inexperienced gaze of the spectator, these close-ups undermine attempts to wholly understand the horrors of war and its effects on its participants. Yet, by showing us an image that is at once unknowable and conscious of its unknowability, *The Master* goes beyond the anaesthetising potential of anti-representational models. Departing from the Adornian–Lyotardian model of ethical aesthetics, I have articulated the strangeness of *The Master* from a position of radical alterity akin to the writing of Emmanuel Levinas. Faces present a site unique to the subject, at once visible but uncontainable, relatable but distinct. I have attempted to articulate Levinasian cinematic ethics as an anti-psychological position of spectatorship, wherein the schematic tendencies of formalist theories are undermined from a position of radical alterity. This position allows war cinema to avoid the default charge of 'unrepresentability'.

As a contemporary American film, *The Master* is in many ways a product of 'the classical Hollywood cinema'[5] that is usually aligned with comprehension and linearity. Like other films I have referred to, however, it poses far more riddles than it solves. Rather than offer a reading of the puzzling narrative along these lines, I have chosen to focus on Quell's close-up to highlight its unknowability. As we have learned from a number of media theorists, the digital age has increased the volume of images that pretend to *know* war.[6] *The Master* implicitly objects to such a notion; Quell's unknowable close-up image returns throughout, challenging the authenticity of appearances. Unlike media representations, genre fiction, documentary investigations, photographic and journalistic reportage, this face does not want to be understood, nor does it want to negate understanding – it simply *is* this way. Looking back to the post-World War II, pre-Cold War, Vietnam, Gulf War era, from an America engulfed in perpetual war, *The Master*'s close-ups embody a dual position of omniscience and ignorance. A warning from the past that is told from the present, these images say: 'You cannot know how I feel. You cannot know who I *am* or what I think. But you do know, really, what caused me to be this way.'

NOTES

1. Dodd uses this word to describe Quell a number of times.
2. This is a key component of Balázs's argument on sound film's threat to the potentiality of close-ups.
3. Examples include the work of Richard Maltby (1995) Murray Smith (1995) and David Bordwell (2002).
4. 'Motor mimicry and facial feedback may occur with any close-up . . . The viewer may actually "catch" some of the emotion the character is thought to be feeling through processes of mimicry and emotional contagion' (Plantinga 2009: 126).
5. Bordwell (1985).
6. The careers of Baudrillard and Virilio are exemplary in this regard, but we might note more contemporaneous examples in Mitchell (2011) and Tulloch and Blood (2012).

BIBLIOGRAPHY

Adorno, T. (1983), 'Cultural criticism and society', in *Prisms*, trans. S. M. Weber, Cambridge, MA: MIT Press, pp. 17–34.

Balázs, B. (2010), *Béla Balázs: Early Film Theory: Visible Man and The Spirit of Film*, trans. Erica Carter, London and New York: Berghahn Books.

Baudrillard, J. (2003), *The Spirit of Terrorism and Other Essays*, London and New York: Verso.

Bordwell, D. (1985), *The Classical Hollywood Cinema: Film Style and Mode of Production to 1960*, London: Routledge.

Bordwell, D. (2002), 'Intensified continuity: visual style in contemporary American film', *Film Quarterly*, 55.3 (Spring), pp. 16–28.

Buckland, W. (ed.) (2014), *Hollywood Puzzle Films*, New York and Abingdon: Routledge.

Deleuze, G. (1986), *Cinema 2: The Time Image*, Minneapolis: University of Minnesota Press.

Gershkoff, A. and S. Kushner (2005), 'Shaping public opinion: the 9/11–Iraq connection in the Bush Administration's rhetoric', *Perspectives on Politics*, 3 (September), pp. 525–37.

Levinas, E. (1999), *Totality and Infinity: An Essay on Exteriority*, Pittsburgh, PA: Duquesne University Press.

Loshitzky, Y. (ed.) (1997), *Spielberg's Holocaust: Critical Perspectives on 'Schindler's List'*, Bloomington: Indiana University Press.

Lyotard, J.-F. (1991), *The Inhuman: Reflections of Time*, Stanford: Stanford University Press.

Maltby, R. (1995), *Hollywood Cinema*, London: Wiley Blackwell.

Mirzoeff, N. (2004), *Watching Babylon: The War in Iraq and Global Visual Culture*, Abingdon and New York: Routledge.

Mitchell, W. J. T. (2011), *Cloning Terror: The War of Images 9/11 to the Present*, Chicago: University of Chicago Press.

Mueller, J. (2004), *The Remnants of War*, Ithaca: Cornell University Press.

Plantinga, C. (2009), *Moving Viewers: American Film and the Spectator's Experience*, Berkeley and Los Angeles: University of California Press.

Rancière, J. (2006), *Film Fables*, London: Berg.

Rivette, J. (1961), 'De l'abjection', *Cahiers du Cinéma*, 120 (June), pp. 54–5.

Smith, M. (1995), *Engaging Characters: Fiction, Emotion, and the Cinema*, Oxford: Clarendon Press.

Tulloch, J. and R. Warwick Blood (2012), *Icons of War and Terror: Media Images in an Age of International Risk*, Abingdon and New York: Routledge.

Vidal, G. (2002), *Perpetual War for Perpetual Peace: How We Got to Be So Hated*, New York: Nation Books.

Walker, J. (2005), *Trauma Cinema: Documenting Incest and the Holocaust*, Berkeley and London: University of California Press.

CHAPTER 7

Visible Dead Bodies and the Technologies of Erasure in the War on Terror

Jessica Auchter

The contemporary visual technologies of the war on terror are as much about invisibility as visibility, as much about what is moved out of sight or rendered visually taboo, as about what images are circulated and rendered hyper-visible. This chapter seeks to conceptualise erasure, by focusing on how images of dead bodies circulate in the war on terror. Rather than focus on soldier bodies, as often form the basis of such framing, I seek instead to understand the framing of what is seen and unseen in dead enemy bodies.

Why should we look at images in the discussion of erasure? Discussions of photography frequently focus on understanding how images are made and the narratives of what is left out in the decisions surrounding what is visually depicted (Sontag 2001, Sliwinski 2011). Beyond this, securitised images become dispersed through the schemas of viewing associated with cinema and other mechanisms of display, which often act as a filter for what can or should be viewed. From Facebook to Twitter, contemporary technology has shifted the frame, wherein war is rendered hyper-visible; at the same time these visualities are managed via a technology of erasure that blurs parts of images, and removes others from our line of sight, so as to manage the context under which the visual encounter occurs.

This chapter uses the cases of Muammar Qaddafi and Osama bin Laden to explore the purposes for which particular dead bodies are rendered (in)visible, and further, the visual politics of the encounter with the bloody body in a political context where bodies are often key sites inscribed with and resistant to power. To do so, I argue that obscenity is mustered as a visual and political tool, to both place a taboo on the viewing of certain dead bodies, and invite the viewing of others. Obscenity here provides the framing concept for visual engagement, precisely because what constitutes or is suggested to constitute the obscene is a political decision, one which generates particular erasures and legitimates particular narratives.

A further note on obscenity itself is necessary here. David Campbell (2007: 369) has noted that the news media is reluctant to portray 'unvarnished horror'. He describes the way it has become conventional wisdom to argue that media depictions of the obscene are commonplace, but in actuality displays of death are not very common (Campbell 2004). Thus, decisions around what is shown, what is considered too obscene or acceptably so, and what we view, are significant beyond just journalistic conventions, which themselves reflect larger social norms. Indeed, Barbie Zelizer (2010: 22) characterises graphicness as a 'moveable, serviceable, and debatable convention, dependent on those who invoke it and for which aim'. She argues that it is deemed acceptable to show Rwandan skulls, but not the victims of American airstrikes in Iraq, for example.

That is, norms surrounding what we 'should' look at are very much culturally based. Obscenity as a framing concept here is more than simply viewing a bloody body or a dismembered corpse. It is about degrees of visuality, and how something becomes too visible such that we no longer want to see it, even as we are visually encountering it. In the cases I discuss below, this is usually by replicating images of these corpses and managing the circumstances and warnings and framings under which they are viewed. In this sense, there is a failure involved in the very existence of these obscene dead bodies and this is what we encounter visually: the political effects of the failure of 'normal' corpse management. And when it comes to non-normative corpses, you can do certain things to them that may otherwise be considered taboo. The examples I discuss below are examples of such a visual encounter with a non-normative corpse (or corpses).

Beyond this, there is a postcolonial dimension at play here that instrumentalises particular foreign bodies. While the bodies of one's own soldiers are entitled to what is considered visual dignity, often involving privacy or even invisibility, the bodies of one's enemies or foreign bodies are deemed visible, either in the service of a humanitarian narrative that paints them as non-agents needing external assistance, or in the service of a dehumanising narrative that depicts their bodies as material trophies or reifies them as things. To this end, the 'we' that composes the audience of these images and bodies of the dead matters.

Images of the obscene dead invoke a political community made up of the viewers, viewing the body of the other rather than the body of one of their own.

THE OBSCENE DEAD: WITNESSING DEATH OR CELEBRATING SUFFERING?

Trauma studies has focused on the immediate present display of the bloody body, a horror that is considered disruptive of subjectivity. In contrast, the focus of this chapter is largely the circulation and display of images of dead bodies as replications of these immediate traumas, which raises the question of how the visual engagement with bloody bodies is managed. The display of a body involves active decision-making, but there are more decisions involved in the circulation of and encounter with images of the body. There is a transgression of a norm when a dead body is made visible outside of display in a funerary rite, thereby offering an indicator of how identities and communities form through the display of corpses deemed to be non-normative. Beyond this, the role of the cinematic in the way bodies are depicted both in images and in popular culture, such as film, offers ways of thinking about the disappearance, reappearance, visibility and invisibility of dead bodies in war.

In this context, these decisions surrounding which dead bodies are rendered visible are political ones that reference moral priors: that is, we are told that viewing images of the dead is necessary for humanitarian purposes in some instances, and that viewing images of the dead is a threat to our security in other instances. For example, in March 2015, photographs defined as 'graphic', depicting the tortured, bloodied and bruised dead bodies of civilians killed by the regime of Bashar al-Assad in Syria went on display in the halls of the United Nations (UN) building in New York. They are accompanied by warning signs to indicate the graphic nature of their subject, and some have argued that they are too graphic to be displayed. However, their display occurs in a context of awareness, which seems to be accompanied by an impetus to look.

'We know that it is far easier to walk rapidly down this corridor, far easier to look away,' Michele J. Sison, the US deputy representative to the UN, told the gathered crowd of diplomats and journalists. 'These images are the graphic depiction of how the Assad regime treats its citizens. It is imperative that we at the United Nations not look away'. (Jalabi 2015)

The images, part of a collection taken by a former Syrian military photographer who defected, were originally taken to act as evidence within the Syrian government that the regime had indeed killed the person they had reported as dead.

In describing the exhibit, UN representatives emphasise the moral imperative associated with looking. In a world where cultural norms often dictate that dead bodies should not be viewable outside of the funerary industry, especially when they are graphic by virtue of a bloody and violent death, these images of dead and tortured bodies are instead accompanied by a command to look. The images are themselves imbued with some sort of humanitarian power, implying that simply by looking, we can make things better, thereby inculcating a particular relationship between the viewer and the image, placing the viewer in a position of power to effect change.

Even as we are instructed to look at and engage with these images, portions of the images considered too graphic for display have been blurred. That is, even as the obscenity of the images provides a basis for their power to effect change, there is also the notion that some things are simply too obscene to be shown. Again, the audience here matters, as the viewers of these images at UN Headquarters are those visiting this building in New York, many of whom are classified as humanitarian actors with the power to bring about change simply via their visual consumption. Other viewers include Western audiences of the media outlets that circulated these images. As another example: in 2012 images and video were released of American soldiers urinating on Afghan corpses. The reporting of the act focused largely on the soldiers, and not the unnamed Afghans whose corpses were desecrated. As I have noted elsewhere, these corpses were simply props supplementary to the main attraction: the soldiers (Auchter 2015a). Most of the websites reporting the story blurred out parts of the images, including the crotch area of the soldiers, and the soldier's faces, before their names were released to the media. But the faces of the dead bodies on the ground were not blurred. By virtue of their visibility, because they were rendered visible, a political statement was made about their lives and deaths; they were both biologically and ontologically dead. Their visibility, at times contrasted with the invisibility of those enmeshed in multiple biological processes with them, rendered them the objects of American military agency even in their death. That is, there seems to be a difference between images we are 'supposed' to engage with and those we are not. The viewer is told by the UN exhibit that viewing these images is necessary, that the images hold some kind of humanitarian power. But other images, the ones we are not supposed to look at, pose some kind of threat to security, whereby simply looking at them renders all of us more insecure.

These two initial stories gesture to the framing through which it may be useful to think about the visibility of the dead: obscenity. The images of Syrian torture victims are intended to spur action on the part of the international community by making obscenity visible. On the other hand, images of dead American soldiers are characterised as too obscene to be part of the visual spectrum of the war on terror. Beyond this, the examples I will address below gesture to the idea that obscenity can allow specific encounters with specific bloody bodies, such as that of Qaddafi, as a means to consume the body as a site inscribed with the power of democratic revolution. But these examples are enmeshed within the wider discourse of images of the body in pain, primarily associated with purported ethical dilemmas with regards to war photography.

Indeed, much of war photography centres on displaying images of suffering, at times obscene, as a means of showing the horrors of war so as to avoid them. Yet the cases I discuss are not intended to support a narrative about the horrors of war. They rather tell us that obscenity can be part of the triumphs and successes of war. If, as Susan Sontag (2003: 21) notes, 'something becomes real by being photographed', then the way these obscene images circulate may tell us something significant about how we are not horrified by the effects of some kinds of violence. Beyond this, though, the examples discussed in this chapter examine the functioning of obscenity in the technologies of erasure. It examines the uses of obscenity framing to legitimise viewing, as in the case of the dead body of Qaddafi, to decide on which parts of images to blur, as in the case of US soldiers posing with dead bodies mentioned above, and to legitimise the disappearance of particular images in the service of security narratives, as in the case of the dead body of Osama bin Laden. As Elizabeth Dauphinee (2007: 140) has noted, the 'drive to make *visible* the body in pain often evokes a particular kind of seeing, which ultimately works to further the Cartesian rupture between self and other'. If this occurs even when the aim of the circulation of the image is to cultivate empathy, we can imagine how this takes effect and is exacerbated when the image is circulated for the purpose of disseminating a dehumanising narrative that instructs the viewer to engage with the photograph, and the body depicted therein, not as a suffering, vulnerable human, but as a 'body part' worthy of serving as a trophy or souvenir.

That is, most work on the body in pain looks at the ethical gap in our ability to receive and witness the suffering of others (Dauphinee 2007).

But what if we are directed, by the context and content of the image, to engage with it, or perhaps to consume it for a particular political agenda? It is important here to move beyond the oft-privileged notion that witnessing pain automatically translates into (at least the struggle involved in) representing suffering, and ask questions about celebrating death rather than mourning it, especially in the context of visual interactions and the visuality of obscenity.

Conflict, natural disasters and global health crises all produce dead bodies en masse. But, as Barbie Zelizer (2010) outlines, media are much more likely to show about-to-die photos than those of dead bodies. Though debated in terms of the political work they do and the narratives surrounding conflict photos, these images are considered more appropriate for depicting horrific events and atrocities. But photos of dead bodies seem to violate an unsaid norm about our schemas of viewing. For example, David Campbell (2007) traced media coverage of Darfur in the *Guardian/Observer* news photographs. Out of forty-eight photographs published across two years, only one depicted a dead body, despite the fact that the very problem being addressed in this time frame was the deaths of thousands of people. That is, death was the matter of the story, yet it was deemed unfit for photographic depiction. Thus, the instances in which dead bodies are made visible are significant. What is it about death that makes it appropriate for description with words, but not photos? And what is it about certain lives and deaths that render them acceptable for viewing, even amidst a general sense that it is undignified to show them and to look at them, especially when the images are obscene due to the graphic and violent nature of the deaths?

There is something specific about taking and viewing images of enemy dead that comes into play here. Michael Sledge has detailed a long history of the emergence of various legal structures to dictate what can be done with dead soldier and dead enemy bodies. He states: 'how a government views the corpses of its soldiers is indicative of how it views its citizens' (2005: 26). That is, the degree to which a government values the material protection of its soldiers, and their dignity when dead, tells us a lot about identity and the formation of political community; one's community forms around the memorialisation and mourning of one's national dead. Similarly, treatment of enemy dead reflects the attitudes towards the enemy's social and cultural system, he argues. Much of his analysis is devoted to the attempted repatriation of soldier dead, but he also addresses enemy corpses. He lays out a long history of abuse of enemy corpses, focusing on those cases committed by Americans, including decapitations of Japanese and Vietnamese soldiers during World War II and the Vietnam War, carving bones into letter openers, and other such abuses. All of these cases perform a specific conception of how that body is envisioned or elided within a particular social structure and performs certain meanings and identities.

The examples I address, then, seek to interrogate the way visual images are often portrayed. They are usually referred to in one of three ways: as evidence of atrocity and suffering that will make humanitarian efforts more likely by cultivating empathy, as part of securitising narratives that justify specific policies (Heck and Schlag 2013), or as able to resist securitising narratives (Hansen 2011). But more work needs to be done on the visual politics of when bodies are seen and when they are erased or rendered unseen. As Susan Sontag (2003: 72) notes, 'the other, even when not an enemy, is regarded only as someone to be seen, not someone (like us) who also sees.' Elizabeth Dauphinee (2007: 144–5) has spoken of this in the context of the Abu Ghraib images: 'the gaze enabled by the photograph also works as a sort of "hooding" of the subject, maintaining the inherently violent fantasy that we can see without being seen.' In this sense, the instrumentalisation of the dead body depicted in the image can work to dehumanise and de-subjectify the subject of the image, as seen in the case of Qaddafi's corpse.

'MAD DOG' ON BLOODY DISPLAY: VIEWING QADDAFI'S DEAD BODY

What are the politics and ethics of viewing the dead, bloodied, body of a dictator, of engaging with it visually, of walking past it as it lies on the ground, of consuming the image on the front cover of the newspaper? What does it mean to encounter the obscene, swollen face of a dead man, one whose face was so parodied in life and now has been so widely dispersed in death? The treatment of Qaddafi is not one isolated case of dead body treatment, but indicative of a larger social structure and discourse of what can be done with dictators. The story of Qaddafi, then, does not end with his death. Rather, his dead body is as vital a political symbol as his living body, and what is done to it gestures to the complex assemblages in which the dead body is enmeshed.

Thousands of Libyans and foreign journalists lined up to see Qaddafi's body, displayed in a cold storage unit in Misrata. Even after removal, photographers were permitted to take pictures of his rotting corpse on its way to be buried.[1] One photograph of Qaddafi's dead body, taken by media sources, shows his bloodied corpse with hands in the foreground of the shot holding cell phones to take photographs of it: a photograph of photographing, a reproduction and re-presentation of the logic of image creation that revolved around this singular figure (see Figure 7.1).

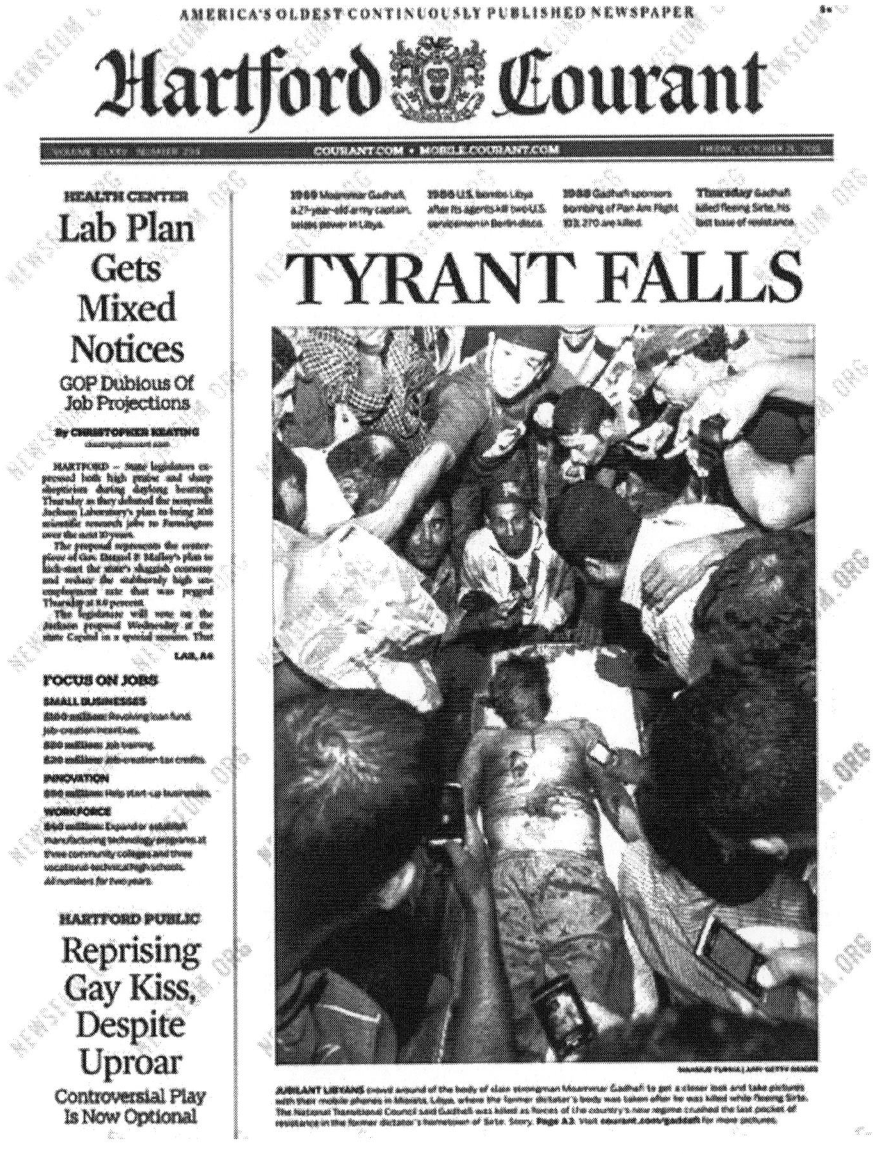
AMERICA'S OLDEST CONTINUOUSLY PUBLISHED NEWSPAPER

Hartford Courant

COURANT.COM • MOBILE.COURANT.COM

HEALTH CENTER

Lab Plan Gets Mixed Notices

GOP Dubious Of Job Projections

TYRANT FALLS

FOCUS ON JOBS

HARTFORD PUBLIC

Reprising Gay Kiss, Despite Uproar

Controversial Play Is Now Optional

Figure 7.1: The cover page of the *Hartford Courant* newspaper announcing the death of Muammar Qaddafi.

This brings up the issue of the ethics of a body on display. The etymology of the word display speaks to its meaning: scatter, unfold, spread out, reveal, exhibit. Thus Qaddafi's body is not simply rendered visible, it is also unfurled in such a way as to convey its essential meaning as the body of a dead dictator, subject to portrayal as a bloody corpse. There is an ethics associated not only with the display but also with the viewing that must be acknowledged. My analysis must engage with this ethical dilemma then: of how to assess a particular set of discourses surrounding this display, draw attention to the way they were replicated and circulated by traditional and social media, yet myself avoid replicating and re-presenting the meanings which are potentially ethically problematic. That is, even as I look at the photographs of Qaddafi's corpse, I am implicated in its display and the ethical questions therein. As Susan Sontag (2003: 42) notes, 'the gruesome invites us to be either spectators or cowards.' If I too am a spectator of the gruesome image, then the onus is on me to be self-reflexive on the silence, invisibilities, asymmetries, such a relationship engenders. Yet there is also something problematic about this dichotomy that I hope to interrogate: the notion that if not looking is cowardice, there is something courageous about looking at the obscene, or the idea that not looking is representative of a fear of engaging with the image rather than a denial of such an engagement. Indeed, as Sontag herself notes (2003: 95), 'images of the repulsive can allure', thus the relationship of viewing must be further complicated than the dichotomy between spectating and cowardice. Exploring how, when, and why images of Qaddafi dead or dying were circulated is the first step towards problematising this dichotomy.

It is important to examine how various media sources portrayed and depicted Qaddafi's death. The *New York Post* had perhaps the most creative, though not entirely accurate, headline, which would appeal to their viewership: 'Khadafy Killed by Yankee Fan: Gunman Had More Hits than A-Rod'. Along with the headline was a photograph of Qaddafi's bloody face as he was dragged through the streets before his death (Fisher 2011). Many news sources chose similar photographs to show in the wake of the death announcement on 20 October 2011, including the *Guardian*, with their headline: 'Death of a Dictator', Washington, DC's *Express,* New York's *Daily News*, the *Washington Post,* and others. It was only later that the images of his dead body on display appeared, mostly on internet media sources, indicative of the dispersion of viewing in an era of democratised technology access. On the day after Qaddafi's death only seven out of 424 print newspapers in the US used large images of his dead body on the cover, for example, though additional ones printed smaller photos of his dead body (Moos 2011). On 21 October the UK's *Mirror* was one of the international papers that showed a picture of Qaddafi's dead body on their cover, with the headline: 'Don't shoot, Don't shoot', Qaddafi's alleged last words. His face is bruised and bloody, swollen with death, and his chest is marked with traces of his own blood. The text that accompanies the

photo reads, 'For 42 years Colonel Gaddafi terrorised his own people
. . . and the world. Yesterday, he died as he lived, shown no mercy as
he pleaded for his life.' Supplementary text refers to him as 'Mad Dog',
which recirculates connections between obscenity and madness that tell
us it is more acceptable to look at a non-normative corpse, and fetishises madness so as to cultivate a distance between the viewer and the
obscene corpse (Auchter 2015b).

The *Daily Mail* similarly reiterates Qaddafi's last words in their
headline on 21 October 2011, but displays a bloody picture of Qaddafi
before his death. The text reads, 'Battered and bloody, the tyrant of
Libya pleads for his life. Moments later, he was dead – executed with a
bullet to the head.' The UK's *Independent* shows a montage of photos
of a bloody Qaddafi being dragged through the street before his death,
with the headline, 'End of a Tyrant'. *The Times* and the *Daily Telegraph*
have a similar headline and photo. *Metro*'s image is of the same heavily
filmed and photographed journey Qaddafi took from his hiding place
to his death. The language of their headline is illuminating: 'A mad dog
in life but a cowering rat in his last, brutal moments'. The reference to
a rat dehumanises Qaddafi after his capture, justifying the measures
taken to kill him. The *Daily Express* shows the same iconic picture of
Qaddafi, bloody, in the streets, before his death, and the headline and
subheading reads: 'Gaddafi gunned down in sewer: Murdering rat gets
his just deserts.' But the *Sun* is perhaps the most dramatic in terms of
justification of Qaddafi's death, with their 21 October headline over a
picture of Qaddafi's bloody face: 'That's for Lockerbie.' The preview of
the table of contents at the bottom of the front page alludes to a story
about Qaddafi in hell with Hitler.[2] This fits with some of the statements
made by Lockerbie family members. Kathy Tedeschi, whose husband
was killed in the Pan Am plane, said in response to Qaddafi's death:
'I hope he is in hell with Hitler' (Usborne et al. 2011).

It is useful to contrast these English and American headlines and
images with those from around the world, to emphasise the cultural
specificity and postcolonial dimension noted above. English and American newspapers were more likely to use the images of Qaddafi, bloody,
being dragged through the streets, or even his dead body, whereas
papers from other regions of the world were likely to use similar headlines about Qaddafi's last words, but to include old photographs of him
before his capture and death. Such papers include *Pakistan Today,* and
a selection of Sri Lankan and Chinese newspapers.[3] France's *Le Figaro,*
Portugal's *Publico*, Poland's *Gazeta* and Canada's *National Post* all
showed an old picture of Qaddafi, some in military uniform and others
not (Moos 2011). Tabloid-type papers were also on the whole more

likely to show photos of his dead body, which legitimates the notion that there is something prurient about viewing the obscene body (Tait 2008). This is also framed by the textual warnings surrounding the images themselves, which depict the fantasy of the dead dictator and allow the reader to become a privileged witness to the obscenity of Qaddafi's violent death. Even descriptions of Qaddafi's death in the media utilised dramatic descriptions of his death and body, whether they chose to show the images or not.

Tiffany Jenkins draws attention to the contrast between Qaddafi's dead body and that of Osama bin Laden. Bin Laden's body was not displayed, photographs were not shown and his burial at sea was intended to keep his grave site from becoming a shrine. Qaddafi, on the other hand, was displayed and paraded, photographs were splashed around the internet and his bloodied body was dragged through the streets. As Jenkins (2011) notes:

> [T]he contrast between the careful concealment of bin Laden's body, and the public parading of Gaddafi's tells us something. The weakness of Gaddafi's position before he died meant he was easier to dominate when dead; bin Laden, on the other hand, was feared until the end, and his supporters are still considered extremely dangerous. Even in death, he remains a threat.

However, what Jenkins omits from her assessment is the discursive work at play here. Osama bin Laden needed to continue to be a threat even from beyond the grave in order to legitimate an ongoing war on terror and the broad criteria for carrying out drone strikes in Pakistan and Yemen, and his body was enmeshed in a wider story about al-Qaeda revenge for the death. Thus bin Laden's body is disappeared within a narrative enabled in the service of a particular policy, as will be explored further below. Qaddafi, on the other hand, is not a dead terrorist, but a dead dictator, and his dead body and its display enable a different conversation about the illegitimacy of the dictator and the lack of threat he poses to democratic forms of governance. In this sense, obscenity as a framing concept becomes particularly useful because it can be imagined both as the obscenity of seeing too much, and as the obscenity of seeing too little. Osama bin Laden was the body that was too obscene to be shown, as I detail further below, while Qaddafi's was just obscene enough to shock on display, and cause some ethical discomfort and debate, while still acting as a triumphant display of a win for Western democracy.

Several news stories and commenters drew attention to the ethical discomfort in viewing Qaddafi's body. For example, Chloe, from London, in a comment on the *Daily Mail* website on the story which shows the picture of a dead Qaddafi, remarks, 'Is it necessary to see these visuals? What are we teaching our children as justice? It's medieval! Kill the man, but don't splash his bloody corpse all over the papers' ('Ignominious End'). This comment is an interesting one because it separates Qaddafi's death from the display of his dead body, implying that justice can be an extrajudicial killing, yet cannot be a visual engagement with the result of such an act, a notion that recurred in the context of the display of the image. Indeed, both were situated within the same larger logic. It is precisely the notion that it was acceptable to kill Qaddafi that rendered the display of his body the logical next step. It is precisely the display of his body which reinforces the justification for killing him: that he is less-than-human and thus not entitled to the same cultural and even legal protections, when alive or when dead.

The very display of the body in this instance evokes a certain paradox about death itself. Death is usually mourned, but what are the politics when a death is celebrated? Jonathan Jones aptly critiques the responses by Western media as hypocritical in that they rushed to publish photographs even while claiming to be concerned about the ethics of displaying the photographs of a dead body. Though it should be noted that not many of the newspapers that published images explored the ethical dilemma of publishing them. Rather, Qaddafi was visual fodder for the story of revolution, and the viewers of the images drew attention to the ethical questions at hand. The display of the body has also co-opted the democratic revolution itself. He writes:

The Arab Spring became The Autumn of the Patriarch, as his dead body haunted the new era. No wonder a Libyan was quoted as saying he has given more trouble dead than alive. Yet the main trouble dead Gaddafi has given is to expose the fundamental shallowness and sentimentality of the Western democracies' support for Arab revolution and in particular our military intervention in Libya. To get upset by photographs of the dead Gaddafi is to pretend we did not know we went to war at all. It is to fantasise that our own role is so just and proper and decent that it is not bloody at all. (Jones 2011)

Thus Libyans are ultimately painted as bloodthirsty even in their strive for democracy, while Western democracies can consider themselves to have clean hands in the matter, reaping the benefits of democratisation without paying the bloody cost, or as Jones says, enacting a fantasy of war based on just war theory that depicts war as 'utterly righteous, from which we emerge with no guilt on our hands, not even the killing of a brutal dictator'. Thus we can claim both the triumph of democracy over dictatorship yet also distance ourselves from the brutality of war that led to the death of Qaddafi and is represented by his body on display: 'a day in the life of hell, also known as war: a corpse photographed for souvenirs, displayed to satisfy the oppressed, in a moment of violent gratification.' Yet I disagree with Jones on the matter of widespread concern about the photographs of Qaddafi's body. Indeed, most of the responses amounted to the fact that he got what he deserved. And even those that considered the photographs problematic attempted to disassociate that from the death itself. That is, there is a politics behind the notion that we are not horrified by the rotting corpse of the dead dictator. In fact, this imagery sustains democracy itself by positing the dead dictator as display-able. This is a politics/ethics of horror, which is biologically grounded in the human body. We are not horrified by the dead bodies of international politics, even when they are rendered overtly visible to us, perhaps because of the politics of visibility at play. If certain bodies do not count as bodies, if certain deaths are not considered grievable (Butler 2010), then perhaps the standard rules of corpses do not apply? That is, the death itself is not any less obscene than viewing it. Encountering the obscenity of the image is one way of deferring the obscenity of the death itself, of making the image the iconic representation so as to not have to reckon with the larger context of the event.

THE VISUAL POLITICS OF OSAMA BIN LADEN: SECURING THE DEAD TERRORIST

In 2011 a dead body was produced, but we were not allowed to look at it. The death of Osama bin Laden after a long search was celebrated as a victory for the US and indeed global security more broadly. Immediately, T-shirts were made celebrating the death, linking it to the 9/11 attacks which bin Laden was so infamous for orchestrating. I also recall seeing a bumper sticker in the aftermath that said 'Navy SEALs 1, bin Laden 0'. This reference to a game score emphasised the ease with which his death was accepted and celebrated by the US. Photos of bin Laden's face, or what was reportedly his corpse, mutilated from the shots that killed him, began to circulate. But those were soon discredited, and photographs of the body, and indeed the body itself, were not released to a demanding public. The body was buried at sea so as to avoid creating a shrine for Osama bin Laden. The body was disappeared in the service of a particular security narrative: we were told that to be secure, we must not look upon this particular corpse, that this dead body was itself still a security risk due to the power it held as a symbol. As US President Barack Obama noted shortly after the mission that killed Osama bin Laden: 'It is important for us to make sure that very graphic photos of somebody who was shot in the head are not floating around as an incitement to additional violence, as a propaganda tool'. (McConnell and Todd 2014)

Yet without the body, the question of memory is put into disarray: how to remember Osama bin Laden without the physical evidence of his death? We can see this in the public demands for the body itself, or at least to see the photographs as synecdoche of the body. There was so much demand for the release of the photos that several Freedom of Information Act (FoIA) requests were filed to get the photos released. Yet at the same time, internal orders were given to destroy the photographs.

> In an e-mail dated May 13, 2011, then-Vice Adm. William McRaven wrote the following: 'One particular item that I want to emphasize is photos; particularly UBLs remains. At this point . . . all photos should have been turned over to the CIA; if you still have them destroy them immediately or get them to the [redacted]'. (McConnell and Todd 2014)

Judicial Watch, a conservative watchdog group, sued the Obama administration to get the photos released, claiming that it was not a security risk for US intelligence services to release the images (Wing 2014). They argued that 'the government had failed to demonstrate how all of the images, even the non-graphic ones, would reasonably be expected to "cause identifiable or describable exceptionally grave damage to national security", as the government suggested they would' (Reilly 2013a). Justice Department lawyer Robert Loeb, in stating the case of the administration, noted a difference between the photos of Uday and Qusay Hussein, which were ultimately publicly released, and Osama bin Laden.

> 'While the US was concerned that releasing photos of the bodies of Saddam Hussein's sons could spark riots, officials determined the release was necessary to assure the Iraqi people they were dead,' said Loeb. 'That wasn't the case with the bin Laden photos,' he argued. (Reilly 2013a)

But there was precisely such a demand for evidence of his death in the days following the raid that killed him.

Indeed, the film *Zero Dark Thirty* depicts this tension nicely. It both satisfies the demand for a visual representation of the death of Osama bin Laden, to present his body on screen to posit a counterpoint to the invisibility of his dead body, as the film centres on finding and identifying, indeed *visualizing* bin Laden, and yet offers lingering questions, as the body's identifying features remain off-screen in the scene where bin Laden's dead body is depicted (see Figure 7.2). In that sense, it both assuaged the desire to see, and maintained the dominant narrative that the American public did not actually want to encounter the obscenity of the overly recognisable death of Osama bin Laden.

One of the important features of this case is the multiplicity of ways the dead body functions. That is, it has sentimental value to loved ones, political value to various states and the international community, and evidentiary value to those demanding to see it. Indeed, according to court papers from the lawsuit mentioned above, one of the main reasons the photographs of Osama bin Laden's corpse existed in the first place was so that the Central Intelligence Agency (CIA) could conduct facial recognition analysis to confirm that it was indeed bin Laden rather than a body double (*Daily Mail*, 'Bin Laden Death Photos' 2013). As in other instances where the dead body is made visible, there is a tension between the dignity often attributed to the dead human body, and the potential value it can have to tell the story of its own death. This dead body was central to political stories about the heroism of American Special Forces, the lack of cooperation with Pakistani authorities and as evidence of the fact that this powerful figure was in fact dead and thus no longer a threat to global and American security. The dead body, then, acted as the symbol that insecurity was alleviated, that the world had been made a safer place.

This recurred in the court narratives with the decision about the release of the photographs. A US appeals court ruled that the CIA did not need to release the photos. The decision to go against FoIA was legitimised by reference to security: the imminent security threat to US 'interests, citizens, and personnel' around the world that would be created by releasing the images, and presumably the assurance of their security by not releasing these images. As the panel decision notes:

> This is not a case in which the declarants are making predictions about the consequences of releasing just any images. Rather, they are predicting the consequences of releasing an extraordinary set of images, ones that depict American military personnel burying the founder and leader of al-Qaeda. (Reilly 2013b)

Thus the debate is one about the security risk of an extraordinary dead body. In a context where the dead body is both the product of a mission to secure (the Abottabad raid that killed Osama bin Laden) and the nexus for potential future insecurity (a propaganda tool for future terrorist recruitment), what the singular dead body means remains hotly contested.

It is impossible to fully conceptualise the relationship between terrorism and security without addressing the way the dead body of the terrorist is produced. That is, labelling terrorism as a key threat to security implies a policy to end terrorism; this has taken the form of targeting terrorists, of causing their deaths. Their dead bodies thus become the symbols of the end of a security risk or threat, but at the same time, their dead bodies are complex things: they are sites for generating future terrorist recruitment, bodies enmeshed in religious discourses about proper body disposal, someone's loved one, the material evidence that a security threat has been eliminated. This raises important questions about who is being secured, and whose dead bodies represent the achievement of additional degrees of security.

Ultimately, then, these images play with notions of how bodies are rendered visible and consumed. I return to the scene of Osama bin Laden's death in the film *Zero Dark Thirty*. The scene takes place in the dark, and the face of bin Laden is never shown, as at the point he is shot the camera pans to display instead the bullet holes on his body (see Figure 7.2). The mismatch of not actually being able to see the face, even while the obscenity, the graphic part of the death, is shown,

Figure 7.2: A still from the film *Zero Dark Thirty* (2012) of the moment when Osama bin Laden is killed, with his face remaining off screen and never visible.

works to construct a narrative about threat and death and security with regards to the dead terrorist. The dead dictator, in the body of Qaddafi, is enmeshed within its own stories about visibility and threat, but both take place within a visual and cinematic context that is not intended to cultivate empathy for the dead, but rather to inculcate a certain type of seeing in the war on terror, a contemporary technology of seeing war that instructs the viewer via framing mechanisms how to see and consume certain kinds of dead bodies.

CONCLUSION: THE FUNCTIONALITY OF ERASING THE BLOODY DEAD BODY

The rules of body display are not set in stone: each dead body story offers up one visualisation of the technologies of erasure, in service of a particular narrative. The existence of a dead body can be a failure of the system, as in natural disasters where bodies crop up in places they should not be, demanding to be managed and reincorporated within mechanisms of body management. However, the existence of a dead body can also be indicative of a success of the system, that a body has been rendered into a corpse so as to enhance security, as with the death of Osama bin Laden, and the demands to materialise his corpse a means to narrativise the security threat itself.

As I have described, images of violently dead bodies have been circulated and mobilised in the service of the war on terror. Some bodies are rendered hypervisible, such as that of Qaddafi, so as to enable a story about the triumph of democracy over dictatorship, and the madness of a dictator that continues beyond his death. Other bodies are displayed in a complex schema of visuality, as in the command to look at Syrian victims, or to look at pieces of blurred images of atrocities committed by soldiers. Still others are deemed too volatile to be displayed, as in the case of the corpse of Osama bin Laden. The images are part of a wider discourse, used strategically and to specific effect. Circulating images of Qaddafi reinforced the notion of the inevitable failure of dictatorship, supporting a policy of democratisation. The body of Osama bin Laden, on the other hand, represented a success of the war on terror, but its visibility was considered a security risk that could further heighten tensions and provoke retaliatory attacks by al-Qaeda.

Judith Butler, in the context of the Abu Ghraib photos, has argued that what we see when we look at these photos is ourselves seeing. To paraphrase, she notes that we are the photographers to the extent that we live within the visual norms in which the prisoners are rendered abject and beaten. But the individuals depicted are indifferent to us (Butler 2005: 826). This is similarly the case in the photographs I have described here, most importantly because in a structural sense, there is no way the dead body can see back at us as we consume it visually. Butler has argued that this sort of depiction tells us that certain kinds of seeing are memorialised in the photograph. These ways of seeing do not depict human suffering because the visual framing does not conceive of the subject of the photograph as human. She lays the framework, then, for considering images of suffering and obscene atrocity that are not intended to, or are unable to, provoke moral outrage precisely because they represent a rupture in symmetric seeing.

The visual asymmetry of viewing the dead inculcates a particular relationship of consumption such that specific non-normative bodies are consumed rather than simply viewed. Beyond this, the privileged act of seeing at a distance is often equated with witnessing, yet it also inculcates a model wherein we experience modern war by proxy, and this framing shapes understandings of what war is via which images of war are deemed legitimate grounds for visual consumption. Obscenity provides a means of generating a spectacle out of dead enemy bodies, both in their display and in the way they are visually erased. It does so through technology: the editing of images, the pixellation of parts of obscene images as a means to blur and remove certain images, thereby visually managing them and their meanings. That is, in thinking about the technologies of erasure in the war on terror, what matters may be questions surrounding who is seen and how, but also who is seeing and how.

NOTES

1. One example can be found in the article 'Ignominious end for Gaddafi' in London's *Daily Mail*.
2. The *Daily Mirror* posts a collection of these images of newspaper front pages at <http://www.mirror.co.uk/news/uk-news/gaddafi-dead-how-colonel-gaddafis-275437> (last access 10 August 2016)
3. See <http://www.mirror.co.uk/news/uk-news/gaddafi-dead-how-colonel-gaddafis-275437> for a selection of photographs (last accessed 10 August 2016).

BIBLIOGRAPHY

Auchter, J. (2015a), 'Corpses', in M. Salter (ed.), *Making Things International*, Minneapolis: University of Minnesota Press.
Auchter, J. (2015b), '@GaddafisGhost: on the popular memoro-politics of a dead dictator', *Journal for Cultural Research*, 19.3, pp. 291–305.

Butler, J. (2005), 'Photography, war, outrage', *PMLA*, 120.3, pp. 822–7.

Butler, J. (2010), *Frames of War: When is Life Grievable?* London: Verso.

Campbell, D. (2004), 'Horrific blindness: images of death in contemporary media', *Journal for Cultural Research*, 8.1 (January), pp. 55–74.

Campbell, D. (2007), 'Geopolitics and visuality: sighting the Darfur conflict', *Political Geography*, 26, pp. 357–82.

The Daily Mail (2011), 'Ignominious end for Gaddafi as he is buried with son Mutassim in unmarked desert grave at dawn', 25 October. Available at <http://www.dailymail.co.uk/news/article-2053110/Gaddafi-burial-Dictator-son-Mutassims-dead-bodies-unmarked-grave.html> (last accessed 10 August 2016).

The Daily Mail (2013), 'Bin Laden death photos will not be released as US court rules they must stay classified', 22 May. Available at <http://www.dailymail.co.uk/news/article-2328948/Bin-Laden-death-photos-NOT-released-U-S-court-rules-stay-classified.html> (last accesed 6 June 2016).

Dauphinee, E. (2007), 'The politics of the body in pain', *Security Dialogue*, 38.2, pp. 139–55.

Fisher, M. (2011), 'Fact check: New York Post's Qaddafi headline almost certainly wrong', *The Atlantic*, 21 October, Available at <http://www.theatlantic.com/international/archive/2011/10/fact-check-new-york-posts-qaddafi-headline-almost-certainly-wrong/247141/> (last accessed 6 June 2016).

Hansen, L. (2011), 'Theorizing the image for security studies: visual securitization and the Muhammad cartoon crisis', *European Journal of International Relations*, 17.1, pp. 51–74.

Heck, A. and G. Schlag (2013), 'Securitizing images: the female body and the war in Afghanistan', *European Journal of International Relations*, 19.4, pp. 891–913.

Hellmich, C. and A. Behnke (eds) (2012), *Knowing al-Qaeda: The Epistemology of Terrorism*, London: Ashgate.

Jalabi, R. (2015), 'Images of Syrian torture on display at UN', *The Guardian*, 11 March. Available at <http://www.theguardian.com/world/2015/mar/11/images-syrian-torture-shock-new-yorkers-united-nations> (last accessed 6 June 2016).

Jenkins, T. (2011), 'Gaddafi: body politics', *Prospect Magazine*, 24 October. Available at <https://www.prospectmagazine.co.uk/magazine/gaddafi-body-politics/> (last accessed 6 June 2016).

Jones, J. (2011), 'The West wrings its hands over dead Gaddafi photos, but war is always hell', *The Guardian*, 25 October. Available at <https://www.theguardian.com/commentisfree/2011/oct/25/dead-gaddafi-photos-war-hell> (last accessed 10 August 2016).

Marlin-Bennett, R. and J. Walton (2010), 'Commodified cadavers and the political economy of the spectacle', *International Political Sociology*, 2.2, pp. 159–77.

McConnell, D. and B. Todd (2014), 'Admiral's email on photos of Osama bin Laden's corpse: "destroy them"', *CNN*, 12 February. Available at <http://www.cnn.com/2014/02/11/politics/e-mail-photos-destroyed-osama-bin-laden/> (last accessed 6 June 2016).

Moos, J. (2011), 'Few US front pages feature dead Gadhafi, many international papers show body', *Poynter*, 21 October. Available at <http://www.poynter.org/2011/few-us-front-pages-feature-dead-gadhafi-many-international-papers-show-body/150386/> (last accessed 10 August 2016).

Reilly, R. J. (2013), 'Osama bin Laden photo release considered by appeals court', *Huffington Post*, 10 January. Available at <http://www.huffingtonpost.com/2013/01/10/osama-bin-laden-photos_n_2444717.html> (last accessed 6 June 2016).

Reilly, R. J. (2013), 'Dead Osama bin Laden photos don't have to be released by CIA, Appeals Court rules', *Huffington Post*, 21 May. Available at <http://www. huffingtonpost.com/2013/05/21/osama-bin-laden-photos_n_3312970.html> (last accessed 6 June 2016).

Sledge, M. (2005), *Soldier Dead: How We Recover, Identify, Bury, and Honor our Military Fallen*, New York: Columbia University Press.

Sliwinski, S. (2011), *Human Rights in Camera*, Chicago: University of Chicago Press.

Sontag, S. (2001), *On Photography*, New York: Picador.

Sontag, S. (2003), *Regarding the Pain of Others*, New York: Picador.

Tait, S. (2008), 'Pornographies of violence? Internet spectatorship on body horror', *Critical Studies in Media Communication*, 25.1, pp. 91–111.

Usborne, D., K. Sengupta, P. Walker, C. Milmo and R. Hall (2011), 'Gaddafi killed in Libya', *Fraser Coast Chronicle*, 21 October. Available at <http://www.frasercoastchronicle.com.au/news/gaddafi-killed-libya/1145560/> (last accessed 10 August 2016).

Wing, N. (2014), 'US troops unloaded "over a hundred bullets" into Osama bin Laden's dead body, sources claim', *Huffington Post*, 13 March. Available at <http://www. huffingtonpost.com/2014/03/13/osama-bin-laden-death-shooting_n_4958147. html> (last accessed 6 June 2016).

Zelizer, B. (2010), *About to Die: How News Images Move the Public*, Oxford: Oxford University Press.

CHAPTER 8

Ambiguity, Ambivalence and Absence in *Zero Dark Thirty*

Lisa Purse

Zero Dark Thirty, Kathryn Bigelow's 2012 film about the ten-year hunt for Osama bin Laden, has provoked competing accusations: that it is either anti-war or pro-war, anti-torture or pro-torture, and left wing or right wing in its political convictions. The heat of the assertions on either side of the debate (Naomi Wolf (2013) famously accused Bigelow of being 'torture's handmaiden') illustrates the extent to which the film's subject matter – the post-9/11 counter-terrorism strategies deployed by the US military and government agencies – itself continues to provoke vociferous political and cultural discussion. Not for the first (or last) time in American cinema history, a film becomes the site at which a nationally felt ambivalence – in this case, about US actions carried out in the name of the so-called 'war on terror' – is explored. *Zero Dark Thirty* has caused controversy not only because of its subject matter, but because of its ambiguity. The debates around the film have focused most intently on key elements of what is presented on screen: the scenes of torture, the character of Maya (played by Jessica Chastain), and the killing of bin Laden. These have provoked strikingly contrasting interpretations, drawn from the same film-making decisions, and the same screen details. Thus *Zero Dark Thirty* has become what Frank Tomasulo once, in relation to a different war film, called a 'national Rorschach test' (Tomasulo 1990: 147).[1] In this essay I want to unpick these ambiguities, to consider if *Zero Dark Thirty* gives voice to or counters a felt ambivalence about the war on terror, by examining what has sometimes slipped from view in the heated discussion of its scenes of torture and killing. That is, what absences might the compelling presences of *Zero Dark Thirty* obscure?

AMBIVALENCE AND PRESENCE: LOCATING AMBIGUITY

The film's moments of ambiguity – moments whose intended import can be interpreted in more than one way – are numerous, and I will examine some of these in what follows. Such a preponderance of ambiguity has the effect of producing political ambivalence at the structural level: that is, the film itself literally becomes a container for contradictory ideas and interpretations, allowing spectators who hold contrasting views to each see their convictions reflected in the text itself. Where *felt* ambivalence generally describes an individual or group's misgivings about a subject, *structural* ambivalence is simply the state of containing or permitting more than one viewpoint or interpretation at once. Structural ambivalence is often designed into American films that wish to address controversial subject matter without alienating parts of their audience, a strategy that, as Richard Maltby points out, 'displaces responsibility for the interpretation of a movie's content onto its audience' so that studios themselves are not accused of holding partisan political views (2003: 275; see also Tomasulo 1990: 147). One of the questions that *Zero Dark Thirty* prompts is how far one might perceive a felt ambivalence in the film's presentation of its subject, in addition to the structural ambivalence that has been designed in.

The presence that seems most compelling for reviewers and commentators is that of Maya, the composite CIA agent who succeeds, in the film, in finding bin Laden. First encountered in the opening torture scenes, and positioned as participant in or behind-the-scenes instigator of almost every scene that follows, Maya is the central protagonist through which the spectator accesses the events the film depicts, and it is her persistence in the face of sceptical colleagues and superiors that is shown to win out in the hunt for bin Laden. Maya is herself a kind of Rorschach test, because her impassive demeanour is the embodiment of ambiguity, prompting a variety of interpretations of the character's motivations, psychological state(s) and emotional arc that serve contrasting readings of the wider movie. Two key moments are repeatedly cited in the attempt to 'read' Maya: her reaction to the torture of Ammar (Reda Kateb), an al-Qaeda money man implicated in the financing of the 9/11 attacks, which is spread across three sequences in the first third of the movie; and the film's final shot, in which, after the culmination of the operation to locate and kill bin Laden, Maya sits silently in an empty aircraft and cries.

Significantly located at the beginning and end of the character's narrative arc in the film, these moments have generated confident assertions of Maya's emotional and intellectual responses from some quarters. For example, for Nick James, the final close-up of Maya in the aircraft shows she is undergoing the realisation 'that shooting bin Laden has achieved nothing much' (2013); for Michael Boughn, she is experiencing the 'recognition of the irreparable wound the war has inflicted on the nation's soul' (2013: 26). Yet in fact the performance and framing of the scene resists clarification. Maya has boarded the plane, declining to enter into a conversation with the pilot. His practical question, 'Where do you want to go?' prompts a further silence. Maya starts to breathe more quickly, her brow wrinkling as her eyes fill with tears. Permitting herself to cry, she closes her eyes, then opens them, looking off screen left and right and then forward again as the tears pass (see Figure 8.1). There are no words to clarify why she is crying, and no strong facial indicators of a particular emotion taking hold above others. Instead, multiple possibilities emerge: Agniezska Piotrowska's summation of Maya's state of mind at this moment, as 'reflective, tired, tearful but defiant' (2014: 154), seems most accurate precisely because it lists all of the emotions that are possibilities based on the performance. Ambiguity in the performance is matched by a narrative framing that also withholds: Maya is in a state of suspension, between question and answer, one mission and another, one direction and another, past and future, a suspension that does not resolve before the credits roll (see Burgoyne 2014: 197).[2]

Figure 8.1: Maya in a moment of contemplation at the end of *Zero Dark Thirty* (2012).

Commentators' readings of Maya's reactions in the film's torture scenes evidence a similar pattern of confident interpretation based on ambiguous performance cues. These scenes are perhaps the most controversial presence in *Zero Dark Thirty*. Inaugurating and located within the chain of events that will lead to bin Laden's discovery and death, and viewed 'with the benefit of hindsight' that shows that the 'intelligence is accurate', the torture scenes accrue, for some commentators, an undeserved and troubling legitimacy, or enact a problematic normalisation of so-called 'enhanced interrogation techniques' (Westwell 2013: 87, see also Maas 2012; Wolf 2013; Zizek 2013). In the torture scenes Maya watches, and eventually assists, Ammar is subjected to hooding, beating, waterboarding, sound torture, sleep deprivation, food deprivation, sexual humiliation, light deprivation, is forced to wear a dog collar and is confined to a box. *Variety*'s Peter Debruge characterises Maya's body language in the torture scenes as child-like, and uses this as a basis for a straightforward assertion that Maya is '*clearly uncomfortable* with the waterboarding and sexual humiliation that were common practice in the morally hazy rendition era' (2012: para. 5, emphasis added). Michael Boughn offers a similarly confident summation of her state of mind: 'Young, naive, idealistic and female, she is compelled to prove herself in what is *clearly a challenge to her moral sense*' (2013: 24, emphasis added). The film offers some narrative information to contextualise Boughn and Debruge's characterisation of Maya as young and inexperienced but 'compelled to prove herself': Maya has just arrived, and wears inappropriate clothes to the interrogation; her resolve is indicated by her refusal of a coffee break mid-interrogation; she didn't ask for the transfer to Pakistan but Washington deems her a 'killer' CIA agent. But there is little narrative or dialogue indication that she is morally challenged.

Like in the final shot of the film, the performance cues that Debruge and Boughn are attempting to read are marked by an absence of thick emotional information. As Maya, Chastain at first looks down and away from Ammar as he is tortured, but later she directs her gaze more persistently at the spectacle of torture before her. Two traditionally self-comforting gestures (arms folded across the body as Ammar is waterboarded, hand massaging wrist as he is forcibly disrobed) convey the possibility of a felt discomfort, one that seems to be confirmed by an occasional swallowing or momentarily clenched jaw. Yet the absence of more communicative facial expressions or pointedly directed looks makes it difficult to locate the source of and motivation for Maya's discomfort; can one be confident, with Boughn, that this is a moral discomfort, or could it be, as Shohini Chaudhuri suggests, a baser revulsion towards a dehumanised Ammar (2014: 30)?[3] Boughn's and Debruge's takes on Maya's feelings in the torture sequences exceed the performance cues presented by Chastain, betraying not just the commentators' own need to 'read' Maya as a psychologically rounded character, but their impulse to 'read' Chastain's performance in a manner that reflects their view of the wider film: in their cases, that *Zero Dark Thirty*'s portrayal of torture is responsible rather than legitimising.

Across the film, Maya – and Chastain – are studiously impassive in ways that exceed narrative requirements. A certain steeliness of demeanour might be required in her professional, male-dominated, environment, for example, but Maya is equally inscrutable in private moments (watching television, eating alone). Her dialogue, too, is obfuscatory about the emotional dimensions of her experience: she only speaks about the mission. As if to underscore this inscrutability, the film occasionally obscures Maya's face behind light-suffused car windows, or toilet cubicle screens; more frequently it holds Maya's inexpressive face in close-up, as if, if one looked for long enough, she would reveal a clarifying emotional response. There is, then, a Kuleshovian structuring absence at the heart of Maya's characterisation.[4] Manohla Dargis claims that Maya's 'vacant face' provides a platform for the spectator's productive questioning of the events and actions the film depicts, an embodiment of the film's progressive credentials: 'it is an article of faith,' she argues, 'that viewers are capable of filling in the blanks, managing narrative complexity and confronting their complicity' (2012: paras 2, 6). Yet does this automatically follow? As we have seen, Boughn's and Debruge's readings emerge more from their own convictions, than from the evidence of the performance itself, implying that the absence at the heart of Chastain's performance does not necessarily move the spectator towards the wider contemplation or questioning of geopolitical realities that Dargis imagines. Indeed, Susan Carruthers suggests that instead it is Maya around which any questioning clusters: 'To the extent that *Zero Dark Thirty* instigates curiosity,' she observes, 'it's largely directed toward conjuring an inner life' for Maya, at the expense of, for example, questions about the efficacy and legality of torture, or the ethical and legal dimensions of extrajudicial killing (2013: 52). Herein lies the risk inherent in the film's most visible presence/absence – Maya's face – and the compelling mystery of the unclarified inner life it emblematises: that it directs the spectator away from other kinds of questions and other kinds of absences.

NARRATIVE PATTERNS AND PERSPECTIVES:
LOCATING ERASURE

Kathryn Bigelow has explained that the goal of *Zero Dark Thirty* was 'to make a modern, rigorous film about counter-terrorism' (Bigelow 2013: para. 1), and she argues that this is a film that expresses a felt ambivalence about those counter-terrorist activities: 'I think that it's a deeply moral movie that questions the use of force. It questions what was done in the name of finding bin Laden' (cited in Winter 2013: 32). The construction of Maya suggests that Bigelow is interested in deploying ambiguity to prompt such questioning, but as we see from the contrasting readings cited in the previous section, what can result is a structural ambivalence that affirms rather than challenges spectators' wider convictions.[5] It is possible that Bigelow's moral ambitions were overtaken by events. She and screenwriter Mark Boal originally set out to make a film about the failed attempt to apprehend Osama bin Laden in the Tora Bora mountain caves of Afghanistan in December 2001, drawing on Dalton Fury's book *Kill Bin Laden: A Delta Force Commander's Account of the Hunt for the World's Most Wanted Man* (2008), a focus that would have lent itself much more obviously to a thematic questioning of 'what was done in the name of finding bin Laden'. However, as the discovery and killing of bin Laden in a compound in Abbottabad, Pakistan on 2 May 2011 came to light, Bigelow and Boal decided to alter the screenplay to accommodate the new events. The resulting film's truth claim in its opening title card ('The following motion picture is based on first hand accounts of actual events') obscures the process of selection and omission that Bigelow and Boal went through to compress this new, longer time frame into a workable feature narrative: that the 'first-hand accounts' would be *only* from American CIA agents, keen to give a positive account of their own and their agency's involvement.

As a result, the narrative framework in which Maya's characterisation sits is less ambiguous than Bigelow might have originally intended. The film opens with a black screen and the sounds of rising panic in the voices of people calling from the World Trade Center before its collapse on 11 September 2001. This gut-wrenching invocation of terrorist-inflicted collective trauma is followed by the first 'enhanced interrogation', notably of someone with a proven connection to those attacks, a move that seems to connect the two events in a causal chain structured around ideas of retribution and revenge, rather than a questioning of torture's efficacy. This pattern is repeated across the first half of the film, as the CIA's surveillance and interrogation activities alternate with a series of terrorist attacks in Saudi Arabia, London, Pakistan and Afghanistan. In a rich account of the film, Robert Burgoyne has suggested that *Zero Dark Thirty*'s 'expanding, widening loop' of violence offers a critique of the 'cycle of revenge in war' and its deleterious consequences (2014: 191–2). However, the opposite may also be true: the affective thickness of these moments, as the spectator's own embodied memories of their responses to specific real-world terrorist attacks converge with their sense of the implications for the fictional CIA agents they are watching, may move the spectator towards sympathy for the 'payback' principles that drive this cycle of violence. Jonathan Lighter captures the spectator's challenge well: 'You're left to form your own opinion,' he observes, 'which may be complicated by the scenes of al-Qaeda bombings and machine-gun attacks and Bigelow's prefatory, black-screen audio of wrenching phone calls from the burning Twin Towers' (2014: 6). The narrative patterning here risks producing a causal chain that exchanges moral and geopolitical complexities for reductive mythology: that there exists a 'unified Islamic fundamentalist world' (Khatib 2006: 175), and that terrorist attacks should provoke death-dealing in turn.

This narrative patterning is also structured by omissions of pertinent aspects of the historical record – omissions that seem at odds with Bigelow's stated aspirations for the film, since their absence means that the reductive mythology that I have suggested is potentially readable in the narrative framing is not explicitly challenged within the film's dramatic action. For example, no mention is made of the public and political debates around the war on terror, the wars in Afghanistan or Iraq, the US drone programme, Guantanamo Bay or the prisoner abuses at Abu Ghraib. These omissions challenge the spectator's ability to see the events of the film in a wider geopolitical context, or from different points of view. If a narrow focus on counter-terrorist activities connected to the hunt for bin Laden might be presented as the motivation for such absences, a more striking omission elides the debates that were actually taking place within government agencies during the period the film covers, about the efficacy and legality of torture, debates which resulted in high profile resignations and the pulling out of FBI staff from interrogation sites. There is also no mention of the scores of detainee deaths during interrogation activities, or of the traumatic effects of torture not just on the detainees but also on the torturers themselves (McSweeney 2014: 39, 41). In this way, the opportunity to portray the felt ambivalence of either individuals or organisations about torture (a part of the extant historical record) is not taken up, and in its place, as Guy Westwell points out, 'the film's neat, chapter-like structure and the way in which the dogged, difficult work of the CIA investigation is set against a backdrop of repeated terrorist attacks . . . lends a purifying coherence to the chaos and contingency of the recent past' (2013: 86).

If the project of the film is to encourage the spectator to count the costs and consequences of violence, then it does so through a persistently American lens that produces its own erasures. The film spends the majority of its running time in the CIA's offices, screening spaces and conference rooms in the US embassy in Pakistan, as well as government corridors in the US, and the forward operating base in Afghanistan from which the attack on bin Laden was launched. This means that exterior spaces – outside the US embassy in Islamabad, or in the bustling streets of Rawalpindi, or the quieter locale of Abbottabad – are also viewed from a US perspective, often from inside the 'US' spaces, or through windows, monitors, and camera and gun sights. These 'non-US' spaces are filled, in the film, with citizens who may at any moment break into violence, from the passers-by-turned-gunmen that shoot at Maya's car as she tries to leave the Islamabad office to the noisy crowd that amasses outside the Abbottabad compound during the raid. A scene featuring a demonstration against the CIA chief in Pakistan, whose identity has been revealed by the family of the victim of an American drone attack, is indicative of what this American perspective implies and elides. After some brief exterior whip pans in which the rowdy, chanting crowds fill the frame, a cut into the interior of Maya's vehicle shows Maya flinching as protestors surround and repeatedly hit the car, intercut with some glimpses through the windscreen from her point of view. Aligned spatially and narratively with Maya, the crowds are difficult for the spectator to individuate, their banners and the motivations behind them difficult to discern clearly. As Shohini Chaudhuri has noted,

> [as] presented in the film, the demonstrators are threatening, potentially violent terrorists filled with anti-American sentiment. There is no sense that protest against the drone policy could be justified, though reports have suggested that drone strikes routinely kill substantial numbers of civilians. (2014: 31)

The lived quotidian spaces and routines of non-violent civilian experience in these regions are rendered invisible, in their place a paranoid 'imaginative geography' (Said 1978) of threatening perpetrators and touchpaper environments.

The intense, detailed focus on procedures of intelligence gathering, surveillance and detective work, 'maintains a conceit of historical neutrality' (Zimmer 2015: 210), but in fact perpetuates the negative framing of spaces and peoples identified above in the film's imaginative construction of space. Glimpsed in clipped segments from longer conversations, mediated through grainy footage from surveillance cameras or video screens, the network of detainees displayed in the interrogation videos Maya sifts through are depersonalised and decontextualised. Their visible connections to family, community and region are literally moved out of frame. The constrained focus of the interrogation questions (further constrained by their compilation into repetitions of key questions and answers by the film) additionally means that these detainees cannot speak about the circumstances in which they have become radicalised or misidentified as a terrorist suspect. Indeed, the film even obscures the possibility of misidentification: the detainees Maya confronts face-to-face are all confirmed in the film as connected to terrorist networks (even though some of them are not 'fulsome' in their replies, as she puts it), another choice that confirms the association of particular nationalities and ethnic groups with terrorism, and which also suppresses curiosity about these figures' wider contexts: their families, livelihoods and lived experiences. If, as Steven Shaviro notes, Zero Dark Thirty is to be lauded for making the 'nightmare of liberal proceduralism . . . visible at a time when its sheer ubiquity might otherwise leave us to take it for granted' (2013), there are signification portions of that 'nightmare' that remain resolutely out of frame, out of earshot and out of mind.

SOMATIC PROVOCATIONS, LIMINAL MOMENTS: LOCATING FELT AMBIVALENCE

So far in this chapter I have interrogated Zero Dark Thirty's strategy of studied ambiguity, showing how it serves a box-office-friendly structural ambivalence,[6] and how it works less to promote active questioning and more to reflect the spectator's own position on the subject matter. Moreover, I have suggested that elements of the film's narrative framing move beyond this achievement of structural ambivalence to perpetuate negative and partial representations of Middle East citizens and spaces, and to erase wider geopolitical contexts and the historically documented, felt ambivalence of individuals and organisations about aspects of counter-terrorist operations. In this final part of the essay, I want to argue that Bigelow's film occasionally displays traces of an opposing movement: towards a legible, felt ambivalence about the counter-terrorist activities depicted. These traces can be excavated in the formal characteristics of certain moments of transitory pause in the film, pauses whose liminality thematises the idea of ethical witnessing: one during the torture of Ammar, the others during the searching of bin Laden's compound.

I have already argued that the torture scenes are situated within a narrative oscillation between terrorist attacks and counter-terrorism measures that suppresses contextual information, confers an impression of causality and frames the torture scenes within a logic of revenge and retaliation. The shot patterns used in the torture scenes do nothing to disrupt this framing: an absence of shots from Ammar's point of view, as well as a relative absence of his reaction shots, and a preponderance of non-verbal responses in the scripted performance, contribute to a marginalisation of his subjectivity. The sensorially textured rendering of the physical degradation of Ammar might evoke pity, but when viewed alongside the dynamic physical and verbal expressivity of interrogator Dan (played by Jason Clarke) in the same shots, and heard alongside Dan's forceful invocations of Ammar's guilt and repeated rationalisations of torture ('If you lie to me I'm gonna hurt you'), it cannot in itself interrupt Ammar's dehumanised depiction (Chaudhury 2014: 30; Carruthers 2013: 51). Yet what does develop is a growing discomfort on the part of the spectator, which is rooted in the torture scenes' somatically acute register. Haptic close-ups of Ammar's sweating, bleeding, beaten-up body, and the equally uncomfortable sounds of him choking, pleading and crying out in pain, invite an intensifying somatic recognition that is sustained over long moments of screen time. The wish to withdraw from these vividly depicted sights and sounds of physical pain is strong, and it is a wish that the film purposefully declines to meet, instead offering us the nightmarishly endless cycle of Dan's performative shifts from violent insistence to sympathy and back again, his disturbingly fluid interrogator's patter contrasting with Ammar's guttural non-verbal pain responses.

In the third torture scene, there is a pause in this regularised violation of the body, as Dan leaves Ammar, stripped humiliatingly from the waist down, alone with Maya while he fetches another torture instrument. In the midst of his own mortification and suffering, Ammar appeals to Maya for help (see Figure 8.2). In a medium shot Ammar says quietly: 'Your friend is an animal,' before a cut to Maya shows her declining to respond in a shadowy medium shot of her own. 'Please,' Ammar asks, now in close-up, 'help me, please.' In a medium-wide shot that gradually reveals itself to be positioned just behind Ammar's shoulder, Maya walks slowly and silently forward. Significantly, we are spatially much more closely aligned to Ammar than Maya in this sequence, and while we don't share Ammar's optical point of view,

Figure 8.2: Ammar asks Maya to help him during a torture scene in *Zero Dark Thirty* (2012).

we are given full access to his emotional state through his expressive intonation and the close-ups of his face, and are brought into spatial alignment through the 'over the shoulder' camera set-up that arrives just before Maya replies. Just for a moment, then, Ammar is permitted to achieve Murray Smith's conditions for character alignment: 'spatio-temporal attachment and subjective access' (1995: 83). Moreover, as a result of the spectator's accumulated, uncomfortable experience of the preceding torture scenes, he or she is likely to be aligned, at a personal, literal level, with Ammar's keenness that the torture be stopped. As Ammar and the spectator wait for Maya to answer, the moment becomes intensely liminal, and infused with possibility: how will Maya answer? In his appeal to Maya's humanity, Ammar demands from her an ethical form of witnessing, one that recognises his subjectivity and hers: what Kelly Oliver, in her Levinasian formulation, calls 'response-ability'; in other words, the attempt to respond in ways that 'continually open and reopen the possibility of response' in others (2001: 19, see Levinas 1981). Given the historical record that the spectator might be aware of – initial denials of certain forms of 'enhanced interrogation', and the destruction of video recordings of interrogations to deny wider acknowledgement of controversial interrogation practices – this call to witness takes on a particular significance.

Maya, Ammar and the spectator are caught in a liminal state, between past and future action, and between different possible responses. Does

Maya's impassivity denote a felt ambivalence that means she might show leniency, or at the least allow Ammar to cover himself? Will his pain and humiliation (and the sights and sounds we are being subjected to as a result) be alleviated, even if just for a moment? This few seconds' pause in the cycle of violence allows the spectator to dream of a longer, more permanent pause. Yet when Maya does move forward to respond, she stops, right in the middle ground of the shot, declining the opportunity for physical proximity, for a spatial intimacy on which one might build dialogue and acknowledgement (see Figure 8.3). Her verbalised response, the aggressively dogmatic statement, 'You can help yourself by being truthful,' the puritanical phrasing and intonation, and Chastain's rigid physical performance, emphatically shut down the possibilities of the liminal pause. The spatial arrangement of the bodies in the shot – Maya in the mid-ground, Ammar and the spectator aligned in the extreme foreground – analogises Maya's refusal to meet Ammar's demand for acknowledgement, understanding or compassion, her refusal of 'response-ability' and its potential to open up intersubjective communication. She fails to move beyond 'seeing others with the objectifying gaze of a self-sufficient subject examining, subordinating, or struggling with the other', to use Oliver's words (2001: 19). Maya's act of witnessing does not produce a transformation of her subjectivity or an understanding of the brutalised other, or, at the literal level, a stepping-back from government sanctioned brutality. But

Figure 8.3: The camera frames Maya from behind Ammar's shoulder as she declines to help, in *Zero Dark Thirty* (2012).

the film invites the audience to feel the absence of this trajectory, the loss of this possibility, in this liminal pause between bouts of torture. In this way, the film invites the spectator to become the ethical witness that Maya has failed to become. In E. Ann Kaplan's words, the film constructs a position for the spectator that 'enables attention to the situation, as against attention merely to . . . individual suffering, and this positioning thus opens the text out to larger social and political meanings' (2005: 125).

This invitation to 'attend to the situation' is, as this essay has tried to suggest, not commonplace in *Zero Dark Thirty*, but it returns in the final section of the film, in the depiction of the invasion of bin Laden's compound, where once again the formal strategy of the liminal pause appears. Here the pause is combined with a form of visual and dramatic redundancy: the spectator is forced to witness an action that seems to exceed what the situation requires in some way, and is forced to witness it in more than one shot. Crucially, this juxtaposition of pausing and redundancy centres around the act of killing.

As the Navy SEALs invade the compound and make their way through doors, down corridors and up stairs, they kill a number of the compound occupants, some of whom are clearly shooting at or about to shoot at the soldiers, others not. At a number of points in this final portion of the film a pattern of pause and redundancy emerges. The first death of the operation occurs when Abu Ahmed al-Kuwaiti (Tushaar Mehra) shoots through a door just as the soldiers are trying to breach it. They return fire, and the shooting stops. Pushing through the door, they find the man lying on the floor. In a pause in the soldiers' forward momentum, the soldiers circle the body, assessing the situation. A close-up shows he is bloodied and unresponsive, but it is at this moment, when the spectator has been shown that he is no longer a threat, that the soldiers fire more bullets into his body, their impact documented in the same close-up that has already declared them unnecessary. The second killing occurs as the soldiers gain entry into another part of the compound. Abrar al-Kuwaiti (Noureddine Hajjoujou) is hiding behind an internal wall and raises his weapon to fire, but the SEALs have spotted him using their infrared goggles, and several fire on him, continuing to shoot as he falls forward and onto the floor, dead. His wife Bushra (Nour Alkawaja) falls upon him, screaming, and picks up his rifle – perhaps involuntarily, or to move it out of the way, or to fire it, it is not clear. The weapon means that she, too, is judged as a threat, and is shot. In a lingering point of view shot through the infrared goggles of one of the soldiers, it becomes clear that both are dead: the prone woman's eyes are open in a death stare, the man's eyes shut, but his immobility

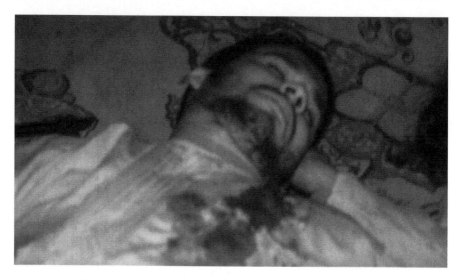

Figure 8.4: The dead Abrar al-Kuwaiti seen through a soldier's infrared goggles in *Zero Dark Thirty* (2012).

and the extent of his chest wounds evident (see Figure 8.4). Once again redundant extra shots are fired into their bodies, captured in a cut to a gloomy medium close-up from a different position. The minimal lighting in this shot plunges the couple's heads into the shadows, stripping them of any identifying features, depersonalising them as if to underscore the transition from living tissue to dead matter, from personhood to absence.

A pattern thus emerges: an initial flurry of activity as shots are fired, then a pause, as the soldier assesses whether the felled target is moving. A close-up shows, apparently incontrovertibly, that the person is dead, yet the soldier then fires further shots into the body. As non-specialists, it is difficult for the spectator to judge whether the extra shots are redundant in terms of military strategy, but the audience feels their redundancy in the somatic impact of watching a lifeless body momentarily reanimated by a penetrating bullet. This redundancy is most vividly displayed in the killing of Osama bin Laden (Ricky Sekhon) himself. SEALs approach a doorway, and spot movement inside the room, firing off a shot as the soundtrack conveys the thump of a body hitting the floor. As the camera moves with the soldiers into the room, bin Laden is shown lying just beyond the threshold, inert. The camera follows the soldiers as they jump across the room to subdue two screaming women, and off-screen two further shots, presumably into the body of bin Laden, are heard. While the women continue to scream in the background, a soldier twice stands over the stilled body and fires off further shots. We witness the bullet impacts – that is, the unsettling redundancy of these repeated actions – in even closer framings that we did earlier: just the shirt-clad torso, extant bullet holes clearly visible. The pattern of pause and redundancy gains force through the spectator's accumulated experience of the compound scenes, as well as through the specificities of the depiction of each moment; in each case the pause, motivated by the soldier's need to complete a threat assessment, is a liminal moment between shooting and not shooting, more or less bullet holes, a more or less intact body; in each case (after the first) the possibility of *not* shooting again is thrown into relief by the next redundant bullet, the sense of the waste of this war on terror compounded with each extra unnecessary pull of the trigger. Moreover, the unnecessary bullet impacts are themselves captured in closer and closer views, as if the film wants to press the point home through unasked-for and repeated proximity to the haptic textures of the breached, dead body.

It is in these moments of pause, between stillness and action, that the film's felt ambivalence comes productively to the surface, pushing beyond the wider tendency towards inert ambiguity, to depictions that promote and demand reflection on what is possible, as well as what was done. Interrupting *Zero Dark Thirty*'s structural ambivalence, and its hermetic diegesis that elides non-American perspectives, geopolitical contexts, and so much of the historical record, these moments can perhaps be seen as the trace of Bigelow's original ambitions for the film. In *Zero Dark Thirty*'s landscape of erasure, absence and ambiguity, these are the presences that complicate, that problematise, that demand thought and reflection on this most complex of stories. Yet their force is blunted by the contexts in which they sit: the film itself, and beyond it a world powerfully shaped by ideologically loaded and heavily politicised rhetorical oppositions between 'us' and 'them', and a US film industry equally powerfully shaped by economic imperatives that compel film-makers to prioritise maximising audiences over overt political complexity.

As this essay has shown, the film constructs a causal chain that begins with the 9/11 atrocities and ends with the capture and death of their architect, a choice that provides a genre-familiar revenge trajectory and a forceful narrative closure, even as the final shot of the film (of Maya in the plane) tries to work against these elements.[7] Restating the juxtaposition between frame and moment that has characterised much of my analysis in this essay permits reflection on the challenge that *Zero Dark Thirty* faces, and the ways in which it fails this challenge. A narrative framing whose shape is familiar from public and political discourse, as well as from film genre conventions, exerts a gravitational force that pulls the spectator away from attending to the nuances of the strategies that Bigelow's moral project seemed to put in play. In his positive account of the film, Michael Boughn notes that art should raise 'questions that propel the mind not toward answers but toward questions' (2013: 19), but this essay has argued that the partisan 'answers' supplied by *Zero Dark Thirty*'s narrative frame speak more loudly and more consistently than the moments that seek to invite a questioning response. Such analysis raises a wider question for ethically minded cultural producers: is there any longer a place for ambiguity and ambivalence? The lesson provided by *Zero Dark Thirty*'s conflicted form might well be that, at a cultural moment filled with the heat and noise of polarised and polarising post-9/11 geopolitics, and in a cultural product designed for the lay spectator, the invitation to ask questions must surely be posed as forcefully as the many 'answers' that noisily circulate in public, media and political discourse.

NOTES

1. Tomasulo was discussing *Apocalypse Now* (Francis Ford Coppola, 1979).
2. Indeed Robert Burgoyne suggests that the final shot makes explicit a 'theme of suspension' that has characterised the earlier scene of Osama bin Laden in the body bag: 'This devastating scene undercuts any sense of triumph or blood satisfaction . . . In some ways we are suspended here, without resolution, without the climax that the film has prepared from the beginning' (2014: 197).
3. Susan Carruthers concurs with Chaudhuri's reading, arguing that '*Zero Dark Thirty* may not "glorify" torture, as Greenwald charged, but its shit-smeared verisimilitude directs disgust more toward the victim than the perpetrator' (2013: 51).
4. Here I am referring to the 'Kuleshov effect,' which offers an interesting perspective on Maya's performance and responses to it. The term derives from V. I. Pudovkin's famous, but perhaps apocryphal, 1929 account of fellow Russian film-maker Kuleshov's montage experiment:

> Kuleshov and I made an interesting experiment. We took from some film or other several close-ups of the well-known Russian actor Mosjukhin. We chose close-ups which were static and which did not express any feeling at all – quiet close-ups. We joined these close-ups, which were all similar, with other bits of film in three different combinations. In the first combination the close-up of Mosjukhin was immediately followed by a shot of a plate of soup standing on a table. It was obvious and certain that Mosjukhin was looking at this soup. In the second combination the face of Mosjukhin was joined to shots showing a coffin in which lay a dead woman. In the third the close-up was followed by a shot of a little girl playing with a funny toy bear. We showed the three combinations to an audience which had not been let into the secret; the result was terrific. The public raved about the acting

of the artist. They pointed out the heavy pensiveness of his mood over the forgotten soup, were touched and moved by the deep sorrow with which he looked on the dead woman, and admired the light, happy smile with which he surveyed the girl at play. But we knew that in all three cases the face was exactly the same.' (Pudovkin 1929, cited in Holland 1992: 79–80)

5. Screenwriter Mark Boal seems to equate structural ambivalence with the success of his and Bigelow's moral project: that is, the inclusion of scenes in which torture seems to work, and scenes in which it doesn't prove valuable. For Steve Coll, these kinds of 'on-the-one hand, on-the-other forms of argument about the value of officially sanctioned torture represents a victory for those who would justify such abuse' (2013).

6. This question of the impact of the imperative to maximise audience share on film-making choices is one that Janet Harris returns to in Chapter 9 of this volume.

7. The narrative trajectory of revenge and retribution is one that spectators familiar with Hollywood genre films (such as Westerns, action movies, detective thrillers, and so on) will readily recognise.

BIBLIOGRAPHY

Bigelow, K. (2013), 'Kathryn Bigelow addresses *Zero Dark Thirty* torture criticism', *LA Times*, 15 January. Available at <http://articles.latimes.com/2013/jan/15/entertainment/la-et-mn-0116-bigelow-zero-dark-thirty-20130116> (last accessed 1 May 2016).

Boughn, M. (2013), 'The war on art and *Zero Dark Thirty*', *CineACTION*, 91, pp. 19–26.

Burgoyne, R. (2014), 'The violated body: affective experience and somatic intensity in *Zero Dark Thirty*', in David LaRocca (ed.), *The Philosophy of War Films*, Lexington: University Press of Kentucky, pp. 189–98.

Carruthers, S. (2013), '*Zero Dark Thirty*', *Cineaste* (Spring), pp. 50–2.

Chaudhury, S. (2014), *Cinema of the Dark Side: Atrocity and the Ethics of Spectatorship*, Edinburgh: Edinburgh University Press.

Coll, S. (2013), 'Disturbing and misleading', *New York Review of Books*, 7 February. Available at <http://www.nybooks.com/articles/2013/02/07/disturbing-misleading-zero-dark-thirty/> (last accessed 1 May 2016).

Dargis, M. (2012), 'By any means necessary: Jessica Chastain in *Zero Dark Thirty*', *New York Times*, 17 December. Available at <http://www.nytimes.com/2012/12/18/movies/jessica-chastain-in-zero-dark-thirty.html?_r=0> (last accessed 24 August 2016).

Debruge, P. (2012), 'Review: *Zero Dark Thirty*', *Variety*, 25 November. Available at <http://variety.com/2012/film/reviews/zero-dark-thirty-1117948801/> (last accessed 1 May 2016).

Holland, N. N. (1992), 'Film response from eye to I: the Kuleshov experiment', in J. Gaines (ed.), *Classical Hollywood Narrative: The Paradigm Wars*, Durham, NC and London: Duke University Press, pp. 79–106.

Hornaday, A. (2012), '*Zero Dark Thirty* and the new reality of reported filmmaking', *The Washington Post*, 13 December. Available at <https://www.washingtonpost.com/entertainment/movies/zero-dark-thirty-and-the-new-reality-of-reported-filmmaking/2012/12/13/3630ce2c-4548-11e2-8e70-e1993528222d_story.html> (last accessed 1 May 2016).

James, N. (2013), 'Zero tolerance (editorial)', *Sight and Sound* (February), p. 9.

Kaplan, E. A. (2005), 'The ethics of witnessing: Maya Deren and Tracey Moffatt', in E. A. Kaplan (ed.), *Trauma Culture: The Politics of Terror and Loss in Media and Literature.* Piscataway, NJ: Rutgers University Press, pp. 122–35.

Khatib, L. (2006), *Filming the Modern Middle East: Politics in the Cinemas of Hollywood and the Arab World*, London: I. B. Tauris.

Levinas, E. (1981), *Otherwise than Being or Beyond Essence*, trans. Alphonso Lingus, The Hague: Martinus Nijhoff.

Lighter, J. (2014), 'Zero Dark Thirty: a review', *War, Literature & the Arts*, 26: pp. 4–6.

Maas, P. (2012), 'Don't trust *Zero Dark Thirty*', *The Atlantic*, 13 December. Available at <http://www.theatlantic.com/entertainment/archive/2012/12/dont-trust-zero-dark-thirty/266253/> (last accessed 1 May 2016).

Maltby, R. (2003), *Hollywood Cinema*, 2nd edn, Oxford: Blackwell.

McSweeney, T. (2014), *The 'War on Terror' and American Film: 9/11 Frames Per Second*, Edinburgh: Edinburgh University Press.

Oliver, K. (2001), *Witnessing: Beyond Recognition*, Minneapolis and London, University of Minnesota Press.

Piotrowska, A. (2014), 'Zero Dark Thirty – "war autism" or a Lacanian ethical act?' *New Review of Film and Television Studies*, 12.2, pp. 143–55.

Said, E. (2003 [1978]), *Orientalism*, London: Penguin.

Shaviro, S. (2013), 'A brief remark on *Zero Dark Thirty*', *The Pinocchio Theory*, 18 January. Available at <http://www.shaviro.com/Blog/?p=1114#comments> (last accessed 1 May 2016).

Smith, M. (1995), *Engaging Characters: Fiction, Emotion, and the Cinema*, Oxford: Oxford University Press.

Tomasulo, F. P. (1990), 'The politics of ambivalence: *Apocalypse Now* as pro-war and anti-war film', in L. Dittmar and G. Michaud (eds), *From Hanoi to Hollywood: the Vietnam War in American Film*, New Brunswick, NJ: Rutgers University Press, pp. 145–58.

Westwell, G. (2013), 'Zero Dark Thirty', *Sight and Sound* (February), pp. 86–7.

Westwell, G. (2014), *Parallel Lines: Post-9/11 American Cinema*, London: Wallflower Press.

Winter, J. (2013), 'Kathryn Bigelow: the art of darkness', *Time*, 181.4 (4 February), pp. 30–7.

Wolf, N. (2013), 'A letter to Kathryn Bigelow on *Zero Dark Thirty*'s apology for torture', *The Guardian*, 4 January. Available at <http://www.theguardian.com/commentisfree/2013/jan/04/letter-kathryn-bigelow-zero-dark-thirty> (last accessed 1 May 2016).

Zimmer, C. (2015), *Surveillance Cinema*, New York: New York University Press.

Žižek, S. (2013), 'Zero Dark Thirty: Hollywood's gift to American power', *The Guardian*, 25 January. Available at <http://www.theguardian.com/commentisfree/2013/jan/25/zero-dark-thirty-normalises-torture-unjustifiable> (last accessed 1 May 2016).

CHAPTER 9

Invisible War: Broadcast Television Documentary and Iraq

Janet Harris

Christopher Booker writes: 'Even today few people in Britain realise the extent to which our intervention in south-eastern Iraq was an abject failure' (North 2009: 1). The dominant narrative of the British military occupation of Iraq and Afghanistan in broadcast television media has been one of emotion, of valiant fighters and of underfunded victims betrayed by politicians, but also of a military strategy, purpose and consequences that are rarely questioned. The media constructs war in a narrow and specific way that leads to an assumption that there is only one way to look at war. Aspects such as the rational analysis of war, the causes of war and, most importantly, the political nature of war disappear.

In this chapter I look at the coverage of a British military operation in Iraq in 2004 in two different British television documentary series, *Andy McNab's Tour of Duty* (ITV4, 2008, ep. 2) directed by Tom Peppiatt, and *Soldier, Husband, Daughter, Dad* (BBC1, 2005, ep. 7), which I directed for the BBC. By comparing extracts of what was shown on screen in each documentary, and discussing what techniques the films use to keep the viewer watching, I reflect as a film-maker how these television documentaries about war can make other realities invisible. I also look at how certain functions particular to British television documentary render invisible aspects of war, including how documentaries 'claim the real' (Winston 1995). I examine the specific way that reality is represented and constructed, and suggest that the demands of the cognitive modes of visual and psychological realism allow the spectre of past war and emotion to hide a more rational analysis of events, thus blocking an understanding of how war has changed. The demands are in part driven by the craft of the film-maker, who has to construct war in a way that is recognisable and plausible to a British television audience who has no experience of war, so builds on what is familiar, that is, the spectacle, the visual and a reaching towards an emotional truth in what is shown. The magnitude of the subject matter and the search for an antecedent truth also affects what is, and is not, shown. Past representations and expectation are a spectre 'haunting what can be said or written' (Nichols 1991: 291). Other 'ghosts' in the construction of a television documentary about war are the demands of the broadcast organisation, the specific brief of the commission and the professional conventions of documentary (Zoellner 2009). I examine these using my own experience as a documentary director.

DOCUMENTARY REALITY

Grierson stated that 'documentary was from the beginning . . . an anti-aesthetic movement' (1942: 249) and Nichols includes documentary as a 'discourse of sobriety' (1991: 3), along with science, economics, politics, foreign policy, education, religion and welfare. He writes: 'Discourses of sobriety are sobering because they regard their relation to the real as direct, immediate, transparent, where its power lies in its claims to record the indexical image' (ibid.: 13). Documentaries enable a viewer to witness a real event, and hear a verbal testimony of that event (Winston 1995). In this function they can be argued to play a similar role to news. However, Grierson also formulated the description of documentary as 'the creative treatment of actuality' (1933: 8), where 'creativity' could include the third influence on documentaries, the use of aesthetic devices. Paget writes that 'Grierson documentary film actively embraced an artfulness that was always likely to be at odds with "actuality"' (1998: 117). The techniques of 'artfulness' communicate another reality, one which is sensory: what is felt and experienced can be conveyed by aesthetic strategies, by the excitement and appeal of cinematic art (Corner 2005: 49). The documentary must offer storytelling which is exciting and dramatic, and offer attraction which is spectacular, shocking or extraordinary. It is in the construction of these other functions that the film-maker as the author of the film has recourse to the expressive or aesthetic function, and 'the greater the expressive power of the piece, that is the more vividly the film communicates, the more likely an audience is to feel persuasion, educative value or revelation' (Butchart 2013: 346). Different operative proofs are manipulated to emphasise the 'real' and elicit attention, not only to persuade an audience of the argument you are making, but to persuade them to continue to watch the programme.

Renov (1993) states that the documentary 'truth claim' is the baseline of persuasion for all non-fiction texts, and for a documentary maker the vividness of the film, and its power to communicate are intrinsic to the film's ability to keep the audience watching, so are a powerful influence on the construction of the film. At issue is the film's vivification, rendering felt what representations only allude to (Nichols 1991: 234). It is not just what you film, but what techniques you use, including storytelling and attraction, to persuade the audience that what they are seeing is not only 'the truth', but a 'bums on seats' truth. So a director uses different techniques of realism 'to make an argument about the historical world persuasive' (Nichols 1991: 165). Nichols suggests there are three types of realism in documentary film: 'empirical, psychological and historical' (ibid.: 170). In the analysis of the two selected documentaries, I examine how these types of realism are used by a documentary director both to try to get at the truth of a situation in some way, but also to use this 'truth' to keep an audience watching.

Zoeller notes a shift in television documentaries towards the 'extreme' where commercial factors which drive the all-pervasive demand for audience figures have pushed television documentary away from the traditional intentions of education and information towards a more 'entertaining, attention-grabbing, hybrid approach to the genre' (Zoellner 2009: 527). She lists four desirable programme conventions in this commercially driven mode of documentary programme making: 'originality, angle, case study and extraordinariness' (ibid.: 532)[1], which affect what is filmed and how the documentary is made, and to which I would add budgets and the practicalities of filming. The result of these pressures is a film where in the conveying of emotional, psychological and historical truths, and in the application of techniques to make the film vivid, persuasive and extraordinary, aspects of the reality of war disappear.

EMPIRICAL REALISM

Meunier posited that all cinematic representation is modified by 'our personal and cultural knowledge of an object's existential position as it relates to our own', since the object itself is absent (Meunier cited in Sobchack 1999: 241). A director knows that for most viewers of a documentary on war, it's not only the object which is absent, but any direct knowledge of the object. However, both the director and audience have 'existential and cultural knowledge' of war from past representations of war, and from cinematic war films; thus audiences come to the Iraq war with an expectation of what 'war' should look like (Sobchack 1999: 243). The preferred media for information about the 2003 Iraq war was television (Worcester 2003), but it was television coverage that incurred much criticism of how it represented the war in Iraq. As North concluded, the media in general 'failed in its most fundamental task of reporting the news, and its analysis was too often trivial or non-existent' (North 2009: 251).

The British occupation lasted until 2009, before the era of social media had really taken hold, so unlike Syria and Gaza, images of the conflict were scarce. Most of the footage which appeared in television documentaries about the British military was filmed by camera teams, or by militia cameramen. When I made a documentary for the BBC for the tenth anniversary of the invasion of Iraq, I found myself re-using footage from my old BBC programmes shot in 2003 and 2005, since there was little other (copyright-free) material of 'the enemy'. It was very difficult to film outside the safety of the military camps, and the nature of the war made it almost impossible to film Iraqi militia. In 2004 a DVD of militia footage was on sale in downtown Basra. The DVD included dramatic pictures of Iraqis firing or carrying rocket-propelled grenades (RPGs) and mortars, running, in the backs of sport utility vehicles (SUVs) or dancing round captured British armoured vehicles, as well as sermons by Muqtada al-Sadr. I obtained a copy and came to the conclusion that many other news teams had also got one, as the repetitive images of the militia from this DVD appeared in many other documentaries and news about the British military in Iraq.[2]

In this situation, then, much of the dramatic sensational footage is not actually from the same time period as that filmed for the documentary. It is thus neither evidence of the actual event being reproduced, nor of the location that provides that event's temporal and geographical context. It is filmed from other times and places and is a kind of 'collage' of an event built around what film-makers and their audiences expect militia to look like and behave like. The documentary producer and viewers learn nothing from the audio-visual content of the actual event, who the people are in the footage, what the battle seen is about and thus why they are fighting. The images of the militia in the television documentaries are used to represent the danger that the soldiers face, and the fear they elicit. As in drama documentaries, they satisfy the need to 'ratify emotionally' what has been understood intellectually (Paget 1998: 89). The director thus resorts to another tool, the aesthetics of drama, to convince the audience both to continue to watch and that what they are seeing is credible.

THE AESTHETICS OF DRAMA

The empirical realism that Nichols (1991) lists as being utilised by documentaries to persuade viewers of the truth of what they are seeing thus becomes weakened. The visuals of the insurgents become a representation of the 'enemy', rather than a reproduction, so they become a strategy of the spectacular, used to 'attract, shock and fascinate viewers' (Ekström 2000: 468). Beattie writes that documentary display 'startles and excites in ways which produce pleasure' (2008: 5). So, Nichols's third influence on documentary, that of 'modernist fragmentation', or aesthetic appeal, becomes predominant in many documentaries on the Iraq war, superseding those of scientific realism or narrative analysis. Sensation becomes the primary vehicle of cognition, and there is a shift in emphasis from journalistic to entertainment priorities. We don't understand who the insurgents are, or why they are fighting, but we feel a frisson of fear and excitement when we see fragments of an insurgency, so want to know what happens to the soldiers who are also feeling this sensation, and we keep watching. We also have experienced fear and excitement, so connect with that particular reality.

It is here that Grierson's 'creative treatment of actuality' needs further consideration. Paget writes that this phrase 'first celebrates documentary's splitting off from fictional forms, then binds documentary practice to invention of various kinds' (1998: 117). For Paget, documentary is 'reactive' to dominant narrative forms, and the influence from drama cannot only be seen in the look of the film (the different camera angles, use of close-ups), but in the construction and creation of a narrative around the individual or small group, where 'the spectator is sucked into the frame through the cathartic power of identification with a fictional "other"' (ibid.: 119, 16). As in drama, the spectator identifies and becomes emotionally bound to the character in the film. This means that such television documentaries display the same elements that Michalski and Gow suggest inform dominant moving image media treatments of warfare: a 'focus on individuals or small groups, the dominance of the striking image over information of other kinds, the emphasis on action and emotion, rather than reflection and reasoning, that derives from the nature of the medium' (2007: 16). A third of the British television documentaries on the British military in Iraq[3] were about the soldier as a victim of war and of the political system that was supposed to look after soldiers who had fought for that system (Harris 2012). These were told as personal individual stories with an emphasis on the soldiers' emotions and feelings, a strategy that is becoming increasingly commonplace in Western-made documentaries about war. Thus here we see Zoellner's 'case study' convention in practice: a focus on small groups or individuals to elicit emotional attachment through personalisation (Zoellner 2009). The sensory affect of emotions aroused and felt by characters in the documentary becomes a rhetorical strategy used to persuade the viewers of the psychological realism of the war they are watching and a means of persuading viewers to stay.

PSYCHOLOGICAL REALISM

Psychological realism 'conveys the sense of a plausible, believable and accurate representation of human perception and emotion' (Nichols 1991: 172). This poses as a 'transparency between representation and emotional engagement, between what we see and what there is' (ibid.: 173). The experience of war is beyond most people's own experience so it is difficult to find 'truth' in the identification of the empirical; therefore it is the psychological or emotional that the director has to manipulate for her documentary to be believable and watchable. Watt (1957) believed that realism depends on the senses and experience of the individual, so the 'reality' of war can be conveyed not only through an individual's personal experience of war, but the reality of the emotion experienced by the viewer of the documentary about war. The increase in emotionalism is one of the factors noted in the blurring of boundaries between programme genres, not only between drama and documentary, but between documentary and news, in the rise of soft news (Nichols 1991), and in the increase in stories which are softer, safer and which deal with human interest and crime stories (Anderegg 1991). One of the developments noted by Pantti and Wahl-Jorgensen is the rise of what they call 'emotional reporting', which is seen as part of a larger social trend that is shifting public discourse away from matters of the common good and towards a preoccupation with the intimate and affective (2007: 4).

However, there is a consequence of this type of personalisation. The audience might empathise more for a soldier in this type of programming, but if his situation is not explained, nor contextualised, the care is merely a concern for the individual soldier or the group of individuals that he represents. There is no cause given to care for those the damaged soldier killed, or care to understand why any of this happened. Writing of the later war in Iraq, Robert Hariman argues that war's emerging visual vocabulary consists of 'fragmentation', where the lack of political purpose given to the fragments of images means that one's affective response to the images is pitched into mere emotionalism and as a result, 'We have banality instead of drama, traces instead of things, objects instead of people and ruins as a product rather than the by-product of war' (2014: 140). Many of the television documentaries about the British military in Iraq were narratives about the effects of the Iraq war on the soldiers,[4] but the war itself, either as an occupation or as a counter-insurgency, was not examined.[5] The dominant framing was of soldiers as victims, a framing with historical precedence, both from the trauma dramas of past television series, but also from documentaries and feature films about the Vietnam War. It is this frame, and the similar images filmed, which perhaps combines the emotional reality with Nichols's third realism: historical reality, where the fusion of the personal memory and the media memory create a powerful connection with past wars, and past films about war, both in documentary and fiction. Memory is evoked by the visual, which draws on the fusion of the personal memory and the media memory to create a powerful connection with the past. But as we have seen, this historical realism can produce a number of problematic omissions.

HISTORICAL REALITY AND MAGNITUDE

A director draws on visual connections to the familiar iconography of past wars and war representation, to emphasise a 'truth' of recognition of the war being covered. If the scene looks like a past war, then it conveys a sense that this is a 'real' war. Fiske writes that 'realism is defined by the way it makes sense of the real, rather than by what it says the real consists of' (1994: 24). The sequence of images tells a story which is shaped by the director's sense of what the story should be, and so the narrative, as well as the visuals, fits into familiar discourses of war. Zelizer writes that news photography does not so much document war, but constructs a highly conventionalised myth of war that harkens back to another militarised past, commenting that journalists strike parallels between wars 'for no better reason than the surrounding mandates for interpreting them resemble each other' (2004:131). This can also be said of both the visuals and narratives of war documentaries.

Hallin (1989) believes that these practices are a cultural response to collective war trauma. He suggests that the media is governed by a powerful mythology born in part out of the trauma of earlier wars.

The subject matter of war and its rider death, carry enormous ideological and historical associations and cannot be dealt with lightly. Nichols (2010) points out that human beings hunger for metaphorical representations to help us understand what values to attach to social practices, including war, and in storytelling there is a logical narrative which has to equate the social practice, in this case war, with the values attached, in this case bravery, honour and courage. Young concurs, noting that 'war stories . . . vary by geography, but they always tell the same story: death, fear, brotherhood. Bravery, courage and the capacity to commit atrocities are not determined by the cause in which they are displayed' (2003: 21). It is these underlying 'universal truths' of war which documentary makers also seem to draw upon. For many programme makers and viewers, the causes of the Iraq war did not seem to have sufficient moral worth to justify or explain the values that were traditionally part of the discourse of the representation of war, so emotion filled the gap and created its own logic. Yet finding stories which represent 'universal truths' about war and which fit into an accepted 'war' narrative also exclude certain versions of war. For example, television war documentaries seldom cover the reality of the tedium of war, the mundane events of war, the day-to-day life of those who suffer from war and the aftermath of war.

CONTEXTS OF PRODUCTION

It is not just these conventions which affect a television documentary. The demands of the commissioners, the schedule slot in which the programme will be broadcast and the channel also have an impact. *Andy McNab's Tour of Duty* series, which I analyse below, was first commissioned by ITV from Flashback Productions as a six-part series of one-hour episodes. Flashback is a major independent television company which has made a significant number of historical and drama documentaries, but in addition to their own approach, they would have had to take into account that for a commercial broadcaster like ITV, viewing figures are extremely important and the programme would also have had to be structured in relation to commercial breaks. I have made films about soldiers and war for Sky TV, MBC, BBC1 and BBC2,[6] and the audience the programme is expected to attract and speak to is a key influence on audio-visual style. For example, the programme I made for Sky TV (*British Army Be The Best?* 2006), and the BBC documentary series I analyse below, were aimed mostly at young males, so corresponding music and a quicker editing style were adopted.

With regards to the BBC series, the difference between a BBC1 and BBC2 audience had also to be considered, the latter being perceived as able to cope with more complex issues. Caldwell argues that negotiated and collective authorship is a determining reality in contemporary film and television production (2008), and as a director whose film had already been commissioned, most of my negotiation about my films was not with the broadcaster, but the series producer (if it was a series) or the executive producer, who was informed of what was being filmed but whose presence was mainly felt in the cutting room.[7] The final viewings often felt like a committee meeting as the series producer, the executive producer, sometimes the head of the independent company who had the commission, and the broadcasting commissioner all had their say on what the film should look like. It could be an incredibly debilitating experience, with one executive demanding things be cut or inserted, then another asking for other changes which the first executive then disagreed with.

In the analyses of television documentaries that follow, I do not look specifically at the production of the programmes, that is, funding, briefs and shooting methods. I look instead at the transmitted programmes, but from the perspective of a film-maker who knows the intent behind one of the productions under discussion. I use this knowledge to assess how Nichols's theory of documentary realism manifests in both programmes, and how this affects the representation of war. I also pay attention to audio-visual style, or what Hoskins and O'Loughlin, following Kress and Van Leeuwen (2001), call the 'multi-modal' discourse of television, that is, its visual, verbal and aural aspects (Hoskins and O'Loughlin 2007: 5). It is not just what pictures are used, but how they are put together, and so editing emerges as a site of particular importance. Schaefer notes that news and expositional documentaries tend to be cut in a naturalistic mode of continuity editing which is characterised by 'transitions between shots recorded at a single site and without any apparent breaks in action' (1997: 74). On the other hand, editing techniques such as dissolves, jump cuts, montages and fades as transitions convey a sense of artificiality (ibid.). Such cinematic techniques are arguably used for dramatic purposes, to excite and stimulate the audience to stay watching, but they also elide: the impression of no 'breaks in action' is, of course, an illusion. I will be looking at how the film-maker represents the 'real' in two television documentaries which both cover the same incident from the occupation of Iraq, at the techniques which are used to persuade the viewer that what she is being presented with is real, and also at the techniques used to persuade the viewer to keep watching. Through this comparative approach, I hope to show how both these pressures can hide the realities of war.

TWO DOCUMENTARY TAKES ON ONE INCIDENT

In August 2004 a group of soldiers from the 1st Regiment Royal Horse Artillery (1RHA) were on patrol in Basra, the city in southern Iraq under British occupation. They came under fire, had to abandon their two Snatch Land Rovers and were besieged in a house in the city, coming under very heavy small-arms fire from insurgent militia. The incident took place at a moment when Muqtada al-Sadr's Mahdi militia were on the verge of taking Basra. The British military were encircled in a few locations in the city and were making forays out to establish their presence. The small group of British soldiers managed to escape with no loss of the regiment's lives.

I want to look at two television documentaries that focused on this situation. The first is *Andy McNab's Tour of Duty*, episode 2, 'Face to Face' (ITV4, 2008), directed by Tom Peppiatt. The series was commissioned in a bid to increase the channel's audience share, and target the channel toward a demographic of twenty-five- to forty-four-year-old men (Thomas 2008), so the director would have had this demographic in mind when making the programme. The other television documentary I look at is 'The Price of Peace', episode 7 of an eight-part series *Soldier, Husband, Daughter, Dad* (BBC, 2005), transmitted on BBC1 in January 2005. I directed this episode, and there was no specific brief from the commission apart from the directive that it had to be about the story of the regiment in Basra but also about the effect of war/separation on both soldiers and their families. Both television documentaries presented their directors with a recurrent problem when making films about war: how do you capture the indexical reality, that is, pictures of fighting, when you and the cameraman are not present when the action happens?

In the Andy McNab account of the siege, they use dramatic reconstruction of the event, intercut with interviews from two of the soldiers involved in the incident as witnesses, who give a step by step account of the incident from 2004. In an interview for *Broadcast*, the executive producer, Taylor Downing, states: 'never reconstruct anything that has been shot for real . . . find those moments when no cameraman has been able to operate, such as under intense fire, and recreate them' (Downing 2008: 28). None of the events of the siege of the house that was besieged by the Iraqi militia was filmed, so the whole battle was reconstructed, much of it looking like a war video game with British soldiers depicted in close, hand-held shots, having to take cover from incoming fire, shooting insurgents as they try to access the house and picking out insurgents who are shooting from

neighbouring buildings. This culturally familiar mode of reconstructing battle becomes the main frame through which the viewer accesses
the event. Arabic-sounding music is also added to give an authentic
feel to the scenes where Andy McNab talks about being on the streets
in Basra. Conventional sound design techniques from cinema are
used to enhance dramatic suspense, such as slow drum beats which
rise to a crescendo to signal a growing danger when the soldiers talk
about the increasing numbers of insurgents surrounding the besieged
house, and rock music is laid over action shots. Images are sensa-
tionalised, and emotions aroused by the addition of dramatic sound
effects and music, such as the laying of the sound of a horn (as in a
hunt) as background to militia footage of the destroyed Snatch Land
Rovers, and the sound of guns firing and explosions as a background
to witness accounts. The footage sounds like war, or what we know
of war from the cinema, so it must be war, and like cinema the drama
and pacing of the narrative keeps us firmly attached to our seats in
front of the television.

The dramatic reconstructions are intercut with the footage from the
militia DVD that I mentioned above, of militia firing RPGs and AK47s
on the streets of Basra. The editing is fast paced, with seamless transitions between militia footage and close-ups of the reconstruction of
soldiers acting out the events from the incident, giving the impression
that there is a spatio-temporal continuity between the different types
of footage. The action sequences then cut back to shots of the 1RHA
uniformed soldiers giving their account as participants in the event. The
'real' soldiers are located in a background similar to the reconstruction,
the actor soldiers and real soldiers all wear camouflage, and the colour
is graded to give the different types of footage the same 'look'. The
real soldiers' voice-overs transition from their accounts of the action
into DVD militia footage and the dramatic reconstruction, binding the
different images together. Andy McNab's commentary, which gives a
'voice of god' explanation of what is going on, lends his authority to
this form of expository documentary, and further knits all the sources
into a coherent whole. This has the effect of melding the mechanics of
the storytelling into one compelling dramatic narrative, where a viewer
is not sure what is re-enacted and what is not. Knowledge of the event
is not only gained through the 'record of external events', but also the
'simulated reality of acted events' (Paget 1998: 81), and it is this 'reality'
which is dominant here.

The re-enactment is shot like a drama, with intimate close-ups of
faces, cutaways showing details of weapons, or a splash of blood on
the wall from an Iraqi being shot (see Figure 9.1). This dramatic textual

Figure 9.1: Dramatic reconstruction in *Andy McNab's Tour of Duty*, episode 2 'Face to Face' (ITV4, 2008).

detail lends immediacy to the scenes, enhancing their reality effect. Historical realism – what a war should look like – is reconstructed by the director to resemble other representations of war familiar from news reports, war games and war films. It is thus itself a war representation which both reconstructs what we know and reinforces an imaginary war that we don't. Betraying its drama influences, the television documentary invokes recognisable emotions to convince us that what we see is real, often through use of the documentary convention of commentary. Andy McNab explains why one of the soldiers shot an insurgent: 'Having never fired a shot in anger, Covidi now had to kill if he wanted to see his wife and children again', and of another soldier in the siege: 'Like every man in the building, Matt's thought turned to his loved ones at home.' The inclusion of the emotions of the soldiers also brings reality to the story. Covidi talks about the kill saying:

> you can see their fear or their anger or something, when they are firing at me. I was a bit scared there though, the first time during a contact; the picture that came into my mind was my son – he'd just turned one when I left. I was praying, telling God if he's an angel just to protect me from the worst.

In addition to these techniques, the Andy McNab programme forefronts the melodrama of the narrative by framing the event only as a story of a siege, where the 'good guys' are surrounded by the enemy, and that they manage to get out with some suffering, but no loss of lives. This is a familiar narrative of fiction films with a satisfying closure where no questions about their fate need to be asked. There is also no account of the role of the soldiers in the wider context, or their reason for being in Basra. The explanation presented is the only story from the exploits of 1RHA, and it is told from their point of view. The rest of the series follows a similar pattern of telling the story of exploits of the war in Iraq and Afghanistan told from the perspective of individuals or small groups, a framing also favoured by narrative cinema. Stewart writes that war films focus on the exploits of a few soldiers or sailors, even though the film may revolve round battle scenes that depict thousands, and contemporary politics are removed, so allowing the representations of the military to 'function more freely as a metaphor for the nation' (1996: 76).

The dramatic framing of this construction of events draws on the reality of the witnesses, but one has also to question the extent to which it is achieved for sensation, to keep 'bums on seats', rather than 'to provoke debate about the significance of the events' (Paget 1998: 82). Whether this elicitation of empathetic personalisation for the soldiers and aesthetic pleasure in the excitement of war fits Grierson's conception of documentary, which Bill Nichols argues 'is to preserve the status quo' (Nichols 2001: 600), it evokes feelings of nationalism and sympathy for the military, and encourages viewers not to question this given version of war, or wonder about other versions.

The BBC does not have the same demands as commercial television, but was also searching for a younger audience, and to justify the licence fee with higher audience figures. The series *Soldier, Husband, Daughter, Dad*, of which the second television documentary example I will analyse is a part, was commissioned by BBC1. BBC1's remit is 'to be the BBC's most popular mixed-genre television service across the UK, offering a wide range of high quality programmes', and the brief for the series, which was to focus on families of the regiment, was intended to widen the audience demographic beyond young males who were perceived to be the main audience for documentaries about war. The series follows the six-month progress of the same regiment (1RHA) on its tour in Iraq and the stories of their families in the UK. The sequence I want to focus on in the episode I directed, 'The Price of Peace', involves the same soldiers from the siege incident reconstructed in the ITV4 programme. It draws on two sources: the filmed account by the soldiers to an non-commissioned officer (NCO) (who has been featured in previous episodes in the series) when they come back from the siege[8] intercut with the same militia DVD footage that seeks to represent the insurgents involved in the fight. The soldiers are sitting down and the sequence cuts from mid-shots of those talking to wide shots of others from the group listening. The shots are cut in a naturalistic mode of continuity editing,[9] the camera following the flow of conversation to give a sense of the reality of the situation; the soldiers' tone is measured, and there is no dramatic non-diegetic music. When the soldiers describe the action of the insurgents, the sequence cuts to the DVD footage of a kneeling figure firing an RPG, balaclava-clad men running and carrying machine guns, and a boy scrunching up a plastic union jack flag. The footage is labelled as 'local footage'.

There was no filmic representation of the action of the British, but it is interesting that the soldiers themselves refer to the reality or unreality of the situation in their testimony. Ollie:

> We was [*sic*] in this house and these were real bullets with people actually trying to kill you, and these people firing back and shooting were actually going down and were being killed, and it didn't seem real until actually getting back.

Paradoxically, for the soldiers involved in war, their perception of the reality of war is often also based on whether it is similar to what they have seen in video games or war films. In the *Andy McNab's Tour of Duty* episode discussed above, this reality/game comparison is also made by the programme itself, as Andy McNab's voice-over says of the soldiers' predicament, 'it is not a game.'

There is a larger point here about the witnessing war and how it is processed, which has implications for how one should represent it. Ellis writes that the witnessing of distant suffering depends for its efficacy on what we witness in much more mundane audio-visual encounters (2012: 130). Everyday mundane witnessing underpins exceptional moments of audio-visual shock, so that 'televisual witness involves a complex to and fro between seeing, believing and feeling among today's active viewers' (ibid.: 131). In this context there is a responsibility to present not just the 'shocks' but also the more mundane aspects of war.

In the sequence in which the soldiers verbally recount the siege, I was trying to show the event as a bureaucratic accounting for bullets and bodies spent, where the matter-of-fact attitude of soldiers towards their job of killing was as much a part of war as the drama of the killing and the fighting their way out of the siege. The sergeant in charge of the platoon, Terry, describes shooting someone who fell and was dragged away, whereupon someone else took up his position. Terry

Figure 9.2: Battery Sergeant Billy Bebb in *Soldier, Husband, Daughter, Dad,* episode 7 'The Price of Peace' (BBC1, 2005).

confirms he 'dropped him' (the replacement combatant), and then verbally confirms four other killings. The young captain taking notes asks the sergeant, 'What's the tally on the KIA [killed in action]?' The battery sergeant, Billy Bebb, replies, 'fifteen, possibly sixteen . . .', and Ollie adds, 'These are close quarter kills' (see Figure 9.2). The conversation is filmed in relatively long takes, and the measured pace of the editing, documenting an unemotional verbal account of the incident, is very different from the Andy McNab dramatic reconstructions of blood being splattered on walls and soldiers storming around with guns. Yet Terry, the NCO in charge of the group of soldiers, also talks about the fear of not seeing his wife again, and familiar emotions of fear and fear of losing loved ones are also shown being expressed, in order to connect the audience to the filmed characters, and to emphasise the reality of what happened. Ellis notes that 'witnesses have to recognise the other as being like themselves if they are to experience empathic emotions . . . the empathy can be intellectual or emotion or a combination of the two' (2012: 131). Both the participant/witness to the event, and the viewer of the mediated event, have to draw on truths that they recognise and to communicate these to others, and know that they will be recognised. We can apply this both to the soldiers' attempts to communicate to each other, and the programme's choice to retain these parts of the footage of the soldiers' conversation in the final cut.

Both documentaries stress familiar emotional 'truths' in their soldiers' experiences (fear, family bonds) that could be recognised by the audience, but Ellis's note about empathy quoted above also raises questions about the other participants in the incident. In both sequences under discussion, the militia have a visual 'reality', in that they are represented on screen, although it is important to note that this is not via a direct, empirical recording but via a process by which fragments of older, unrelated militia DVD footage stands in for the militia involved in the incident. This means that the militia do not have a psychological or historical reality: the images lack personal Iraqi militia testimony to draw them together, and so construct a one-dimensional enemy, with no narrative or expressed cause. When in Basra, I was very conscious that we were not getting any Iraqi voices, but the security situation meant it was impossible to venture outside the British compounds without a military escort, and when we went out with them, it was to film what the British were doing. I filmed some of the political discussions between the colonel and the Iraqis, but could not include them in the cut film, as these political manoeu-vrings lay outside the family-focused brief of the programme, and I suspected were not 'familiar' (in Zoellner's terms (2009)) to the executive producer's expectations of 'war', so were excluded. Ulti-mately, the BBC programme gave perhaps a more 'realistic' version of the tedium of war, perhaps to the tedium of the audience. It also gave an insight into the personal lives of soldiers which elicited an emotional response from an audience who could empathise with feel-ings of fear, missing a loved one, home-sickness and the importance of both the regimental and social family. However, like the ITV4 series, it made invisible the difficult questions about the occupation and militia attacks, questions which might have rocked the status quo so prized by Grierson.

CONCLUSION

Both films find a universal and historical truth (Nichols 1991) about the courage and bravery of war, where soldiers as family men fight for their lives against an overwhelming, faceless foe. Both films rely heav-ily on the emotional truth of the fear of losing loved ones, of fear of the enemy and of excitement of danger. The Andy McNab documentary relies more heavily on overt artistic strategies designed to dramatise and sensationalise the action, thus ensuring continuing engagement with the documentary and an attentive audience, but perhaps missing a truth that the BBC programme tried to present. However, for both series, questions about what sort of war these soldiers are fighting, their reasons for fighting (other than survival) and the reasons behind the engagement of the Iraqi militia are not considered. The nature of the occupation, its political character and possible explanations for Iraqi opposition to a foreign invasion and occupation are not discussed. I had to cut out the political dimensions of the colonel testimony about the mission in Iraq, not for specific security reasons, but because the rest of the episodes in the series did not deal with these issues, and the series brief was about family and war. The politics had been erased for BBC1 family viewing, illustrating clearly how commissioning briefs can, unwittingly or otherwise, channel ideological erasures. The aspects of occupation that were not dramatic or 'war-like' were also not shown, unless the drama came from personal relationships between individual soldiers and their families. Traditionally war on television is not about meetings, about administration and accounting. It is not about soldiers painting schools or looking at date plantations, or about tedium or the aftermath of war for Iraqi soldiers and their families. The changing nature of the enterprise from war to occupation and the role of the soldiers is not examined, nor is the nature of the insurgency and counter-insurgency efforts discussed.

At the heart of this account lies the battle between the necessity to keep the audience watching, and the claims of the real: of whether the aesthetics of attraction become dominant, or whether more critical forms of analysis or a journalistic need to inform the audience of what is happening take precedence. In the effort to persuade people to stay watching, many realities of war disappear. When commissioners' main concerns are audience numbers, war on British television documentaries becomes a war that can be seen, but not seen; it can be felt, but not understood. This narrow understanding of war also means that it is mainly documentaries which can promise 'war fighting' that get commissioned on television, and nothing new is presented. An emphasis on the sensory and the emotional silences rational analysis and so there is no complete television documentary account of the British military failure in Iraq. Clausewitz (2007) wrote that war is the continuation of politics by other means, and it is often politics and other means that end wars.[10] If we do not understand this, the view that war is the only way to resolve political debate becomes entrenched and the public are more likely to support a government's decision to bomb or fight as they think that's the only way to resolve an issue. With little appetite for understanding what was happening politically in Iraq, television documentary itself becomes complicit in the public blindness about alternative forms of conflict resolution.

NOTES

1. Zoellner (2009: 527) argues that originality means the ideas have to be presented in a way that is 'headline-grabbing and extreme', through case studies and contributors 'where documentary makers achieve personalisation which provides viewers with identification and emotional attachment'. The angle gives the perspective of the programme, that is the 'particular way of looking at a topic' (ibid.: 524).
2. This footage was used in the documentaries *Soldier, Husband, Daughter, Dad*, BBC1, 2005; *Dispatches: Iraq: the Reckoning*, C4, 21 November 2005; *Panorama: the Battle for Basra Palace*, BBC1, 10 December 2007; *Panorama: Soldiers on the Run*, BBC1, 23 June 2007; *Panorama: Basra – the Legacy*, BBC1, 17 December 2007; *Andy McNab's Tour of Duty*, ITV4 and Sky, 2008.
3. My previous research looked at the eighteen documentaries and two UK television documentary series about the British military in Iraq that aired between 2004 and 2015, a third of which framed the soldiers as victims of war or betrayed by politicians and the Ministry of Defence (Harris 2012).
4. *Real Story with Fiona Bruce*, BBC1, 29 November 2004; *Sweeney Investigates: Death of the Red Caps*, BBC2, 10 February 2005; *Panorama: Bringing our Boys Home?* BBC1, 19 March 2006; *Dispatches: Battle Fatigue*, C4, 22 May 2006; *When our Boys Came Home*, BBC2, 1 June 2006; *Tonight: War Wounds*, ITV1, 30 October 2006; *Panorama: for Queen and Country?* BBC1, 19 February 2007; *Panorama: Soldiers on the Run*, BBC1, 26 March 2007; *Dispatches: Iraq – the Betrayal*, C4, 17 March 2008; *Despatches: Iraq: the Legacy*, C4, 13 December 2008; *The Fallen: Legacy of Iraq*, BBC4, 19 June 2009; *Iraq 2003–2009*, BBC1, 9 October 2009; *Dispatches: Battle Scarred*, C4, 7 September 2009.
5. Some of the theatrically released documentaries about the war in Iraq did examine the war as an occupation from the point of view of the Iraqis, and these were mainly shot in Baghdad. I did not come across any documentaries which looked at the governance and co-governance of Iraq by the British and American military.
6. *This World: Did My Son Die in Vain?* BBC2, 2013; *British Army Be The Best?* Sky1, 2006; *The Queen's Cavalry*, BBC1, 2005; *Saddam's Iraq*, MBC and ITV, 2004; *Fighting the War*, BBC2, 2003.
7. Caldwell (2008) writes of the control over scripting and filming by series producers, but this is more difficult in documentary because of the contingency of filming, especially when filming an observational documentary.
8. After every encounter where weapons are fired, British soldiers have to give a detailed description of the ammunition used and bodies killed, for accounting purposes.
9. Paget (1998) calls this a documentary camera rhetoric.
10. In a survey of campaigns from 1900 to 2006, Chenoweth and Stephan (2011) found that campaigns of non-violent resistance were more than twice as effective as their violent counterparts in achieving their stated goals.

BIBLIOGRAPHY

Anderegg, M. (ed.) (1991), *Inventing Vietnam: The War in Film and TV*, Philadelphia: Temple University Press.

Aufderheide, P. (2012), 'Perceived ethical conflicts in US documentary filmmaking: a field report', *New Review of Film and Television Studies*, 10.3, pp. 362–8.

Beattie, K. (2008), *Documentary Display: Re-viewing Nonfiction Film and Video*, London and New York: Wallflower Press.

Butchart, G. C. (2013), 'Camera as sign: on the ethics of unconcealment in documentary film and video', *Social Semiotics*, 23.5, pp. 675–90.

Caldwell, J. T. (2009), 'Screen studies and industrial "theorizing": professionalism and new realities in television production', *Screen*, 50.1, pp. 167–79.

Chenoweth, E. and M. J. Stephan (2011), *Why Civil Resistance Works: the Strategic Logic of Nonviolent Conflict*, New York: Columbia University Press.

Chouliaraki, L. (2006), *The Spectatorship of Suffering*, London: Sage.

Clausewitz, C. von (2007), *On War*, trans. Michael Eliot Howard and Peter Paret, Oxford: Oxford University Press.

Corner, J. (1996), *The Art of Record*, Manchester: Manchester University Press.

Corner, J. (2005), 'Television, documentary and the category of the aesthetic', in A. Rosenthal and J. Corner (eds), *New Challenges for Documentary*, Manchester and New York: Manchester University Press, pp. 48–58.

Cottle, S. (2013), 'Journalists witnessing disaster: from the calculus of death to the injunction to care', *Journalism Studies*, 14.2, pp. 232–48.

Deluca, K. M. and J. Peeples (2002), 'From public sphere to public screen: democracy, activism and the "violence" of Seattle', *Critical Studies in Media Communication* 19.2, pp. 125–51.

Downing, T. (2008), 'On location: *Andy McNab's Tour of Duty*', *Broadcast*, 19 May. Available at <http://www.broadcastnow.co.uk/on-location-andy-mcnabs-tour-of-duty/1379287.article> (last accessed 8 Feb 2016).

Ekström, M. (2000), 'Information, storytelling and attraction,' *Media, Culture & Society*, 22, pp. 455–92.

Ellis, J. (2012), *Documentary: Witness and Self-revelation*, London: Routledge.

Fiske, J. (1994), *Television Culture*, London: Routledge.

Grierson, J. (1933), 'The documentary producer', *Cinema Quarterly*, 2.1, pp. 7–9.

Grierson, J. ([1942] 1976), 'The documentary idea', in R. Barsam (ed.), *Nonfiction Film Theory and Criticism*, New York: E. P. Dutton and Co.

Hallin, D. (1989), *The Uncensored War: the Media and Vietnam*, Berkeley and Los Angeles: University of California Press.

Hariman, R. (2014), 'Watching war evolve: photojournalism and new forms of violence', in L. Kennedy and C. Patrick (eds), *The Violence of the Image: Photography and International Conflict*, London and New York: I. B. Tauris.

Harris, J. (2012), 'A dismal and dangerous occupation: an investigation into the discourses in the television news and documentary coverage of the British military in Iraq from 2004–2009, examining how the coverage plays out in specific genres', PhD thesis, Cardiff University.

Hoskins, A. and B. O'Loughlin (2007), *New Security Challenges: Television and Terror: Conflicting Times and the Crisis of News Discourse*, Basingstoke: Palgrave Macmillan.

Kaplan, E. A. (2005), *Trauma Culture: the Politics of Terror and Loss in Media and Literature*, New Brunswick, NJ and London: Rutgers University Press.

Kress, G. and T. van Leeuwen (2001), *Multimodal Discourse: the Modes and Media of Contemporary Communication*, Oxford: Oxford University Press.

Mellencamp, M. (2006), 'Fearful thoughts: US television since 9/11 and the wars in Iraq' in A. Martin and P. Petro (eds), *Rethinking Global Security: Media, Popular Culture and the 'War on Terror'*, New Brunswick, NJ: Rutgers University Press.

Mestrovic, S. G. (1996), *Genocide after Emotion: the Post-emotional Balkan War*, London: Routledge.

Michalski, M. and J. Gow (2007), *War Image and Legitimacy: Viewing Contemporary Conflict*, London and New York: Routledge.

Mitchell, W. J. T. (2002), 'Showing seeing: a critique of visual culture', *Journal of Visual Culture*, 1.2, pp. 165–81.

Nichols, B. (1991), *Representing Reality: Issues and Concepts in Documentary*, Bloomington and Indianapolis: Indiana University Press.

Nichols, B. (2010), *Introduction to Documentary*, Bloomington and Indianapolis: Indiana University Press.

North, R. (2009), *Ministry of Defeat: The British War in Iraq 2003–2009*, London: Continuum.

Paget, D. (1988), *No Other Way to Tell It: Dramadoc/Docudrama on Television*, Manchester: Manchester University Press.

Pantti, M. and K. Wahl-Jorgensen (2007), 'On the political possibilities of therapy news: media responsibility and the limits of objectivity in disaster coverage', *Studies in Communication*, 1 (March), pp. 3–25.

Renov, M. (1993), *Theorising Documentary*, New York and London: Routledge.

Sancho, J. (2003), *Conflict around the Clock*, London: ITC.

Seaton, J. (2005), *Carnage & the Media: the Making and Breaking of News about Violence*, London: Allen Lane.

Schaefer, R. J. (1997), 'Editing strategies in television news documentaries', *Journal of Communication*, 47.4 (Autumn), pp. 69–85.

Sobchack, V. (1999), 'Toward a phenomenology of nonfiction film experience' in J. Gaines and M. Renov (eds), *Collecting Visible Evidence*, Minneapolis: University of Minnesota Press.

Stewart, I. (1996), 'Presenting arms: portrayals of war and the military in British cinema', in I. Stewart and S. Carruthers (eds), *War, Culture & the Media: Representations of the Military in 20th Century Britain*, Trowbridge: Flick Books.

Takacs, S. (2009), 'The body of war and the management of imperial anxiety on US television', *International Journal of Contemporary Iraqi Studies*, 3.1, pp. 85–105.

Thomas, L. (2008), 'ITV4 re-loads for next assault' *Broadcast*, 7 May. Available at <http://m.broadcastnow.co.uk/1326198.article> (last accessed 10 August 2016).

Watt, I. (1957), *The Rise of the Novel*, Harmondsworth: Penguin.

Winston, B. (1995), *Claiming the Real: the Documentary Film Revisited*, London: BFI Publishing.

Worcester, R. (2003), 'Iraq: public support maintained – the state of public opinion on the war', 8 April. Available at <https://www.ipsos-mori.com/newsevents/ca/180/Iraq-Public-Support-Maintained-8212-The-State-Of-Public-Opinion-On-The-War.aspx> (last accessed 2 April 2016).

Young, M. B. (2003), 'In the combat zone', *Radical History Review*, 85, pp. 253–64.

Zelizer, B. (2004), 'When war is reduced to a photograph', in S. Allan and B. Zelizer (eds), *Reporting War: Journalism in Wartime*, London and New York: Routledge.

Zoellner, A. (2009), 'Professional ideology and program conventions: documentary development in independent British television production', *Mass Communication and Society*, 12, pp. 503–36.

CHAPTER 10

Nine Cinematic Devices for Staging (In)visible War and the (Vanishing) Colonial Present

Shohini Chaudhuri

In a climactic battle in *American Sniper* (2014), the protagonist Chris Kyle and his platoon are confronting rebel fighters as a gigantic sandstorm approaches. The platoon is aided by formidable surveillance: the stream of aerial images from aircraft providing air support, relayed to soldiers monitoring the battle on overhead screens, and the binoculars and riflescope that Kyle uses to line up and successfully fire at his target, an insurgent on a rooftop 2,100 yards away (we even follow the bullet's path). When the sandstorm engulfs them, suspense is generated about how long Kyle's platoon can hold out: visibility lessens and figures become lost in the landscape, hidden by swirling grains of sand. The insurgent's dead body is glimpsed in a final shot, before the sand erases him altogether.

Erasures in media depictions of the 'war on terror' are intensely cinematic. Many people do not even notice them, because the erasures themselves are hidden, like shots produced by visual effects that are meant to be invisible to audiences – here, the VFX sandstorm that transforms a bustling, modern Iraqi city into a desert, devoid of people. It is not accurate to talk simply of erasures, but rather of the heightened visibility of certain people, images and experiences and the reduced visibility of others. Even redactions in official documents, such as interrogation logs for suspected terrorists, are inscribed by this logic: words such as 'waterboarding' remain highly visible, along with detainees' names, while actual details are kept classified. With such 'public secrets',[1] 'things that we all know about, but know we should not know *too much* about'

(Craze 2015: 389), such as torture under the Bush administration and drone warfare during the Obama era, intense focus on so-called 'high-value' suspects forestalls questions about these measures' legality and impact on innocent civilians caught up in the whirlwind: the invisible victims.

In this chapter, I trace the cinematic logic of visibility and invisibility through which these conflicts are produced, drawing on the work of Derek Gregory, who maintains that 'spaces of constructed visibility are always also spaces of constructed invisibility' (2004: 199), and Gil Z. Hochberg's analysis of conditions of visibility in the Israeli–Palestinian conflict rooted in the colonial–settler imagination (encapsulated in the slogan 'a land without people for a people without a land', an erasure of the land's native Palestinian inhabitants) (2015: 5). As Hochberg suggests, states hold the power to conceal their violence and manipulate their citizens' frame of vision, inducing blindness as to what is carried out in their name.

Firstly, I examine seven cinematic devices through which visibility and invisibility are achieved in mainstream Western depictions of recent wars, and which render those wars in terms of an imperial cartography, illustrating this with *American Sniper* and other cinematic examples along with news reporting of conflicts from the 2001 US-led invasion of Afghanistan to the British government's decision to join Western coalition aerial bombing in Syria in 2015. This approach helps to sharpen critical discourses of 'invisible war' developed by Paul Virilio (1989) and Jean Baudrillard (1995), a war operationalised from computer screens, experienced like a video game by combatants. I suggest there is a double regime of (in)visibility: one consisting of carefully staged elements for the domestic audience's benefit that condition us not to see beyond the limits of that imperialistic vision, and another for populations where conflicts are waged. Or, as a banner for activist group Peace of the Action puts it, 'VIDEO GAME FOR US, BLOODBATH FOR THEM' (2000).

Secondly, I turn to two alternative cinematic strategies in *Concerning Violence: Nine Scenes from the Anti-imperialistic Self-defense* (2014), a documentary by Swedish film-maker Göran Hugo Olsson, which explores the reverse perspective of those on the receiving end of the West's actions. Although it deals with decolonisation struggles in Africa in the 1960s, 1970s and 1980s, using archive footage from Swedish state television and text from Frantz Fanon's *The Wretched of the Earth* (1961), it encourages viewers to see beyond the period and connect it to current issues, evoking the 'colonial present' in which violence inflicted on marginalised people continues in new forms.[2]

CINEMATIC DEVICES 1–7

1. Scenario: Good Versus Evil, or Civilisation Versus Barbarism

Orientalism, the term Edward Said (1991) used to describe the West's construction of itself and its 'others', helps to illuminate ways in which conflicts are filtered for domestic audiences. Cinema and news media often promote scenarios of good battling evil, or civilisation facing numerous, barbarous enemies. Focus on evil enemies, along with clear-cut division between 'good' and 'bad' guys, lends itself to many genres, but the Western, steeped in the colonial–settler imagination, establishes the civilisation/barbarism antinomy (see Kitses 1969: 11). Contemporary war films extend these genre tropes. In *American Sniper*, directed by one-time Western star Clint Eastwood, when soldiers arrive in US-occupied Iraq, they are welcomed 'to the new Wild West of the old Middle East'. The Western encapsulates a previous history of occupation along the American frontier, 'a border between established and unestablished order . . . that is not crossed but endlessly pushed back' (Dyer 1997: 33). The frontier image epitomises the imperial task and its imaginative geography of the desert/wilderness that serves as a foil for Western civilisation. American settlers' victory over Native Americans is typically seen as good triumphing over evil, civilisation over barbarism. Furthermore, viscerally pleasurable shoot-outs solidify the narrative that 'an act of violence can sort things out' (Dyer 1997: 34).

The civilisation/barbarism trope plays out in the present by preparing the public to accept war as a justifiable response, exhorting vengeance. Good/evil binaries help to foster prevalent views of Western powers as essentially benevolent actors, founded on amnesia about the colonial past and their ongoing violent interventions in the world. As in the Western and old imperial adventure films, economic and strategic interests are masked by 'redeeming ideas', such as the fight against savagery and fascism (Shohat and Stam 1994: 112). Cases for recent military interventions have been justified as moral imperatives, to save Afghans, Iraqis, Libyans and Syrians from the tyranny of dictators and/or vicious terrorists (whose gross violations and harms are also inexcusable). To claim moral high ground and justify warring agendas, the label 'fascism' has been used for a litany of 'bad guys', from Saddam Hussein to ISIS, a power discourse that forms a binary between (Western) democracy and fascism and helps mask 'the West's part in subverting democracies abroad' (Shohat and Stam 1994: 2). Similarly, the word 'terrorism' is used indiscriminately for any kind of resistance to state power. In Israel, where the state's self-image as a democracy significantly relies on the hypervisibility of Palestinian violence, scrutiny is removed from state actions by casting them simply as responses to terrorist violence.

Government and media regularly magnify public fears of terrorism with reference to 9/11 and other attacks, presenting the West as facing a new evil: radical Islam. The extremist group ISIS has gained high visibility for its videoed beheadings of captives, among them US journalists James Foley and Steven Sotloff. Their highly visible deaths generated mass outrage – US Vice-President John Kerry called Sotloff's execution 'an act of medieval savagery' – and catalysed US-led air strikes against al-Qaeda-related and ISIS fighters in Syria in 2014, which was alleged by a Pentagon official (who was unable to disclose details) to have killed 'lots of bad guys' (Brook and Michaels 2014). As following sections will show, the devices with which mainstream media report on such killings ensure that dropping bombs is viewed as 'civilised', while beheading is seen as 'barbaric'.

2. Focalisation: Embedded with the POV of Western Military and their Weapons/Surveillance Systems

Due to the practice of embedded reporting, pivotal to government policy since the Vietnam War to ensure that journalists support the official line, the public mostly see war from the point of view of Western military. All kinds of news media (TV, print, internet) utilise pictures released by satellite companies and government defence departments, which turn the battleground into an 'abstract, de-corporealised space' of visible targets, showing buildings being destroyed, rather than people (Gregory 2004: 53). As Gregory writes of media coverage of the aerial bombing of Afghanistan, 'American bombs and missiles rained down on K-A-B-U-L [that is, coordinates on a grid or letters on a map], not the eviscerated city of Kabul' (2004: 248). Seeing war from the viewpoint of those firing guns or missiles makes war look thrilling, a focalisation that encourages us to be indifferent (or even sadistic) to those on the receiving end.

Surveying and mapping territories and their resources were crucial instruments of empire. Imperial map-making erased indigenous experiences of land and space. The legacy of this can be seen in the visual logic of military surveillance, in which 'Ground truth vanishes in the ultimate "God-trick", whose terrible vengeance depends on making its objects visible and its subjects invisible' (Gregory 2004: 54). Drone missiles that penetrate buildings, killing those inside, may only leave a small hole in the roof invisible at the level of publicly available satellite pictures, which are much lower resolution than military surveillance images, enabling concealment of state crimes (Weizman 2015: 201).

Hollywood films about recent conflicts are also 'embedded'. Following the restricted viewpoints of soldiers on the battlefield or journalists and CIA agents within securitised zones, which block out the war's wider context, they suture viewers to the occupier's perspective. As in the Western, the viewer is often positioned behind a gun barrel; we see through the gunsights, and cinematic mechanisms of identification (such as point of view (POV), shot scale, sound) make American troops 'the focus of our attention and sympathy', as they 'sally out' against unknown, inexplicably hostile attackers (Stam and Spence 1985: 641). In *American Sniper*, Kyle's riflescope serves as the POV through which we see Iraqis from a distance (see Figure 10.1), with cutaways to other perspectives, such as a rival sniper's POV, only to build suspense about threats that US soldiers are under. As Guy Westwell says of similar cutaway shots in *The Hurt Locker* (2008), 'they remain at all times decontextualised, with no attempt at characterisation' (2011: 27).

This applies even to films overtly critical of the war, such as *Green Zone* (2010), where cross-cutting, together with an edgy, suspenseful soundtrack, make us want American soldiers to succeed in a planned raid on a home where Saddam Hussein's generals are holding a secret meeting (a fictionalisation that elides many ordinary civilian homes raided during the Iraq occupation). In *Good Kill* (2014), we follow Major Tommy Egan as he pilots drones and hunts targets in Afghanistan, Yemen and Pakistan from his base in Nevada. Throughout, our viewpoint on these

Figure 10.1: Iraqis are framed through the viewpoint of Kyle's riflescope in *American Sniper* (2014).

places is from overhead, through a drone's high-resolution sensor, bring-ing the battlefield into heightened visibility and even illuminating bod-ies in the dark. Through identification with drone pilots' POV, viewers can vicariously enjoy the visceral thrill of firing at targets and share that visual mastery, able to attack anyone, anywhere, from a distance, with-out being seen or heard. Momentarily, the film invites us to think what it would be like if such weapons were turned against 'us'. Egan's subur-ban home in the Nevada desert, with its bright-green, artificially-turfed garden, is shown from above, as if from a drone's perspective, but signifi-cantly neither he nor his family are at risk and no on-screen cross-hairs reduce them to targets.

3. Star Quality: Machismo

By going to war, governments claim to provide security, displaying their military force. Ella Shohat and Robert Stam have analysed CNN cov-erage of the Gulf War (1990–1), which was 'machismo-driven from the start': 'through a show of phallic vigor, a senescent America imag-ined itself cured of the traumatic "impotence" it suffered in another war [Vietnam]' (1994: 128). Similar metaphors of virile intervention have played out in media imagery of recent conflicts. For instance, on the first day of official British air strikes in Syria in 2015, UK news media gave high visibility to RAF jets and 'Brimstone missiles', suppos-edly known for their 'low-collateral' (Samuels 2015), their phallic tips pointing suggestively at the camera. In *American Sniper*, Kyle proves himself to be a 'real' man as well as a patriotic hero, saving other front-line soldiers with his long-barrelled rifle, a self-proclaimed protector of the nation. The film's intent to idealise him is reinforced by the fact that it is based on Chris Kyle's biography; as Martin Barker argues of other Iraq war films, the format of fictionalising real people turns characters into 'proposed models of soldiering' (2011a: 47).

The cult of virility ties empire and nationhood to masculine ide-als, its less visible underside being the damaged man. In the Iraq War (2003–11), the media were forbidden to photograph the return of US soldiers' coffins and 'seriously injured troops were flown into Andrews air force base in the dead of the night' (Gregory 2004: 233). However, although they were traumatised by what they saw and the sacrifice of their lives is tragic, these soldiers' experiences are considerably more visible than ordinary civilian casualties.

In understated ways, under his macho exterior, Kyle in *American Sniper* is troubled about his actions, and suffers from combat trauma. Eastwood aims to show that 'War is not pretty and it has an effect on the people we send into conflict' (Jarrett 2015: 56). But deployment of trauma discourses through a POV structure that permits viewers to feel only what US soldiers undergo further reduces war to a quintessentially American experience. Barker observes that trauma in films such as *In the Valley of Elah* (2007) and *The Hurt Locker* makes the murderous behaviour of US soldiers 'excusable', similar to the revisionism of Vietnam War films, which recast the US military as victims instead of perpetrators (2011b: 82). My additional point is that focus on bodily/psychic vulnerability does not change the problem of focalisation noted above. Combat trauma discourse suffers from the same solipsism and is just as confined to soldiers' point of view.

4. Casting Extras as Serial Others

A major consequence of foregrounding US soldiers is that others are reduced to background extras. In Iraq war reports, 'The Iraqi people are distant, fleeting bit players' (Pilger 2010: 6), according to the script of the invasion which insisted they 'remain invisible so their country could be reduced to a series of "targets"' (Gregory 2004: 199). Statistics held by organisations such as Iraq Body Count and the Bureau of Investigative Journalism reveal that thousands of people, many of them civilians, have been killed by coalition troops in recent conflicts, through aerial bombing, indiscriminate firing during raids on homes and public places, and at military checkpoints. Even drones, with their high-precision weapons, have frequently targeted the wrong people through flawed intelligence, human error or the policy of 'double tap' (follow-up strikes that often kill civilians who come to help those blown up in the first attack).

This huge civilian death toll goes largely unreported. Stories of these innocent victims 'are usually buried along with their bodies', 'their suffering unseen and their plight invisible before the gigantic imperative of killing terrorists' (Benjamin 2013: 113, 123). Al-Jazeera and other Arab news media offer contrasting perspectives, not shirking, for example, from reporting the horrors of the coalition bombing of Iraq in 2003. Differences in coverage are not simply, as is often presumed, due to Western media's desire to avoid voyeuristically graphic images, but are also politically motivated. A near blackout in mainstream Western (and Israeli) media helps to produce the impression of high-tech, casualty-free wars; if covered at all, these casualties are given a low priority for fear of undermining public support for wars. In contrast, as witnessed by coverage of 9/11 and the November 2015 Paris massacre, the (far rarer) attacks on home soil against civilians who are their own (or near) compatriots, achieve headline news – generating the perception that 'The real horror happens *here*, not there' (Gregory 2004: 279).

Gregory claims that, in the 'war on terror', both armed opponents and local civilians are reduced to *homines sacri* – Giorgio Agamben's term for those who are 'excluded from politically qualified life' (2004: 212). Placed beyond protections of international law, their deaths, unlike deaths of Western citizens, don't matter. Treatment of victims additionally reflects what Jean-Paul Sartre, in *Critique of Dialectical Reason* (an influence on Fanon's writings on colonialism), calls 'seriality': people made anonymous and interchangeable (Macey 2012: 480). *Good Kill* rehearses the argument that if drone warfare saves 'one American', then the price is worth it – a view that not only reveres American lives more, but makes it acceptable for many of 'them' to die for 'us'. In this 'grisly colonial calculus', the lives of others are left officially uncounted and thus unaccountable; even though coalition forces have technical capacity for 'damage assessment' by their weapons, their 'kills' are 'tanks, artillery, missile launchers – objects – not people' (Gregory 2004: 207, 249).

Such discrepancies are familiar to us in the stagings of Hollywood cinema in which lives of racial others are deemed cheap and expendable. They die, almost invisibly, in the background, disposed of en masse in action sequences. As Michele Aaron notes, 'mainstream cinema works to bestow value upon certain lives . . . in a hierarchical and partisan way . . . [T]hese moving images of death divulge also what is held sacred and which lives reign sovereign in cinema' (2014: 5). Mainstream cinema enacts what Achille Mbembe (2003) calls 'necropolitics', dictating 'who may live and who may die'. According to Aaron, it forms part of 'a much larger mortal economy: that of Western "society", which cinema "merely" reinforces' (2014: 93).

5. War as a Hitchcockian MacGuffin

In a *Guardian* article about UK members of parliament who complained about online bullying regarding their decision to vote in favour of airstrikes in Syria, and in doing so made the issue a psychodrama about themselves, Marina Hyde stated these politicians were in 'danger of reducing a bombing campaign to what Alfred Hitchcock called a MacGuffin – "a plot device that motivates the characters and advances the story", but which is often unimportant in itself' (2015: 41). That war is a MacGuffin can be seen in the way that war quickly disappears from public view. Interest in war soon slips, as it drops from headlines and gets buried under other news. As Medea Benjamin says of US coverage, 'The mainstream media, after cheerleading for war and enthusiastically covering the initial shock-and-awe volley of missiles, quickly become bored with America's imperial exploits . . . especially when there's something important like a celebrity break-up to report' (Benjamin: 2013: 213).

Furthermore, the tactical shift from ground troops to air wars, fought by fighter pilots or drones operated remotely, posing far less risk of casualties to one's own side, helps to remove war from public consciousness. In the US and Britain 'lower enlistment and lower casualties' reduce the need to scrutinise 'whether the wars are worth fighting' and make conflicts 'more obscure' (Benjamin 2013: 150). The covert drone programme allows the US and Britain to attack people in places where they are not officially at war, including Pakistan, Yemen, Somalia, Libya and the Philippines, as well as Iraq, Afghanistan and Syria. In both Iraq and Afghanistan, drone strikes increased just as those wars were officially announced to be winding down, permitting killing to continue behind the scenes even when wars are supposedly 'over'. In Israel/Palestine, too, there is sometimes no need for 'boots on the ground' in order 'to dominate and extinguish – Palestinian life' (Benjamin 2013: 71). Removal of territorial presence, such as Israel's 2005 'withdrawal' from Gaza, helps engender the invisibility of war for the domestic public, creating a semblance of 'normality' in Israel while the Palestinian Territories are continually terrorised by drones.

Because the physical and psychic cost of war to the Western public is very low (though the financial cost to the public purse is not), most people are distanced and isolated from the effects of war. Therefore, war becomes incidental to our lives. As Benjamin writes of the situation in the US, 'The paradox is that while the US military is engaged in more and longer conflicts than ever in our history, fewer people are involved, touched, concerned, or engaged. The public is barely even aware of these conflicts', having simply learned to accommodate and essentially ignore them (Benjamin 2013: 152).

6. Special Effects: Spectacular Violence

In this media economy, 'sudden eruptions of violence associated with large-scale military assaults or terrorist attacks widely circulate, with this type of "spectacular violence" drawing attention to itself as *violence par excellence*' (Hochberg 2015: 13). As well as ISIS beheadings, exemplary instances include 'shock-and-awe' campaigns that demonstrate military force, such as the 2003 coalition bombing of Iraq and the 2014 Israeli bombardment of Gaza. Such campaigns are a tactic of intimidating and terrorising the local population, sending one message to them (flee or surrender), and another to the domestic public, for whom the military violence is displayed as a 'cinematic performance', since it is 'not politically expedient for them to see this as a war *of* terror' (Gregory 2004: 198). In the Israeli border town Sderot, Israeli citizens gathered for front-row seats to watch the assault on Gaza, experienced as a pyrotechnic display against the horizon (Mackey 2014). US and UK citizens were similarly invited to admire the 'shock-and-awe' campaign against Iraq on their TV sets. To lend historical authenticity, *Green Zone* opens with audio of news reports of 'shock-and-awe' over a black screen; however, when visuals appear, revealing Baghdad's nocturnal skyline illuminated by colourful explosions, they merely augment the televisual experience of war, accompanied by a martial soundtrack.

The entertainment format of both mainstream news and cinema favour spectacular violence, gravitating towards dramatic moments, such as explosions or shoot-outs – moments that mainstream cinema often fetishises with lyrical visual effects. This forms a contrast to 'more mundane and persistent types of violence' which, Hochberg argues, stay 'almost *entirely* invisible to external viewers', except when 'reframed and labeled as exceptional and scandalous', such as revelations of torture and abuse of Iraqi prisoners by US soldiers at Abu Ghraib prison during the Iraq occupation (2015: 13–14). When it becomes visible, this kind of 'routine' systemic violence is quickly dismissed as an aberration or tragic mistake, rather than an everyday occurrence, made to seem the fault of a few 'bad apples'. One of the rare instances in which everyday violence against Palestinians in the Occupied Territories gained mainstream media visibility was the burning to death in 2015 of a Palestinian child by Israeli settlers (Buchanan 2015). Israeli politicians rushed to express condolences to the family and vowed to bring perpetrators to justice, as if this was the only instance of settler violence. What also often remain invisible are deaths caused by the legacy of war; for example, after the 2003 'shock-and-awe' campaign, which destroyed vital civilian infrastructure, including water and sanitation systems, thousands of Iraqis perished through lack of clean water and healthcare, adding to the hidden and unseen deaths of the 'war on terror'.

7. Closure: White Redemption

In *Death and the Moving Image*, Aaron observes the repeated 'erasure of black life to guarantee white subjectivity and redemption' (2014: 141). I argue that white redemption forms part of the imperial cartography that erases others in favour of mainly white Western subjects and ensures continuation of the status quo. *Green Zone* elides most aspects of its putative source, *Imperial Life in the Emerald City* (2006), Rajiv Chandrasekaran's account of the follies and ambitions of the US-led occupation of Iraq, and rewrites them in terms of a Hollywood redemption narrative about a noble hero who reveals the 'truth' about the war (simplified as the deception of one corrupt official who falsifies intelligence that led to the war).

Good Kill is likewise critical of the 'war on terror' in its dialogue but not in its other cinematic codes. When Egan tells his wife Molly about his day at work, the scene alternates between the couple outside their suburban Nevada home and flashbacks to Egan's flight over Waziristan (via drone POV), as he first describes blowing up a Taliban commander's home while his family was still inside, then, after following mourners to the funeral, blowing them up too, upon the arrival of the commander's brother. A series of close-ups of the tearful Molly contrast her blonde hair and blue eyes with the dark-skinned, long-robed people that Egan targets. Molly's features mark her exemplary whiteness, according to cultural codings (Dyer 1997: 44) (see Figure 10.2). The tearful wife is the moment that the film's '(racialised and sexualised) normative consciousness' (Aaron 2014: 93) becomes most apparent, helping to explain its structural mirroring between Molly and Suarez, Egan's co-pilot (played by Afro-American actress Zoë Kravitz), a rival love interest, who also sheds tears for victims. Elimination of Taliban suspects and their families allows for tenderness to be expressed for them posthumously, as if the only way to treat them is in the past tense, which condemns them to their fate while dismissing any claims for accountability in the present.

Figure 10.2: In *Good Kill* (2014), close-ups of the tearful wife, Molly, mark her exemplary whiteness in contrast to the people targeted by drones.

The erasure of white redemption is at work again in *American Sniper*, which ends with Kyle's funeral after he has been shot dead by a veteran he was 'trying to help' (as we are informed in the closing titles). As his coffin is carried along, the highway is festooned with American flags and tributes. The film as a whole seeks to 'honour a slain war hero' (Norris 2015: 69). The hero is sacrificed: as Aaron says of this motif in a range of other films, 'his sacrifice eclipses their sacrifice' (2014: 93), here the 160 Iraqis whose lives he took.

TWO ALTERNATIVE STRATEGIES: APPROPRIATION OF THE ARCHIVE AND DIALECTICAL MONTAGE IN *CONCERNING VIOLENCE*

The cinematic devices explored above are products of conscious and unconscious structuring, orientalist habits that have become institutionalised in mainstream Western cinema as part of its imperial legacy.[3] These habits constitute limitations of vision, manifesting a close fit between mainstream cinema and Western news organisations' values and priorities. I am not denying that films have their complexities, but it is important to draw attention to the institutionalised forms through which they structure our viewing experience. One reading of *American Sniper* defends the film by arguing that it 'says one thing and shows another' (Pinkerton 2015: 62), but the problem with this is that the film's cinematic strategies don't support that claim, as shown by the earlier discussion of focalisation through the Western military's point of view. My argument about *Concerning Violence*, on the other hand, is based on the alternative strategies that it adopts.

Concerning Violence revives traditions of 'Third Cinema' described in Fernando Solanas and Octavio Getino's manifesto, according to which critique of the system and its blind spots cannot come from within the system – that can only result in a '"progressive" wing of Establishment cinema' (1976: 45), a 'wing' to which films like *Good Kill* arguably belong. Instead, Solanas and Getino advocate documentary, which 'bears witness to, refutes or deepens the truth of a situation' in ways that 'the system finds indigestible' (1976: 55). However, by this, they do not mean mere documentation or witnessing, though these are important strategies, which today include videos by citizen journalists and monitoring groups that collect data of civilian casualties and deploy visual proof of their suffering. Circulation of such testimonial images, usually via non-mainstream media, constitutes 'an alternative archive of seeing', challenging official accounts of war by exposing what was previously invisible or under-reported (Hochberg 2015: 8).

Concerning Violence does not offer a straightforward presentation of events: though attuned to perspectives of victims of imperial wars, it takes a more indirect approach than either realist fiction film or documentary, which create identification through optical or narrative point of view. In voice-over, US singer/rapper Lauryn Hill reads from Fanon's *The Wretched of the Earth* (1961) as the words often simultaneously unfurl onscreen, layered over rediscovered footage from Swedish archives that shows struggles of colonised people against colonial powers in Africa. The film sets out the violent record of European colonial powers and suggests links with present-day wars, highlighting historical realities erased by dominant representations. Divided into nine chapters, each one dealing with a particular liberation struggle or theme of the coloniser/colonised relationship, it follows the stages of (1) producing perceptual shock, (2) ordering and elaboration of concepts, then (3) knowledge of revolutionary practice, in order to develop Western audiences' consciousness.

Archive footage generally implies evidence excavated from the past, while offering 'something "new" [which] we did not know or had not seen before' (Baron 2014: 6). *Concerning Violence* appropriates archive footage from official sources – Swedish state TV – and places it in a different interpretive context, generating new understandings of both past and present. Sweden's officially neutral position at the time enabled Swedish film-makers and journalists to create these images, which are revealing of their own colonial views and prejudices, despite their sense of solidarity with anti-imperialist struggles.[4] For Jacques Derrida (1996), the archive itself is a form of political power and has erasure at its heart. But this also endows it with possibilities of resistance, particularly relevant when certain images, people and experiences are being erased. The film's archive footage evokes a past world – not the specific reference points with which Fanon deals (mainly Algeria under French rule), but decolonisation struggles in other African countries – in order to provoke thoughts about the present. Though Olsson (2015) contemplated incorporating contemporary footage (specifically mentioning the Gaza war), he decided against it on grounds that it would encourage viewers to focus on those particular events rather than the wider context the film seeks to portray.

Another strategy at play in *Concerning Violence* is dialectical montage which, according to its main theorist and practitioner Sergei Eisenstein, is the most apt formal approach for 'ideologically critical theses' (1998: 110). The full meaning is not contained in a shot but emerges through collision of disparate shots that form new concepts in the viewer's mind. In *Strike* (1925), a bull's slaughter is intercut with troops firing at workers. The association between slaughter and mass shooting both emotionally intensifies the scene and offers thematic comparison between different subjects. As if to declare affinity with Eisenstein's approach, *Concerning Violence* opens with slaughter of livestock, shot by troops firing from helicopters. The point of view shifts from over a soldier's shoulder, as he points his gun at the fleeing animals, to the death throes of a slaughtered bull on the ground. Peals of brass instruments sound warning notes, as Hill begins her voice-over from Fanon's text, superimposed in bold white type on the sky: 'Colonialism is not a thinking machine, nor a body endowed with reasoning faculties. It is violence in its natural state . . .'

The film achieves its effects through selection of archival fragments and the accumulation of associations that they arouse, which produce a stronger effect when experienced as a whole. One result of deploying dialectical montage is that shot content becomes less important and sometimes the text dominates the images, relegating people in them to the background. In its attempt to follow Fanon in making a general statement about colonialism and its legacies, the film risks erasing these particularities.

FANON'S THESIS

Fanon wrote *The Wretched of the Earth* in the midst of the Algerian War and was himself affiliated to the FLN (the National Liberation Front in Algeria). Influenced by ideas about the antagonistic forces of history (the Hegelian dialectic, which he absorbed via Sartre), he argues that the colonial situation is founded upon and perpetrated through violence. That violence is internalised by the colonised, who respond to the original violence of colonialism with their own counter-violence – a thesis that reverses the order implied by mainstream Western media, in which 'civilisation' is attacked by 'barbarism', and state violence is a 'response' to terrorism.

In many ways, the cycle of violence described by Fanon remains unbroken today. However, *Concerning Violence* treats his thesis in a dialectical way that invites us to view it critically. Just as the book has a preface by Sartre, the film, too, has a preface, this time by Gayatri Chakravorty Spivak. Spivak's preface is important, both because of the issues it raises and the dialectical relationship it establishes with the rest of the film. She points out problems in Fanon's text, Sartre's original preface and the film itself. Fanon's view that the colonised cure themselves of their neurosis by armed struggle lends itself to justification of extreme violence by the alienated, an interpretation reinforced by Sartre's preface. However, to see the book as a glorification of violence, Spivak says, misses Fanon's point that the poor resort to violence out of desperation because they lack other means of opposing the legitimised violence of their colonisers. Furthermore, she highlights gender as a blind spot in Fanon's thinking; he was unable to see its invisible structuring presence in histories of colonial domination and resistance struggles. The violence of gendering unites coloniser and colonised, manifesting for Spivak in the endorsement of rape, but also, one could argue, the machismo that underlies violent posturing, even in Fanon's text.

Concerning Violence's use of a female voice to evoke the spirit of Fanon's writing dialectically conflicts with the gendering of the text.[5] Lauryn Hill further brings associations between colonial histories shown in archive footage and black oppression in America. The film presents racial hierarchy as the vehicle for slavery and imperial domination, the legacy of which can be seen in the racial imagery organising today's world, including 'who bombs and who is bombed' (Dyer 1997: 1), as well as differential access to healthcare, housing, education and equitable working conditions. Moreover, the archival images do not merely illustrate Fanon's thesis, but occasionally form a counterpoint, as when visuals linger on a dying colonial soldier in the Guinea–Bissau war of independence, lending a critical slant to Fanon's text about violence as 'a cleansing force'. As Jaimie Baron states, 'images of the human body often undermine the viewer's sense of ironic detachment' (2014: 41), soliciting powerful bodily responses from viewers – in this case, highlighting bodily consequences of violence.

ANTI-COLONIAL RESISTANCE AND COLLECTIVE PUNISHMENT

Whereas Hollywood films take a colonial viewpoint from which all we see is an insurgency and counterinsurgency operations, *Concerning Violence* presents the reverse perspective of resistance fighters seeking to drive occupying forces from their homeland. This is not necessarily an optical or spatial point of view, but rather a political point of view, one rarely seen in mainstream Western media. In a section about the FRELIMO resistance group in Mozambique in 1972 (then a Portuguese colony), the guerrillas are shown as speaking subjects, people possessing their own agency, views and capabilities, not 'extras' in their

own country like Iraqis in Hollywood scripts. Female FRELIMO combatants explain their reasons for taking up armed struggle – namely,
'500 years of slavery', a desire for self-determination, and the fact that
peaceful protest has been ignored.

These archive images show that armed conflict hasn't changed that
much for those on the receiving end of imperial wars, though resistance
groups have adapted to new warfare methods. One enduring measure is
collective punishment, which involved large-scale terror tactics against
colonial subjects in order to facilitate resource extraction and territorial
acquisition; later, the same terror tactics were adopted to prevent decolonisation, justified as defence against 'insurgents'. Unlike mainstream
Western media, *Concerning Violence* gives high visibility to collective
punishments and other coercions that form part of Western powers'
violent record, for example, invasions and coups such as the 1987
French and US-backed coup in Burkino Faso. The Mozambique section
generates multiple associations with recent wars, evoking both Israel/
Palestine, where the Israel Defense Forces (IDF) have specialised in collective punishments on the Palestinian population, and Iraq, where the
US crackdown upon the insurgency and civilian population's support
for guerrillas was inspired by IDF actions in the Occupied Palestinian
Territories, using curfews, heavy tanks, artillery, aerial bombardment
of 'suspected "guerrilla bases"', demolition of homes and 'targeted killings' (Gregory 2004: 243).

In *Concerning Violence*, a male FRELIMO soldier talks about how
the Portuguese imperial power has stepped up psychological actions
against the population, with use of jet aeroplanes, such as the Fiat
G.91 supplied by NATO countries, to terrorise the population and
drop napalm bombs. Menacing sounds and shadows of planes in the
sky are perceived from the ground, where the FRELIMO are gathered.
The colonial power's further tactics, articulated by a Swedish journalist's reportage, include destroying harvests to starve out the guerrillas
and terrorise the local population to undermine their FRELIMO support. The Portuguese army control airspace and seek to occupy territories within the liberated zones. They destroy what locals have built
up in these areas, including schools, hospitals and orphanages, which
become military 'targets' for the colonial authority. Archive footage
shows us bombshells, which have destroyed people's homes, as well
as aircraft mercilessly dropping bombs. Straight afterwards comes a
close-up of a young woman speaking, who, as the focus is pulled out,
is revealed as an amputee, with her arm cut off. Bare-breasted, she
later suckles her baby, also an amputee. Spivak's preface identifies this

as the film's 'most moving shot'. But while victims of Western military actions rarely appear in mainstream media, use of this woman's image for pathos is problematic (though composition and framing suggest she consented to be shown). She remains unnamed and de-individualised: a generic war victim.

STRUCTURAL VIOLENCE

In its exposition of the violent record of Western powers, *Concerning Violence* mostly focuses on the less visible forms of structural violence rather than the spectacular violence of bombing and its aftermath. It presents the struggle for resources and capitalist motives as major factors in imperial wars, screened out of most Hollywood versions. Over archival footage of a quarry, where a crane is lifting earth and transporting it to a conveyer belt for sorting for precious minerals, the voice-over and superimposed words of Fanon's text relate to us former imperial powers' use of their colonies for raw materials and, later, as a market to sell the manufactured goods. Colonial subjects were terrorised into slave (or enforced) labour and worked to death, on assumptions that the labour force was replaceable (a dramatic illustration of the seriality produced by colonialism).

In today's situation, the film goes on, instead of decimating native people, (neo)colonial powers attempt to 'safeguard their own "legitimate interests"'. The words form a counterpoint with archival footage: the images are differentiated from the text yet form productive associations with it, by suggesting links between imperialism past and present. As Ruth Blakeley remarks, upon decolonisation, European powers attempted to retain 'influence in regions they had previously dominated . . . to ensure ongoing access to valuable resources and markets in those regions' and 'maintain political conditions favourable to [their] trading requirements', which involved supporting repressive regimes (2009: 64). In a similar vein, the film tells us that 'For centuries, capitalists have behaved in the underdeveloped world like nothing more than war criminals. Deportation, massacres, forced labour and slavery have been the main methods used by capitalism to increase its wealth' – the wealth of Europe that, Fanon claims, over images of a market replete with exotic products, is stolen from 'underdeveloped peoples'.

As *Concerning Violence* acknowledges in its conclusion, European colonial powers are no longer the biggest players. They have been displaced by America, now linked by 'a vast web of interests' to 'all parts of the former colonial world' (Said 1991: 285). The film's tone darkens, literally, through night footage of rag pickers, as, again through Fanon's text, it indicts the US, a former European colony, which decided to 'catch up with Europe' and 'became a monster, in which the taints, sickness and inhumanity of Europe have grown to appalling dimensions'. This, its most pointed reference to the present, invites audiences to reflect on how the US pursues similar aims to European colonial powers. For example, struggle for resources (oil) has been seen as a motivation for the Iraq War, as it had been in previous conflicts in the region. According to Gregory, it was not the main factor, though the war certainly was an imperial exploit, as 'Decisions were taken to privatize Iraq's industries and award major contracts to American (mainly American) and British companies' (Gregory 2004: 228). While power was eventually handed over to the Iraqis, the US retained economic control – in Naomi Klein's words, 'mass theft disguised as charity' (2003: 14).

OPEN ENDING: A NEW HUMAN BEING

Concerning Violence ends with Fanon's rejection of old models ('Let us not imitate Europe') and call to action. Archive footage fades to black, a *tabula rasa*, while Hill's voice-over, along with the superimposed white text, continues, resolving that 'We must work out new concepts and set afoot a new human being.' Since colonised people are not treated as human, the film (like Fanon's book) asserts the need to create a new, liberated kind of human being, who forms a new consciousness, not organised along ethnic lines. Solanas and Getino's 'Third Cinema' manifesto, itself inspired by Fanon, similarly proposes 'a cinema fit for a new human being' (1976: 63) which decolonises our imagination from old ideas and models like the cinematic devices discussed earlier, which are so familiar we do not even notice their erasures. *Concerning Violence* is structured as a film that promotes the practice of changing the world, rather than perpetuating the status quo; this is why it ends here, opening out to audiences so they can continue it. Olsson (2015) suggests that its archival montage, voice-over and text are available for further remixing: 'My dream is that people will download this film in the future, take the narration and make their own version.'

CONCLUSION

This chapter has explored seven 'cinematic' devices that produce heightened and reduced visibility of certain people, images and experiences in mainstream Western media depictions of recent conflicts: scenarios of civilisation versus barbarism; focalisation through Western troops' point of view; macho star qualities; extras cast as serial others; war as a Hitchcockian MacGuffin; spectacularly violent special effects; and white redemption. These enable erasures that are often unseen and unnoticed because Western viewers tend to take them for granted, affecting our understanding of recent wars by producing amnesia about the colonial past and present. The chapter has considered how *Concerning Violence* addresses these sites of erasure through two alternative cinematic strategies: appropriating the archive and creating a dialectic between images and words from the past and the viewer's understanding of the present. It has also shown how the film itself operates on principles of erasure, sometimes problematically. While its combinations of archival image, text and voice seek to develop viewers' consciousness of colonialism and its present-day legacies, the use of dialectical montage gives less importance to actual shot content which is occasionally overwhelmed by the superimposed text.

Moreover, the act of interpretation rests heavily on its audience, who, in the absence of explicit linkage to contemporary actions, must make sense of the images in relation to their own knowledge of recent events, making comparisons between them. As Eisenstein acknowledged, chains of associations triggered by dialectical montage will differ according to viewers' backgrounds. Although *Concerning Violence* is an important attempt to evoke the complex interrelation between past and present, which mainstream media cause to vanish, the bigger, off-screen picture to which it alludes may be completely missed by some. This matters because, as this chapter has shown, the processes of erasure in the 'war on terror' reflect power interests, permitting concealment of state violence and public blindness to its consequences. Governed by what is deemed politically expedient, the filtering of reality through cinematic devices results in the heightened visibility of certain people, images and experiences and reduced visibility of others. *Concerning Violence* offers a rare alternative to the dominant regime of visibility/invisibility, countering the amnesiac histories of recent wars offered in Hollywood versions and mainstream news. Without a wider understanding of the colonial roots of present-day conflicts towards which *Concerning Violence* gestures, there is a danger that the same blindness will simply continue.

NOTES

1. The term 'public secrets' comes from Taussig (1999: 50–1).
2. I am grateful to Libby Saxton for conversations about *Concerning Violence* which helped me to arrive at the reading unfolded in this chapter.

3. As Shohat and Stam (1994) point out, the advent of cinema coincided with the height of European imperialism in the late nineteenth century.
4. Some have expressed surprise that a Swedish film-maker should confront the subject of colonialism, to which Olsson (2015) has answered that Sweden, too, was an imperial power and, like the rest of Europe, it 'benefited from the fruits of robbery and looting'.
5. There are multiple language versions of *Concerning Violence*. In the Swedish version, Finnish actress Kati Outinen does the voice-over, alluding to colonial relations between Sweden and Finland.

BIBLIOGRAPHY

Aaron, M. (2014), *Death and the Moving Image: Ideology, Iconography and I*, Edinburgh: Edinburgh University Press.
Barker, M. (2011a), '"America hurting": making movies about Iraq', in P. Hammond (ed.), *Screens of Terror: Representations of War and Terrorism on Film and Television since 9/11*, Bury St Edmunds: Arima Publishing, pp. 37–50.
Barker, M. (2011b), *A 'Toxic Genre': the Iraq War Films*, London: Pluto Press.
Baron, J. (2014), *The Archive Effect: Found Footage and the Audiovisual Experience of History*, Abingdon: Routledge.
Baudrillard, J. ([1991] 1995), *The Gulf War Did Not Take Place*, trans. Paul Patton, Sydney: Power Publications.
Benjamin, M. (2013), *Drone Warfare: Killing by Remote Control*, London: Verso.
Blakeley, R. (2009), *State Terrorism and Neoliberalism: the North in the South*, Abingdon: Routledge.
Brook, T. V. and J. Michaels (2014), 'Air war in Syria could last years', *USA Today*, 23 September. Available at <http://www.usatoday.com/story/news/nation/2014/09/23/airstrikes-syria-iraq/16121861/> (last accessed 21 January 2016).
Buchanan, R. (2015), 'Palestinian toddler burnt alive after masked "Jewish extremists" target home in arson attack', *The Independent*, 31 July. Available at <http://www.independent.co.uk/news/world/middle-east/palestinian-toddler-killed-in-arson-attack-by-suspected-jewish-extremists-in-israels-west-bank-live-10429165.html> (last accessed 21 January 2016).
Craze, J. (2015), 'Excerpts from a grammar of redaction', in A. Downey (ed.), *Dissonant Archives: Contemporary Visual Culture and Contested Narratives in the Middle East*, London: I. B. Tauris, pp. 385–400.
Derrida, J. (1996), *Archive Fever: a Freudian Impression*, trans. Eric Prenowitz, Chicago: Chicago University Press.
Dyer, R. (1997), *White*, London: Routledge.
Eisenstein, S. ([1929] 1998), 'The dramaturgy of film form (the dialectical approach to film form)', in R. Taylor (ed.), *The Eisenstein Reader*, trans. Richard Taylor and William Powell, London: BFI, pp. 93–110.
Gregory, D. (2004), *The Colonial Present: Afghanistan, Palestine, Iraq*, Malden: Blackwell.
Hochberg, G. Z. (2015), *Visual Occupations: Violence and Visibility in a Conflict Zone*, Durham, NC: Duke University Press.
Hyde, M. (2015), 'The trolling is vile, but we should not confuse bullying with dissent', *The Guardian*, 4 December, p. 41.
Jarrett, G. (2015), '*American Sniper*', *Cinema Editor*, 65.1, pp. 54–6.

Kitses, J. (1969), *Horizons West: Anthony Mann, Budd Boetticher, Sam Peckinpah: Studies of Authorship within the West*, London: Thames and Hudson.

Klein, N. (2003), 'Bomb before you buy', *The Guardian*, 14 April, p. 14.

Macey, D. (2012), *Frantz Fanon: a Biography*, London: Verso.

Mackey, R. (2014), 'Israelis watch bombs drop on Gaza from front-row seats', *The New York Times*, 14 July. Available at <http://www.nytimes.com/2014/07/15/world/middleeast/israelis-watch-bombs-drop-on-gaza-from-front-row-seats.html?_r=1> (last accessed 21 January 2016).

Mbembe, A. (2003), 'Necropolitics', trans. Libby Meintjes, *Public Culture*, 15.1, pp. 11–40.

Norris, Chris (2015), '*American Sniper*', *Film Comment*, 51.1, pp. 68–71.

Olsson, G. H. (2015), 'Director's Q&A with Sara Myers', special features, *Concerning Violence: Nine Scenes from the Anti-imperialistic Self-defense* DVD, Dogwoof Ltd.

Pilger, J. (2010), 'Why was this event reported as a bloodless victory welcomed by all Iraqis?' *The Guardian*, 10 December, sec. G2, pp. 4–7.

Pinkerton, N. (2015), '*American Sniper*', *Sight and Sound*, 25.2, pp. 62–3.

Said, E. ([1978] 1991), *Orientalism: Western Conceptions of the Orient*, London: Penguin.

Samuels, Jonathan (2015), 'Syria airstrikes', *Sky News Tonight*, Sky, 3 December.

Shohat, E. and R. Stam (1994), *Unthinking Eurocentrism: Multiculturalism and the Media*, London: Routledge.

Solanas, F. and O. Getino ([1971] 1976), 'Towards a third cinema' in B. Nichols (ed.), *Movies and Methods*, 1, Berkeley: University of California Press, pp. 44–64.

Stam, R. and L. Spence ([1983] 1985), 'Colonialism, racism, and representation', in B. Nichols (ed.), *Movies and Methods*, 2, Berkeley: University of California Press, pp. 632–49.

Taussig, M. (1999), *Defacement: Public Secrecy and the Labor of the Negative*, Stanford: Stanford University Press.

Virilio, P. ([1984] 1989), *War and Cinema: the Logistics of Perception*, trans. Patrick Camiller, London: Verso.

Weizman, E. (2015), 'A drone strike in Miranshah: investigating video-testimony', in D. Dufour (ed.), *Images of Conviction: The Construction of Visual Evidence*, Paris: Le Bal–Éditions Xavier Barral, pp. 199–213.

Westwell, G. (2011), 'In country: mapping the Iraq War in recent Hollywood combat movies', in P. Hammond (ed.), *Screens of Terror: Representations of War and Terrorism on Film and Television since 9/11*, Bury St Edmunds: Arima Publishing, pp. 19–35.

CHAPTER 11

Afterword: Reflections on Knowing War

Christina Hellmich

This book has been dedicated to an in-depth examination of 'knowing war' in the post-9/11 world. Specifically, it has used cinema as a case study through which to map those people, images and experiences that are erased from US and European cultural representations of military action connected to the 'war on terror', and to reflect on the effects of these erasures on our understanding of war and its consequences. Against the backdrop of the ongoing academic discussion over the changing nature and alleged 'disappearance' of war, the authors featured in this volume, academics and practitioners working on the intersection of war, politics and film, made a particular effort to suspend their judgement on what war is in order to identify what is moved out of sight and the consequences of these absences for the manifestation of our individual and collective realities of war.

The findings of this investigation are sobering: at a time when the accelerations in media technologisation seem to provide unprecedented and immediate forms of access to distant locations, conflicts and affected communities in places such as Afghanistan, Iraq and Syria, the result of such access is not necessarily a more objective, better informed audience. Orientalist imaginings, far from disappearing, persist, and not in the form of weighty reports written by the likes of Gertrude Bell, but in new, readily available visual manifestations on television, cinema and mobile screens; featuring not sandcastles and exotic harems, but veiled women and inscrutable men stepping out of the shadows of dilapidated buildings in war-torn towns, potentially plotting suicide missions. Modern technology not only provides these neo-orientalist manifestations with an unprecedented presence in everyday lives in the

Western world, but it is deeply intertwined with the all too familiar 'us versus them', 'clash of civilisations' rhetoric of the war on terror, both reflecting and reinforcing a reality borne of shock and fear when the New York twin towers collapsed. Much in the way the political rhetoric left no room for the ordinary others between 'us' and 'them', cultural representations of the war on terror frequently erase the ordinary Arab, the ordinary Muslim man, woman or child and their quotidian ways of living. For example, popular films such as *American Sniper* and *The Hurt Locker*, and the series of Iraq-focused fiction films of which they are a part (including *Stop-Loss*, *The Messenger* and *In the Valley of Elah*, among others), allow the viewer little room to recall an Iraq where people once enjoyed high standards of life with a GDP comparable to Western European countries, and where the presence of fully veiled, impoverished women and children was more of an exception rather than the norm. In the re-imagined civilian spaces of Iraq, ordinary people have been replaced with prospective militants, an air of potential danger overshadowing even the most everyday scenes. At the same time, no explanation is offered as to why these once ordinary people have been radicalised – they just are. The complex, painful reality of loss and suffering in long years of war and sanctions experienced by ordinary Iraqis is not shown or explained.[1] In this imagined Iraq, collateral damage, regrettable as it may be, does not necessarily befall ordinary people, but instead targets militants, rendering both them and the ordinary people their presence elides, ungrievable lives (to use Judith Butler's fittingly pointed phrase). The very notion of innocent civilian casualties – for which accurate numbers still do not exist – quietly disappears.

The erasure of the victims of war, as Cora Goldstein reminds us, is not a new phenomenon but a hallmark of US war films since the early 1940s, with the violence and killing of non-traditional combatants and the devastation of towns, cities and their residents – the collective damage that could have turned locals into fierce (and morally justified) defenders of their homes – limited to a backdrop of rubble and trash. What these past and present depictions of war casualties have in common, and as Jessica Auchter, Tom Gregory, Agniezska Piotrowska, Shohini Chaudhuri and Lisa Purse have shown in their respective chapters, is that in all cases, the suffering, dying and death of civilians remains out of sight, while the legitimacy of the national war discourse remains unquestioned. As Robert Burgoyne observes, a feature of the contemporary moment is a focus on the experience, trauma and loss of US soldiers. Indeed, the privileging of the experiences of US and allied soldiers, at the expense of other dead, stands out as a perennial feature of contemporary US film and other cultural productions. The staggering success of *American Sniper* and its defence as allegedly 'anti-war' and 'intentionally un-political' by director Clint Eastwood and other supporters exemplifies this point (Jilani 2015). Some of the authors in this volume conclude that this lays greater responsibility on both analysts and film-makers to develop an explicitly ethical approach. But public criticism of the national discourse, especially of the fallen heroes in uniform, remains a difficult line to cross. Indeed the extent to which this is possible in popular media production is questionable, given institutional pressures and market forces, as Janet Harris's experience highlighted. Moreover, outspoken critics of *American Sniper* have received a torrent of insults and even death threats (Jilani 2015). Even subtle criticism and ambivalence, as Purse, Piotrowska and James Harvey have shown, are easily lost in the heated cultural and political discourses of 'right' and 'wrong' that swirl around the war on terror and its geopolitical and human consequences.

As a result, the chapters of this volume document a collective failure: one of adequately engaging with the lived reality of war in the post-9/11 world. The different analyses featured offer important insights into the cultural production of war at a distance – cultural production that ultimately has little to say about these distant places and people. Instead, the moving images examined here reveal important insights into the West itself, and the processes by which audiences removed from the actual sites of war and conflict make sense of the world 'out there'. While little is learned about the 'other', we have an opportunity to learn about 'ourselves'. As Steve Smith, former president of the International Studies Association (ISA) passionately argued in 2004:

> All of us in the discipline need to reflect on the possibility that both the ways in which we have constructed theories about world politics, and the content of those theories, have supported specific social forces and have essentially, if quietly and innocently, taken sides on major ethical and political questions. In that light I need to ask about the extent to which IR has been one voice in singing into existence the world that made 9/11 possible. Please note, I mean all of us engaged in the study of war, not just 'them', whoever they are, not just the 'mainstream', whatever that is, and not just the 'US discipline', however that is defined. Rather, I will take this opportunity to ask each and every one of us about our role in 9/11, and thereby reflect on the link between our work, either in writing or teaching, and international events.

More than twelve years later, the extent to which the field of war studies broadly defined has taken these words to heart remains uncertain. Indeed, it might be timely to continue Smith's line of thought by reflecting upon the extent to which more recent research and scholarly activity played a role in creating and perpetuating the post-9/11 world.

While the authors featured in this volume have not claimed, and would not claim, that they themselves have no presuppositions, it is worth noting that, as they seek to analyse the cultural manifestations of a Western worldview, they themselves write in the setting of Anglo-Saxon higher education. As such, they are subject to the pressures and incentives imposed by institutions, departments and disciplinary clusters where invisible forces tend to produce a marked homogeneity of outlook. Yet interdisciplinary dialogue can interrupt these pressures, opening up a space to critically reflect on the findings, methodologies and perspectives of different disciplines. This project, from conversations held at the writers workshop from which this book emerges, to feedback on draft chapters, allowed space for new avenues of thinking to be explored. We hope that readers will experience some of this dialogue in their own journey through the different approaches showcased in the essays, and in the ways in which they speak to each other. In this way, it is hoped that this volume might offer at least a partial response to Smith's request, but its conclusions point to a much greater need: not only for critical reflection, but for the continued creation of spaces and opportunities where this kind of interdisciplinary thinking can be done freely and productively, to allow scholars and civilians alike to question assumptions, and to think differently about the most pressing interdisciplinary challenges: knowing war, and knowing ourselves.

NOTE

1. For a comprehensive overview of the experience of war and sanctions in Iraq, see, for example, Geoff Simons (1998), *The Scourging of Iraq: Sanctions, Law and Natural Justice*.

BIBLIOGRAPHY

Jilani, Z. (2015), 'The ugly truth about "*American Sniper*"', *Salon*, 25 January. Available at <http://www.salon.com/2015/01/25/the_ugly_truth_of_american_sniper_partner/> (last accessed 7 June 2016).
Simons, G. (1998), *The Scourging of Iraq: Sanctions, Law and Natural Justice*, New York: St. Martin's Press.

Index

Note: *italic* page numbers refer to illustrations